D1200401

STUDIES IN PUBLIC EMPLOYMENT AND COMPENSATION IN CANADA

edited by
Meyer W. Bucovetsky

Volume 2 in the IRPP series on Public Sector Employment in Canada

Butterworth & Co. for the Institute for Research on Public Policy/Institut de Recherches Politiques
Montreal
1979

Legal Deposit First Quarter
Bibliothèque nationale du Québec

Canadian Cataloguing in Publication Data

Main entry under title:

Studies in public employment and compensation in
    Canada

(The IRPP series on public sector employment in Canada; v. 2)

ISBN 0-409-88601-7

1. Civil service — Canada — Addresses, essays,
lectures.   2. Canada — Officials and employees —
Addresses, essays, lectures.   I. Bucovetsky,
Meyer W.   II. Series: Institute for Research on
Public Policy. The IRPP series on public sector
employment in Canada; v. 2.

JL108.S88   354'.71'001   C79-094188-0

Butterworth & Co. (Canada) Ltd.
2265 Midland Ave.
Scarborough, Ontario
M1P 4S1

Preface

This is the second in a series of four volumes arising from a study of public sector employment in Canada. This study was commissioned by the Institute for Research on Public Policy in order to help separate myth from reality with regard to a host of issues related to public sector employment and compensation in Canada, at both the federal and provincial levels of government.

This volume contains six chapters, each of which focuses on a single aspect of the study's overall theme. Each chapter addresses a series of questions which have been the subject of hot, public debate in recent years and about which many dogmatic opinions have been expressed. It is hoped that the analysis contained in the chapters of this book will give, for the first time, a solid factual base on which the public debate can continue.

The issues of both the absolute size of government and its rate of growth, the level of wages government employees are paid, both in absolute terms and relative to wages paid in the private sector, and the long-run impact on the Canadian economy of federal and provincial public sector employment and compensation policies are important public policy issues. Clarifying the debate on issues such as these is one of the major purposes of IRPP and the raison d'être for this project.

Michael J. L. Kirby
President
January 1979

Préface

Cet ouvrage est le second d'une série de quatre volumes issus d'une analyse de l'emploi dans la fonction publique canadienne. Cette étude a été entreprise à la demande de l'Institut de recherches politiques, afin de distinguer la légende de la réalité en ce qui concerne une foule de questions reliées à l'emploi et la rémunération dans la fonction publique du Canada, tant au niveau provincial qu'au niveau fédéral.

Ce volume renferme six chapitres. Chacun d'eux aborde un aspect spécifique du thème global de l'étude, traitant d'une série de questions qui ont animé le débat public depuis quelques années et soulevé plusieurs opinions tranchantes. Nous espérons que l'analyse contenue dans ces chapitres fournira pour la première fois une base positive propice à la poursuite du débat public.

La taille globale de l'administration publique et son taux de croissance, le niveau des salaires des fonctionnaires, en termes absolus et relatifs, en regard des salaires versés dans le secteur privé, et les répercussions économiques à longue échéance des politiques d'emploi et de rémunération des secteurs publics fédéral et provincial au Canada: voilà autant de questions majeures dans le domaine des politiques. L'un des principaux objectifs de l'IRP, et l'objet même de ce projet, est d'éclairer le débat portant sur ces questions.

Michael J. L. Kirby
Président
Janvier 1979

Table of Contents

List of Tables and Figures

Executive Summary: Overview of the Studies

by
Meyer W. Bucovetsky

The chapters of this volume were commissioned as part of a broad-ranging investigation of the growth of public sector employment in Canada, undertaken for the Institute for Research on Public Policy by the Institute for Policy Analysis of the University of Toronto. The entire study will have been detailed in four published volumes, of which the present volume is the second.

Like the first volume of studies in this series (Foot, 1978), each chapter of the present volume is a self-contained report on one aspect of public sector employment and compensation in Canada. The first volume, however, had a single, unifying theme: the comprehensive review and analysis of the basic relevant data. The chapters of the present volume are rather more heterogeneous. Each of them extends the basic investigation of public sector expenditure in a different direction. The separate themes, however, are all essential ingredients in any overall judgment on the causes and consequences of public employment trends in Canada.[1] Each chapter of the present volume explores the answers to a particular set of questions that relate to public sector growth, and to pay and employment in particular.

Do public sector employees earn more than their private sector counterparts? And, if they do, to what extent are the differences explained by the 'quality' of the public work force, and to what extent by a different pay policy? **Chapter One** of this volume dissects observed earnings differentials between the public and private sectors in Canada. Morley Gunderson uses data from the Individual File of the Public Use Sample Tape of the 1971 Canadian Census to account for pay differences between workers in the public sector and those in Canadian manufacturing. The technique, essentially, is to decompose the observed earnings differences into two components, one that can be attributed to differences in wage-generating endowments of the employees and a residual that represents pure differences in the pay structures of the two sectors.

If, for example, public sector workers, on average, were better educated than those in the private sector, and if education contributes to productivity, one would expect public sector workers to receive higher pay. Using the private sector pay structure to control for the influence of wage-generating characteristics, like education, training, experience, marital status, and geographical

---

[1] The third volume in this series (Bird, forthcoming) is a summary of judgments reached by the present investigators. The fourth volume (Foot, forthcoming) is a statistical compendium.

location, Gunderson is able to isolate the pure wage advantage (or disadvantage) associated with public employment. He is able to calculate the hypothetical earnings of public sector workers, who have specified characteristics, if they were paid according to the private sector earnings structure. Separate calculations were made for the male and female work force.

Gunderson's finding, in the case of males, is that, on average, government employees were paid 9.3 per cent more in the survey period than were manufacturing employees. About one-third ($245.) of that difference may be attributed to the superior wage-determining endowments of public sector males; about two-thirds of the difference ($492.) arose because of a more generous pay structure in the public sector. Average pay for females was lower than for males in both sectors, but, on average, public sector female employees earned 22.3 per cent more than females in manufacturing. Just under two-thirds ($606.) of the female differential is accounted for by superior wage-determining characteristics; slightly over one-third ($383.) may be attributed to a more generous public sector pay structure.

It also emerges, however, that the pure pay advantage in the public sector occurred mainly because of the payment of a relatively constant premium and not because public compensation was always higher for specific wage-generating characteristics. In consequence, the public sector earnings advantage tended to be largest for the least skilled workers, at the lowest level of earnings. Indeed, the public sector pure differential tended to disappear or become negative at higher levels of earning capacity. The public sector appears to follow a more egalitarian compensation policy, as a result of which one might infer that the public sector may face job-rationing problems at the low end of the pay scale and recruitment problems at the upper end.

Is there any evidence that government is willing and able to substitute outside purchases for directly-employed labour? How much employment and how much personal income are generated by government purchases? The central theme of **Chapter Two** is the generation of 'indirect' government employment: jobs in Canadian private industry that result from government's non-payroll expenditure on goods and services. Public provision of 'public goods' requires both that government hire its own direct labour and that it purchase materials and services in the market. To some degree, then, direct public employment and outside purchases are complementary, and to some degree they are substitute inputs. Shifts in the magnitude and composition of outside purchases indicate something about the nature of public production processes. To the extent that 'jobs in industry' are a necessary ingredient of government purchases, they may be viewed as an employment consequence of public sector spending, auxiliary to the direct public work force.

The research tool used by Meyer Bucovetsky in this chapter is Statistics Canada's 'Open Input-Output Model', covering each of the years from 1961 to 1971, with government spending disaggregated into eight originating sectors. Two of the sectors comprise gross investment in capital goods: Machinery and

Equipment, and Construction. The other six government spending sectors represent operating expenses on account of Hospitals, Education, Defence, 'Other' Municipal, 'Other' Provincial, and 'Other' Federal.

For the latest year studied, 1971, government's indirect labour force amounted to about 644 thousand persons, which was 39.5 per cent of direct government employment, and 7.4 per cent of the total Canadian employed labour force. The last ratio, indirect government employment as a proportion of all Canadian employment, remained remarkably constant over the 11-year period, while the proportion of total employment directly attributable to government had been rising (16.1 per cent in 1961, 19.9 per cent in 1971). Thus, relative to direct government employment, indirect jobs had been declining for government as a whole. Nonetheless, in three individual sectors (Education, 'Other' Provincial, 'Other' Federal) indirect employment grew more rapidly than did direct employment.

Over the same years, the total constant-dollar or 'real' government purchases that gave rise to the indirect employment grew even more rapidly than did direct government employment. (The Hospital and 'Other' Municipal sectors were exceptions.) What apparently was happening over the period was an increasing tendency for governments to substitute purchased inputs for direct labour — perhaps in response to the more rapidly rising unit-cost of direct labour relative to purchases. There was also a notable shift of emphasis in the character of purchased inputs away from tangible goods and toward services.

The author notes two reasons why indirect employment grew more sluggishly than did the causative 'real' government purchases. One reason was rising private sector output per person employed; the other was a growing import-component in the goods and services bought by government.

Finally, Bucovetsky estimates that, taking account of government transfer payments and interest on the public debt, as well as both direct and indirect payroll, nearly 40 per cent of Canadian personal income in 1971 could be attributed to government spending — an increase of about seven percentage points from the proportions that held before 1967.

Is it in any sense 'inevitable' that the share of public sector employment in total national employment must grow over time? Some writers have proposed hypotheses that imply such a secular growth mechanism with respect to relative public sector employment. Is there a systematic explanation for deviations of relative public sector employment around the long-run trend? Again, a number of hypotheses have been advanced that might account for cyclical phenomena in relation to government's employment share. In particular, either (or both) 'economic' or 'political' choices may influence short-term movements around the public employment trend. An economic cycle would be characterized by stabilizing or perverse responses of relative government employment in reaction to the ebbs and flows of general economic activity. A political cycle would be characterized by the reaction of government's employment share to the timing of elections or the perceived popularity of political incumbents.

In **Chapter Three**, David K. Foot scrutinizes the postwar evidence on relative Canadian public sector employment. Growth trends in the employment share of a number of public sector sub-aggregates are examined for their explanatory power. He then tests for a relationship between deviations from trend and an economic cycle variable. Finally, the employment share data are tested against five alternative explanatory variables of a 'political' nature. Two alternative sets of relative public employment data are used. One set, derived from *Taxation Statistics* (Revenue Canada, Taxation, annual), covers relative Federal, Provincial, Municipal, Educational and Institutional employment, over the years 1946 to 1975 inclusive. The second set, derived from quarterly issues of three Statistics Canada publications, *Federal Government Employment, Provincial Government Employment,* and *Local Government Employment*, yields employment shares for those three sectors for the years 1961 to 1976, inclusive.

With respect to the long-run trend, Foot finds that the relative share of *federal* government employment in total Canadian employment has been downward, using either data set. All other public employment categories show rising relative shares over time. There is also strong indication (from the *Taxation Statistics* data) that the share of government 'proper' in total *public* employment (the latter inclusive of education and hospitals) has been falling over time.

The statistical significance of the tests on the 'economic' and 'political' cycle variables is not strong. Federal government employment, however, could be labelled as economically anticyclical (i.e., as stabilizing). With respect to politically motivated public employment cycles, there is evidence that federal employment, since 1961, has tended to rise in relative terms whenever the government's popularity was low (as evidenced by Gallup poll ratings).

To what extent has the Canadian public service become 'professionalized' in recent years? What special problems does professional identification pose for public sector employees and their employers? These questions and the attendant conflicts, tensions and policy issues are covered comprehensively by Morley Gunderson in **Chapter Four**.

Gunderson first marshalls evidence to demonstrate the rising importance of the public sector as employer of professionally-trained labour, between the 1930s and the 1970s. If the public sector is broadly interpreted to include health and education, in 1971 it employed nearly 70 per cent of the Canadian professional labour force. The proportion of all professionals employed in 'government', narrowly defined to include only public administration and defence, was considerably smaller, but as a percentage of the growing government labour force, professionals accounted for over 13 per cent in 1971, nearly double the proportion of 40 years earlier. He observes, further, that many professional jobs in the private sector depend on public spending. In short, the public purse has become the main source of professional income, and the public service has become heavily profession-oriented.

In the bulk of the chapter, Gunderson goes on to explore what he perceives as a growing malaise among salaried professionals in the public service. The problem is rooted in the essential characteristics of professional workers: their specialized training, their sense of identity, the self-governing powers vested in their associations. These defining characteristics often conflict with the authority structure of the public service. The inherent tensions have been aggravated as growth of the public sector has moderated and as competitive pressure has mounted from skilled but non-professional workers. One response to frustrated aspirations of public sector professionals has been increasing recourse to collective bargaining. In turn, this development breeds conflict when professional associations attempt to act both as bargaining agents and as guardians of professional integrity.

Gunderson analyzes the likely impact of professional unions on wages and other conditions of employment, but finds that generalizations are hazardous. The chapter concludes with a number of provocative, if speculative, observations. Among these, the author calls for restriction on the powers of professional governing bodies and the adoption of more market-oriented wage policies toward professionals on the part of public sector employers.

Has Canada caught 'the British disease'? Some authors attribute the economic problems of the United Kingdom in the 1970s to the unbridled growth of public expenditure and the concomitant expansion of public employment. Some interpret the trend of the Canadian public sector as portending economic enervation on the British model. To judge the plausibility of the allegation requires answers to a number of prior questions. Can one judge the consequences of government activity by the size (and growth) of total government spending? Have public sector growth trends in the U.K. (and Canada) been remarkable in an international comparative sense? What are the specific problems of the British economy in the 1970s? These important questions are addressed by Peter M. Jackson in **Chapter Five**.

Jackson first considers the interpretation of measured trends in government 'expenditure ratios' (such as total public spending as a proportion of GNP). He demonstrates that such summary measures are fraught with pitfalls for the unwary, and, in any event, are poor proxies for the influence of government either on economic behaviour or on personal freedom. With this preliminary warning, he compares historical trends in the relevant ratios among the countries of the OECD, and, in particular, those relating to Canada, the United States and the United Kingdom. He finds that the U.K. government does play a more dominant spending role than do the governments of Canada and the U.S.A., but that the British government is no more spending-prone than are those of the other West-European nations. In all countries, when the government expenditure ratio is measured at constant prices, the increase in the relative size of public sectors appears much more modest than when the ratio is measured at current prices.

Jackson next turns to comparative international trends in public sector employment, relating these, in particular, to structural changes in the labour market. He shows that public sector employment has followed an upward trend similar to that of the service sector as a whole. In common with the rest of the service sector, public sector employment growth has been characterized by increased numbers of female employees, especially those employed part-time. He also shows that in Canada, the U.S.A. and the U.K., public employment growth was a sub-national government phenomenon, associated with the shifting composition of public sector outputs. There is no evidence that rising labour demand by the public sector has 'crowded out' private sector employers.

In the final section of the chapter, Jackson turns to an analysis of the British economy in the 1970s. A number of long-term weaknesses are discussed, but Jackson places major emphasis on the relatively low ratio of investment to GNP. In his view, the considerable increase in U.K. public expenditure in the mid-1970s was a reaction to external events that were superimposed on a slow-growth economy. He judges that the structure of the public sector (for example, the rate structure of personal taxes) was not adequate to a period of no-growth and rapid inflation. To that extent, the nature of the public sector was not helpful in ameliorating a crisis, but it was not the fundamental cause of crisis. In order to redress the structural weaknesses of the public sector, a pause in public expenditure growth was called for and has, in fact, been implemented. He concludes that neither in the U.K. nor in Canada are the existing economic problems a consequence of rising government expenditure as such.

Do public servants vote as a massive self-conscious bloc? To the extent that the threat of their bloc-voting behaviour is a real one, do public servants have a disproportionate influence on the decisions of their nominal masters, the politicians? Is that influence exercised in the interests of an ever-growing public service? These questions are addressed by Richard Johnston in **Chapter Six:** the relevant issues are sorted out and those that can be are subjected to empirical verification on the basis of a voter sample survey conducted after the 1968 Canadian general election.

Johnston first notes that the nature of expressed fears about the voting behaviour of bureaucrats has shifted in the course of the present century. Before the Civil Service reforms, early in the century, it was feared that the very insecurity of public service tenure made patronage a powerful weapon for keeping political incumbents in office. Now, many observers feel, an entrenched bureaucracy can and will use the electoral process to assure its own continuing expansion and prosperity. Johnston's own conclusion is that the exercise of monolithic electoral power by Canadian public servants has not been demonstrated, although the available evidence is limited in many respects.

The analysis of the chapter is conducted in terms of five factors that would determine the political effectiveness of public servants in pursuit of their distinctive collective interest. One factor is the relative extent to which public servants participate in elections. A second is the homogeneity of their political preferences. A third factor is their readiness to switch allegiance between political parties. A fourth (relevant in an electoral system based on single-member pluralities) is the geographic distribution of the public service. The fifth factor is the very size of the public service.

As regards participation, the evidence from the sample survey (in which respondents, classified by occupation and other characteristics, were asked whether they had voted in the latest federal and provincial elections) is that public servants are somewhat more likely to vote than are other citizens. The difference, however, is negligible when the higher average educational attainment of public servants is taken into account.

In respect to homogeneity of preferences, Johnston notes possible conflicts within the public service, for example as between those whose personal interest is in career advancement and those who are more comfortable in a stable environment. For this and other reasons, party preferences are unlikely to be monolithic. The evidence, from the 1968 sample survey, is that, in one federal election, public servants were more likely to support the incumbent Liberal party than were other voters. Whether the Liberals were favoured as the party most likely to foster public service growth, or simply because they were the incumbents, is not clear.

The third relevant factor is the relative extent to which the public service vote is available for transfer between parties. The evidence here, from responses to the sample survey, is that public servants are no more nor less available for switching between parties than are other voters.

The fourth and fifth factors do not lend themselves to testing against evidence from any available data. With respect to geographic distribution, from the viewpoint of public service self-interest, an 'efficient' dispersion would be one where its votes were significant in closely-contested constituencies. Johnston speculates that, to increase its popularity in closely-contested districts, an incumbent political party may be tempted to locate government operations in these marginal areas. If that were the case, the location decision would confer enhanced leverage on the public service vote.

As regards the relevance of the size and growth of the public service to its voting effectiveness, Johnston notes several complicating elements. The more numerous the group, the greater its potential political influence, but the larger its numbers, the more diverse its composition and the less cohesive the perceived self-interest of members of the group. He concludes that the assumption that all bureaucrats would agree on the desirability of further public service growth may no longer be warranted.

REFERENCES

Bird, R.M. (forthcoming) *The Growth of Public Employment in Canada* (Toronto: Butterworth & Co., for the Institute for Research on Public Policy).

Foot, D.K., ed. (1978) *Public Employment and Compensation in Canada: Myths and Realities* (Toronto: Butterworth & Co., for the Institute for Research on Public Policy).

Foot, D.K. (forthcoming) *Public Employment in Canada: Statistical Series* (Toronto: Butterworth & Co., for the Institute for Research on Public Policy).

Abrégé: Vue d'ensemble des études

par
Meyer W. Bucovetsky

Le présent volume n'est qu'une partie d'une vaste enquête sur la création d'emplois dans le secteur public au Canada. Les résultats de cette enquête entreprise par l'Institute for Policy Analysis de l'Université de Toronto, à l'intention de l'Institut de recherches politiques, doivent paraître en quatre volumes dont voici le second.

Comme dans le premier volume de cette série (Foot, 1978), chaque chapitre constitue une analyse complète de l'un des aspects de l'emploi et de la rémunération des fonctionnaires publics du Canada. Le premier volume ne portait que sur un seul sujet homogène: l'étude et l'analyse d'ensemble des données fondamentales sur l'emploi et la rémunération. Les chapitres qui suivent sont passablement plus hétérogènes. Chacun d'eux oriente l'étude fondamentale sur les dépenses dans le secteur public vers une sphère différente. Ces divers domaines sont cependant tous essentiels pour porter un jugement global sur les causes et les conséquences de l'orientation de l'emploi dans le secteur public au Canada.[1] On trouvera dans chacun des chapitres de ce volume l'analyse des réponses à une série de questions se rapportant à la croissance du secteur public dans son ensemble et, plus particulièrement, à la rémunération et à l'emploi.

Les travailleurs du secteur public ont-ils un revenu plus élevé que leurs homologues du secteur privé? Si oui, dans quelle mesure peut-on expliquer cette différence par la "compétence qualitative" des travailleurs du secteur public et par une politique de salaires différente? Dans le **Chapitre Un**, Morley Gunderson dissèque les différences salariales qui existent entre les travailleurs du secteur public et ceux de l'industrie au Canada. Pour expliquer ces différences, il se base sur les données du fichier des travailleurs établi lors du recensement de 1971 au Canada. Sa technique consiste à décomposer les différences de salaires observées en deux éléments: le premier serait relié à la valeur marchande plus ou moins élevée des compétences et le second découlerait strictement des barèmes salariaux des deux secteurs.

Si, par exemple, les travailleurs du secteur public ont, en moyenne, un niveau d'instruction supérieur à ceux du secteur privé, et si cette instruction contribue à la productivité, il semblerait raisonnable que les travailleurs du secteur public soient mieux rémunérés. En se servant du barème salarial du secteur privé pour déterminer l'influence qu'exerce la valeur marchande des compétences telles que l'éducation, la formation professionnelle, l'expérience, la situation de famille et

---

[1] Le troisième volume de cette série (Bird, à publier) est le résumé des appréciations auxquelles sont arrivés les auteurs du présent volume. Le quatrième volume (Foot, à publier) est un relevé statistique.

la situation géographique, Gunderson peut établir l'avantage (ou le désavantage) salarial net relié au secteur public. Il peut calculer le revenu hypothétique des travailleurs du secteur public qui ont des compétences précises, s'ils étaient rémunérés selon le barème des salaires du secteur privé. La rémunération des travailleurs masculins et des travailleurs féminins a été calculée séparément.

Gunderson en est arrivé à la conclusion que, durant toute l'enquête, les fonctionnaires masculins recevaient, en moyenne, une rémunération de 9,3 p. cent plus élevée que s'ils avaient travaillé dans l'industrie. A peu près un tiers ($245) de cette différence peut être attribué à une valeur marchande des compétences supérieure chez les travailleurs masculins du secteur public, et environ deux tiers ($492) à un barème salarial plus élevé dans le secteur public. Le salaire moyen des travailleurs féminins était dans les deux secteurs plus bas que celui des travailleurs masculins, mais, en moyenne, le salaire des travailleurs féminins du secteur public était de 22,3 p. cent plus élevé que celui de leurs homologues de l'industrie. Un peu moins des deux tiers ($606) de la différence chez les travailleurs féminins sont attribuables à la plus grande valeur marchande des compétences et un peu plus d'un tiers ($383) est attribuable au barème salarial plus élevé du secteur public.

Nous pouvons aussi voir que le seul avantage du secteur public est dû en grande partie au fait qu'une prime a été versée aux travailleurs de façon presque ininterrompue et non à ce que la rémunération dans le secteur public a toujours été plus élevée pour des compétences spécifiques. Par conséquent, dans le secteur public, les travailleurs les moins spécialisés et situés aux plus bas échelons salariaux se sont trouvés les plus favorisés. De plus, la différence tend à disparaître et même à s'exercer négativement aux échelons supérieurs de salaires. Le secteur public semble avoir une politique de rémunération plus égalitaire: on pourrait en déduire qu'il peut être confronté à des problèmes de rationnement de l'emploi aux plus bas échelons salariaux et des problèmes de recrutement aux échelons supérieurs.

Peut-on démontrer que le gouvernement est disposé à substituer sa propre main-d'oeuvre aux achats externes et qu'il est en mesure de le faire? Combien d'emplois ces achats externes créent-ils et à combien se chiffrent les salaires ainsi payés? Le sujet principal du **Chapitre Deux** porte surtout sur la création d'emplois gouvernementaux indirects: les emplois dans l'industrie privée créés à la suite de dépenses extra-salariales engagées par le gouvernement sur les biens et les services. L'approvisionnement du secteur public en ''biens publics'' nécessite que le gouvernement embauche directement sa propre main-d'oeuvre et qu'il achète ses matériaux et ses services sur le marché. Jusqu'à un certain point, donc, la main-d'oeuvre relevant directement du gouvernement et les achats extérieurs se complètent et sont aussi, dans une certaine mesure, des biens de remplacement. Les changements dans l'ampleur et dans la teneur des achats à l'extérieur révèlent certains aspects des procédés de production du secteur public. Dans la mesure où les ''emplois dans l'industrie'' font nécessairement partie des achats du gouvernement, ils peuvent être considérés comme une conséquence des dépenses gouvernementales et comme auxiliaires à la main-d'oeuvre relevant directement du gouvernement.

Dans ce chapitre, Meyer Bucovetsky s'est inspiré du "modèle ouvert de détermination de la production" de Statistique Canada portant sur chacune des années 1961 à 1971 et sur les dépenses gouvernementales réparties selon huit secteurs d'origine. Deux de ces secteurs comprennent l'investissement brut en immobilisations: l'acquisition de machines et de matériel et la construction. Les six autres secteurs de dépenses gouvernementales se rapportent aux dépenses de fonctionnement relatives aux hôpitaux, à l'enseignement et à la défense nationale ainsi qu'aux "autres dépenses" municipales, provinciales et fédérales.

Dans le cas de la dernière année à l'étude, soit 1971, la main-d'oeuvre employée indirectement par le gouvernement s'élevait à environ 644 mille personnes, soit 39,5 p. cent de la main-d'oeuvre directe du gouvernement et 7,4 p. cent de la main-d'oeuvre active totale au Canada. Le dernier pourcentage, soit la main-d'oeuvre employée indirectement par le gouvernement par rapport à la main-d'oeuvre totale au Canada, a été remarquablement constant au cours de ces onze années, alors que la proportion de la main-d'oeuvre totale relevant directement du gouvernement s'est accrue de 16,1 p. cent en 1961 et de 19,9 p. cent en 1971. Par conséquent, la proportion de main-d'oeuvre employée indirectement par le gouvernement s'est amenuisée dans son ensemble par rapport à la main-d'oeuvre directe. Néanmoins, la main-d'oeuvre indirecte s'est accrue plus rapidement que la main-d'oeuvre directe dans trois secteurs particuliers: l'enseignement, et les "autres dépenses" provinciales et fédérales.

Au cours de ces mêmes années, le total des achats gouvernementaux en dollars constants, ou "réels", procurant des emplois à la main-d'oeuvre indirecte, a augmenté plus rapidement même que pour la main-d'oeuvre directe (à l'exception des comptes hôpitaux et "autres dépenses" municipales). Au cours de ces années, il semble que les divers gouvernements aient plutôt cherché à substituer de plus en plus une main-d'oeuvre privée à la main-d'oeuvre directe, probablement parce que le coût de cette dernière à l'unité augmentait plus rapidement que dans le secteur privé. Un changement marquant dans la nature des achats, de moins en moins caractérisés par des biens matériels et de plus en plus par les services, s'est aussi fait sentir.

L'auteur donne deux raisons pour lesquelles la main-d'oeuvre indirecte s'est accrue plus lentement que les dépenses "réelles" du gouvernement qui la justifient. L'une des raisons est l'augmentation du rendement du salarié dans le secteur privé et l'autre, la croissance de l'importation de biens et de services dans les achats du gouvernement.

Finalement, Bucovetsky croit que, compte tenu des paiements de transfert et de l'intérêt sur la dette publique ainsi que de la main-d'oeuvre payée directement et indirectement par le gouvernement, près de 40 p. cent du revenu personnel des Canadiens en 1971 peuvent être attribués aux dépenses gouvernementales, soit une augmentation d'environ 7 points par rapport aux pourcentages antérieurs à 1967.

Est-il vraiment "inévitable" qu'au cours des ans les emplois créés dans le secteur public augmentent par rapport à ceux de l'ensemble du marché du travail au Canada? Certains auteurs ont émis des hypothèses impliquant ce genre de croissance séculaire de l'emploi dans le secteur public. Existe-il en fin de compte une explication systématique aux écarts des taux d'emploi dans le secteur public? Différentes hypothèses ont été émises pour expliquer les phénomènes cycliques en ce qui a trait à la portion des emplois créés par le gouvernement. En particulier les choix "économiques" ou "politiques" pourraient l'un et l'autre avoir une influence sur les fluctuations à court terme de la courbe de l'emploi dans le secteur public. Un cycle économique se reconnaîtrait par les réactions favorables ou contraires du taux de la main-d'oeuvre en réponse aux flux et reflux de l'économie en général. Un cycle politique serait caractérisé par la réaction de la proportion de l'emploi dans le secteur public au moment des élections ou par la popularité des hommes politiques en place.

Dans le **Chapitre Trois**, David K. Foot analyse l'évolution du taux de l'emploi dans le secteur public au Canada, après la guerre. Il fait l'examen de la courbe de la création d'emplois d'un certain nombre de sous-organismes du secteur public pour les éclaircissements qu'elle apporte. Il tente ensuite d'établir un lien entre les divergences qui s'y trouvent et une variable économique cyclique. Finalement, il compare les données relatives à la création d'emplois avec cinq variables explicatives possibles de nature "politique". Il se sert de deux séries de données sur la proportion de l'emploi dans le secteur public. La première est tirée de *Statistique fiscale*, publié annuellement par la division de l'impôt de Revenu Canada, et porte sur le taux de l'emploi des gouvernements municipaux, provinciaux et fédéral et sur les organismes institutionnels ainsi que sur le domaine de l'enseignement pour les années 1946 à 1975 inclusivement. La deuxième série de données, tirée de trois publications trimestrielles de Statistique Canada (*L'emploi dans l'administration publique fédérale, L'emploi dans les administrations publiques provinciales* et *L'emploi dans les administrations locales*), établit la comparaison entre ces trois secteurs en ce qui a trait à la création d'emplois, de 1961 à 1976 inclusivement.

En ce qui concerne la tendance à long terme, Foot conclut que le taux d'emplois du gouvernement *fédéral* pour l'ensemble du Canada a diminué, quelles que soient les données utilisées. Toutes les autres catégories d'emplois dans le secteur public suivent une courbe de participation ascendante dans le temps. Il existe aussi une forte indication, selon les statistiques fiscales, que la participation "propre" au gouvernement dans l'ensemble du secteur *public* (compte tenu de l'enseignement et des hôpitaux) a baissé au cours des ans.

Les tests des variables des cycles "économique" et "politique" n'ont pas une très grande signification statistique. L'emploi au gouvernement fédéral, toutefois, pourrait être catalogué comme étant économiquement anti-cyclique, c'est-à-dire facteur de stabilisation. En ce qui a trait aux cycles d'emploi motivés par la politique dans le secteur public, il semble bien que l'embauche au fédéral depuis 1961 a eu tendance à augmenter chaque fois que la popularité du gouvernement était à la baisse (comme en font foi les résultats des sondages Gallup).

Dans quelle mesure les employés des services publics au Canada se sont-ils "professionnalisés" au cours des dernières années? Quels sont les problèmes que pose ce genre d'identité auprès des employés du secteur public et de leurs employeurs? L'ensemble de ces questions, les conflits, les tensions et les problèmes d'éthique qui s'y rattachent sont traités en détail par Morley Gunderson au **Chapitre Quatre**.

Gunderson établit d'abord les preuves pour démontrer l'importance croissante du secteur public à titre d'employeur de la main-d'oeuvre ayant reçu une formation professionnelle entre les années 1930 et 1970. Si on englobe dans le secteur public la santé et l'éducation, il employait en 1971 près de 70 p. cent de la main-d'oeuvre professionnelle au Canada. La proportion de tous les professionnels travaillant pour le "gouvernement", ce dernier terme étant pris au sens étroit et ne s'appliquant qu'à l'administration publique et la défense nationale, était très inférieure, mais en tant que pourcentage d'un nombre grandissant d'employés gouvernementaux, le nombre de professionnels s'élevait à plus de 13 p. cent en 1971, soit environ le double de ce qu'il était 40 ans auparavant. Il fait remarquer, en outre, que plusieurs postes professionnels du secteur privé sont à la merci de la dépense publique. En bref, les deniers publics sont devenus la principale source de revenu des professionnels et les services publics ont tendance à se tourner vers eux de préférence.

Gunderson consacre la plus grande partie du chapitre aux symptômes de ce qu'il perçoit comme un malaise croissant chez les professionnels salariés du secteur public. Les caractéristiques essentielles aux travailleurs professionnels, soit leur spécialisation, leur sens de l'identité, les possibilités d'autogestion qu'exercent leurs associations, se trouvent au coeur du problème. Ces caractéristiques entrent souvent en conflit avec la structure de l'autorité dans le secteur public. Les tensions inhérentes se sont aggravées à mesure que la croissance du secteur public diminuait et que la pression de la concurrence augmentait chez les spécialistes non professionnels. Leurs aspirations ayant été déçues les professionnels du secteur public ont, dans certains cas, fait de plus en plus appel aux négociations collectives. Cette évolution fait, à son tour, naître des conflits lorsque les associations professionnelles tentent de représenter leurs membres à la fois comme médiateurs et protecteurs de l'intégrité professionnelle.

Gunderson analyse les répercussions possibles de l'intervention des associations professionnelles sur les salaires et autres conditions d'emploi, en soulignant toutefois qu'il est périlleux de généraliser. Enfin, il termine ce chapitre par un certain nombre de remarques intéressantes, bien qu'hypothétiques. Entre autres, l'auteur demande que l'on restreigne les pouvoirs des organismes professionnels gouvernementaux et que les employeurs du secteur public adoptent des politiques salariales correspondant à celles du secteur privé.

Le Canada a-t-il attrapé le "mal britannique"? Certains auteurs attribuent les problèmes économiques du Royaume-Uni, au cours des années 70, à la croissance effrénée de la dépense publique et l'expansion concomitante de l'emploi dans le secteur public. Quelques-uns interprètent la tendance du secteur public canadien comme étant le présage d'un affaiblissement économique tel que l'a connu l'Angleterre. Pour juger de la vraisemblance de cette allégation, il est essentiel que l'on réponde d'abord à un certain nombre de questions. Peut-on juger des conséquences de l'activité du gouvernement en se fondant sur l'ampleur et la croissance de ses dépenses? La courbe de croissance du secteur public au Royaume-Uni (et au Canada) est-elle remarquable par rapport aux autres pays? Quels sont les problèmes précis de l'économie britannique des années 70? Peter M. Jackson s'attaque à ces questions, lourdes de sens, au **Chapitre Cinq**.

Jackson tient d'abord compte de l'interprétation des résultats estimatifs des "ratios de dépenses" du gouvernement (comme la dépense publique totale par rapport au PNB). Il démontre que ces résultats sommaires fourmillent de pièges si on manque de vigilance et que, de toute façon, ils ne sont que de piètres intermédiaires pour permettre au gouvernement d'influer sur le comportement de l'économie ou sur la liberté personnelle. Compte tenu de cet avertissement préalable, il établit une comparaison entre les courbes historiques des ratios pertinents des pays de l'O.C.D.E. et, surtout, de celles se rapportant au Canada, aux Etats-Unis et au Royaume-Uni. Il estime que le gouvernement du Royaume-Uni joue un rôle prépondérant dans le domaine de la dépense comparativement aux gouvernements du Canada et des Etats-Unis, mais que le gouvernement britannique ne prône pas plus la dépense que les autres pays de l'Europe de l'Ouest. Dans tous les pays, l'accroissement de l'importance relative des secteurs publics semble beaucoup plus modeste lorsque la proportion est calculée à des prix constants que lorsqu'elle est calculée aux prix courants.

Jackson s'attaque ensuite aux tendances comparatives internationales de l'emploi dans le secteur public en les reliant surtout aux modifications structurales du marché du travail. Il démontre que l'emploi dans le secteur public a suivi une courbe ascendante semblable à celle du secteur des services dans son ensemble. Comme dans le reste du secteur des services, la croissance de l'emploi dans le secteur public a été caractérisée par un nombre croissant de femmes, employées surtout à temps partiel. Il démontre aussi que la croissance de l'emploi dans le secteur public au Canada, aux Etats-Unis et au Royaume-Uni n'a été qu'un phénomène de gouvernement infra-national associé à la composition changeante de la production dans le secteur public. Il ne trouve aucune preuve que la demande croissante de main-d'oeuvre dans le secteur public ait "démuni" les employeurs du secteur privé.

Dans la dernière partie du chapitre, Jackson fait l'analyse de l'économie de l'Angleterre dans les années 70. Il y dénonce un certain nombre de faiblesses à long terme, mais il accorde plus d'importance au ratio relativement bas des investissements par rapport au PNB. D'après l'auteur, l'augmentation considérable de la dépense publique au Royaume-Uni au milieu des années 70 était une conséquence des événements extérieurs qui se juxtaposaient à une économie plutôt nonchalante. Il estime que la structure du secteur public (par exemple la structure de l'impôt sur le revenu des particuliers) était mal adaptée à une période de stagnation et d'inflation rapide. De ce point de vue, la nature du secteur public n'aidait pas à réprimer une crise, sans être toutefois la cause principale de cette crise. Afin de remédier aux faiblesses de structure des secteurs publics, on a demandé de freiner les dépenses publiques, ce qui fut fait. Il en conclut que ni au Royaume-Uni ni au Canada les problèmes économiques existants ne sont une conséquence de la dépense gouvernementale croissante comme telle.

Les employés du gouvernement votent-ils consciemment en bloc? Dans la mesure où ce vote représente une menace réelle, les fonctionnaires exercent-ils une influence disproportionnée sur les décisions de leurs maîtres en titre, les hommes politiques? Cette influence s'exerce-t-elle dans l'intérêt d'un service public toujours grandissant? Voilà les questions que pose Richard Johnston au **Chapitre Six**. Les questions pertinentes sont sélectionnées et celles qui peuvent l'être sont soumises à une vérification empirique fondée sur un sondage mené auprès d'un échantillon d'électeurs, après l'élection générale de 1968 au Canada.

Johnston mentionne d'abord que la nature des craintes exprimées au sujet du comportement électoral des bureaucrates s'est modifiée au cours de ce siècle. Avant les réformes du service civil, au début du siècle, on craignait que la durée très aléatoire des services publics ne transforme le "mécénat politique" en une arme puissante pour maintenir en place les représentants du gouvernement. Se basant sur leurs observations, nombreux sont ceux qui croient à présent qu'une bureaucratie retirée peut utiliser et utilisera le processus électoral pour assurer derrière ses retranchements sa propre expansion et sa prospérité grandissante. La conclusion de Johnston est que l'exercice du pouvoir électoral monolithique des employés du gouvernement du Canada n'a pas été démontré, bien qu'à plusieurs égards il ne puisse arriver à en donner une preuve absolue.

L'analyse de ce chapitre se fonde sur cinq facteurs qui détermineraient l'efficacité politique des employés du gouvernement dans la poursuite de leurs intérêts collectifs distinctifs. L'un de ces facteurs est le taux de participation des fonctionnaires lors des élections. Le deuxième est l'homogénéité de leurs préférences politiques. Le troisième est leur facilité à changer d'allégeances politiques. Le quatrième (pertinent dans un régime électoral fondé sur le pluralisme d'un seul député) est la distribution géographique du fonctionnariat. Le cinquième facteur est l'importance même du service public.

En ce qui a trait à la participation électorale et en se basant sur l'enquête par sondage (au cours de laquelle les répondants, classés selon leurs professions et certaines autres caractéristiques, se sont vus demander s'ils avaient voté lors des dernières élections fédérales et provinciales), on a pu démontrer que les employés du service public sont plus enclins à voter que les autres citoyens. La différence est négligeable, toutefois, si l'on tient compte de leur plus grand niveau moyen d'instruction.

A l'égard de l'homogénéité des préférences, Johnston fait mention des conflits qui pourraient exister à l'intérieur du service public, par exemple entre ceux dont l'intérêt personnel est de gravir les échelons et ceux qui préfèrent vivre dans un milieu stable. C'est probablement pour cela et d'autres raisons que les préférences pour un parti ou un autre ne peuvent être monolithiques. D'après l'enquête fragmentaire de 1968, il ressort que les fonctionnaires sont beaucoup plus enclins à voter pour le candidat du parti libéral déjà en place que ne le sont les autres électeurs dans une élection fédérale. Il est difficile de déterminer si leur choix s'est porté sur les libéraux parce qu'ils prônaient la croissance des services publics ou tout simplement parce qu'ils étaient au pouvoir.

Le troisième facteur pertinent est la mesure dans laquelle les fonctionnaires sont portés à changer d'allégeance politique. Les résultats de l'enquête fragmentaire révèlent que les fonctionnaires ne sont ni plus ni moins portés à en changer que les autres électeurs.

Les quatrième et cinquième facteurs ne se prêtent pas à une démonstration fondée sur des données existantes. En ce qui concerne la répartition géographique, du point de vue de son propre intérêt, le fonctionnariat pourrait être "efficacement" présent dans les circonscriptions où les votes font l'objet d'une lutte acharnée. Johnston suppose que pour augmenter sa popularité dans les districts où les votes sont vivement disputés, un parti politique en place pourrait être tenté de situer les activités gouvernementales dans ces régions marginales. Si c'était le cas, le choix de l'endroit pourrait conférer au vote du fonctionnariat une portée plus grande.

En ce qui a trait à l'importance et à la croissance des services publics par rapport à leur efficacité électorale, Johnston fait remarquer plusieurs complications. Plus le groupe est nombreux, plus son influence politique peut être grande, mais plus sa composition est diversifiée et moins la perception des intérêts respectifs des membres est cohérente. Il conclut que l'hypothèse voulant que tous les bureaucrates désirent la croissance de la fonction publique n'a plus de fondement solide.

RÉFÉRENCES

Bird, R.M. (à publier) *The Growth of Public Employment in Canada* (Toronto: Butterworth & Co. pour l'Institut de recherches politiques).

Foot, D.K., éd. (1978) *Public Employment and Compensation in Canada: Myths and Realities* (Toronto: Butterworth & Co. pour l'Institut de recherches politiques).

Foot, D.K. (à publier) *Public Employment in Canada: Statistical Series* (Toronto: Butterworth & Co. pour l'Institut de recherches politiques).

Chapter One

Decomposition of Public-Private Sector Earnings Differentials

by
*Morley Gunderson**

INTRODUCTION

Public sector wages have come under increased scrutiny in recent years in part because of the alleged magnitude of wage settlements in that area. Concern stems from the fact that in the absence of strict market forces, there may be few if any constraining elements to limit public sector wages. The concern is bolstered by the potentially disruptive impact of strikes in the public sector.

While there is legitimate reason for concern in this area, it is important that it be based on accurate information concerning the magnitude of public sector wages, especially relative to wages of comparable workers in the private sector. Newspaper stories and conventional public wisdom to the contrary, it is surprising how little systematic information is available in this area.

The purpose of this report is to provide some systematic information on Canadian experience in this area by attempting to answer the following questions: What is the magnitude of the pure earnings differential between public and private sector workers who are comparable in other respects? How much of the overall earnings differential is due to the different endowments of productivity-related characteristics and how much is due to a pure surplus payment? What is the relative contribution of various wage-determining factors to the public-private earnings differential? Is the differential larger for males or females, and for skilled or unskilled workers?

Editor's Note: **Morley Gunderson** is Associate Professor in the Faculty of Management Studies and Scarborough College, and Associate of the Centre for Industrial Relations, all at the University of Toronto. Some of the results reported in the present chapter were reported in another current paper by the author, entitled "Earnings Differentials Between the Public and Private Sectors".

* The author acknowledges the assistance of the staff at the Centre for Industrial Relations, University of Toronto. He is grateful for research assistance by Marcelle Elhadad, Oleh Ilnyckyj, and Richard Obadiah. Some of the work on this chapter was done while the author was a visiting associate of the International Institute for Labour Studies in Geneva, Switzerland.

In an attempt to answer these questions, separate earnings equations are estimated for public and private sector Canadian workers,[1] separately for males and females. The structural determinants of earnings in each sector are then compared to see if there is a difference in the underlying wage determination process. For each sex, the overall earnings differential is decomposed into its component parts: a portion due to different endowments of productivity-related characteristics, and a portion due to a pure surplus payment for the same characteristics. The related contribution, to the earnings differential, of the various wage-determining characteristics is then presented and the earnings equations are analysed in somewhat more detail so as to shed light on the wage determination process in each sector. Before the empirical work is presented there is a discussion of the explanatory variables, the data and the definition of the public and private sectors, and the technique for decomposing the earnings differential.[2]

VARIABLES, DATA AND METHODOLOGY

Explanatory Variables: Functional Form and Expected Impact

Estimation of earnings equations is by now well established in the literature on labour market economics. The dependent variable — some variant of wages, earnings or income — is usually expressed in logarithmic form. The resulting regression coefficients, when the explanatory variables are in natural units, indicate the percentage change in the dependent variable that results from a unit change in the explanatory variable.[3]

The explanatory variables, depending on the nature of the data, are usually some mix of human capital variables (education, experience, training, etc.)[4] as well as a set of variables designed to control for other wage-determining influences such as short-run demand changes, compensating wage differentials, or desirable labour market characteristics. These control variables often include marital status, residence, region, hours of work and occupation. In addition, we include a language variable to reflect the impact on labour market earnings of knowing only English or French or being bilingual.

In our analyses these control variables are generally included in categorical form; therefore, the estimated regression coefficient indicates the percentage change in earnings that results from an individual being in the given category

---

[1] This approach has been used by Smith (1975, 1976) based on U.S. data, and the results reviewed in Gunderson (1978b).

[2] The underlying theory of public sector wage determination has not been presented here because it has been reviewed in an earlier report, Gunderson (1978b).

[3] In the simple regression $\ln y = \beta x$ where $\exp(\ln y) = y = \exp(\beta x)$; the change in y that results from a unit change in x is $\partial y/\partial x = \beta \cdot \exp(\beta x) = \beta y$ and therefore the regression coefficient $\beta = (\partial y/\partial x)/y = (\partial y/y)/\partial x$.

[4] A weakness in the data on human capital that are used as explanatory variables in this kind of estimation is that they are at best an index only of quantities. The measures used cannot distinguish the variable quality of human capital.

(e.g. bilingual) as opposed to being in the omitted reference category (e.g. English only). The education and experience variable are entered in quadratic form so as to allow the percentage return to an additional unit of human capital to vary with the *level* of human capital. The education and experience variables were also entered interactively (i.e. as education times experience) to allow the effect of education to depend on labour market experience and vice-versa.

Separate regressions were run for males and females in both the public and private sectors to allow for the fact that the wage determination process may be different for males and females in the two sectors. This also enables the calculation of separate public-private earnings differentials for males and females.

Data and Definition of Public and Private Sectors

The data is based on the Individual File of the Public Use Sample Tape of the 1971 Canadian Census and the responses refer to activity during 1970. Only those observations with the following characteristics were included: worked full-time (35 to 44 hours per week) and full year (49 to 52 weeks per year), for pay or profit in a nonfarm location as a civilian whose major source of income was from wages and salary. In addition, observations were excluded if their occupation was in the religion, primary, construction or 'other' occupational groups. This resulted in 1,786 male and 733 female observations in the public sector, and 4,897 male and 1,413 female observations in the private sector.

In our analysis the public sector is defined as the major industry group of 'public administration and defence'. Since only civilians working for pay or profit were included in the sample, the only defence personnel considered would be civilians in the defence industry. Unfortunately, the data did not enable one to separate federal, provincial and local levels of government. For the private sector in our analyses the manufacturing industry group was used, in part because it is generally regarded as our main private sector industry, and in part because it contained a sufficiently large number of observations.

Technique for Decomposing the Earnings Differential

In the earnings equations, the regression coefficients reflect the pay structure for each sector in that they indicate the percentage change in earnings associated with a unit change in the explanatory variables. They measure the returns paid for variation in the characteristics that workers bring to the labour market. The explanatory variables, on the other hand, indicate the characteristics embodied in a given worker. These two factors — the characteristics of workers and the returns to these characteristics — determine earnings.

Once the separate earnings equations are estimated for each of the public and private sectors, the average earnings differential between the two sectors can be decomposed into a portion due to the different pay structures (regression coefficients including the constant) and a portion due to the different wage-generating endowments (explanatory variables) between the two sectors. The latter portion is considered a 'legitimate' differential in that it reflects the returns to the acquisition of human capital such as education or training, or it reflects compensating differentials or short run earnings advantages. The former differential — arising from differences in the regression coefficients — is considered an economic rent or surplus since it reflects a pure pay differential paid for the same characteristics.

The decomposition of the earnings differential can be illustrated formally. Let y denote earnings, β the set of regression coefficients including the constant term, X the set of explanatory variables and the g and c subscripts denote the public and private sectors respectively. The earnings function for each sector can be written as:

$$\ln y_g = \Sigma \, \beta_g X_g$$

and
$$\ln y_c = \Sigma \, \beta_c X_c.$$

In regression analysis the mean of the dependant variable is equal to the regression coefficients times the mean of the explanatory variables. That is:

$$\overline{\ln y_g} = \Sigma \, \beta_g \overline{X_g}$$

and
$$\overline{\ln y_c} = \Sigma \, \beta_c \overline{X_c}.$$

The overall average earnings differential is therefore:

$$\overline{\ln y_g} - \overline{\ln y_c} = \Sigma \, \beta_g \overline{X_g} - \Sigma \, \beta_c \overline{X_c}.$$

Decomposing the right-hand side by subtracting and adding $\Sigma \, \beta_c \overline{X_g}$ yields:

$$\overline{\ln y_g} - \overline{\ln y_c} = \Sigma \, \beta_g \overline{X_g} - \Sigma \, \beta_c \overline{X_g} + \Sigma \, \beta_c \overline{X_g} - \Sigma \, \beta_c \overline{X_c},$$

which reduces to
$$\overline{\ln y_g} - \overline{\ln y_c} = \Sigma \, (\beta_g - \beta_c)\overline{X_g} + \Sigma \, \beta_c(\overline{X_g} - \overline{X_c}).$$

The first term on the right-hand side reflects differences in the pay structure between the two sectors (i.e. differences in the regression coefficients), evaluated for the average characteristics for public sector workers (i.e. $\overline{X_g}$'s). The second term reflects differences in endowments between the two sectors (i.e. differences in the explanatory variables) evaluated according to the private sector pay structure (i.e. β_c's). Together these two components make up the overall average differential as given on the left-hand side.[5]

The earnings equations can be used to calculate the hypothetical earnings of public sector workers if they retained their own characteristics but were to be paid according to the private sector earnings structure. This is computed as

---

[5] It would also have been possible to add and subtract $\Sigma \, \beta_g \overline{X_c}$ to the right-hand side in which case the different pay structures would have been evaluated for the average characteristics of private sector workers and the differences in the endowments evaluated according to the public sector pay structure. This decomposition was not utilized here, however, because the private sector pay structure is the one that is used by the public sector for comparability purposes, and, consequently, it is more meaningful to evaluate the endowment differences according to that standard.

$\Sigma \beta_c \overline{X}_g$. The difference between their actual average earnings $\Sigma \beta_g \overline{X}_g$ and this hypothetical earnings is their surplus payment. That is:

$$\Sigma (\beta_g - \beta_c)\overline{X}_g = \Sigma \beta_g \overline{X}_g - \Sigma \beta_c \overline{X}_g.$$

Similarly the difference between the actual earnings of private sector workers $\Sigma \beta_c \overline{X}_c$ and this hypothetical earnings is the amount due to different endowments, since the pay structures are the same. That is,

$$\Sigma (\overline{X}_g - \overline{X}_c)\beta_c = \Sigma \beta_c \overline{X}_g - \Sigma \beta_c \overline{X}_c.$$

EMPIRICAL RESULTS FOR MALES

Earnings Equations for Public and Private Sectors for Males

Table 1.1 presents the results of the estimated earnings equations for males; Table 1.2 gives the t- and F-statistics for these equations, the F-statistics being the appropriate test for a variable represented by more than one regressor, as is the case with many of the categorical variables and with the quadratic education and experience variables. As the table indicates, the F-statistics were always significant indicating that each of these wage-determining variables, represented by more than one regressor, was a statistically significant predictor of changes in earnings in each of the public and private sectors. The (untabulated) F-statistics on the overall relationship were 60.70 for the public and 86.15 for the private sector, indicating that in both sectors the set of wage-determining variables were significant predictors of changes in earnings. A Chow test on the equality of the slope coefficients in the public and private sectors resulted in a statistically significant F-statistic of 5.17 indicating that the underlying wage determination process, as indicated by the slope coefficients, is different in the two sectors.

Decomposition of Public-Private Earnings Differentials for Males

Based on these estimated earnings equations, average male earnings, in logarithmic terms, are 9.0647 (i.e. $\Sigma \overline{X}_g \beta_g$) in the public sector and 8.9756 (i.e. $\Sigma \overline{X}_c \beta_c$) in the private sector, for a difference of 0.0891 in favour of public sector male workers. In dollar terms this translates into an average earnings figure of $8,645 (i.e. antilog 9.0647) in the public sector, and $7,908 (i.e. antilog 8.9756) in the private sector, for a difference of $737 or 9.3 per cent in favour of the public sector. This gross or unadjusted difference reflects differences in both the endowments (explanatory variables) and the pay structure (regression coefficients) between the public and private sectors.

If both public and private sector workers had the same pay structure — in this case the private sector pay structure, since this represents the private sector

TABLE 1.1

EARNINGS EQUATION FOR PUBLIC-PRIVATE SECTORS FOR MALES, 1971[1]

Variable Name[2]	Public[3]			Private[4]		
	Mean $\bar{X}_g$	Coefficient β_g	Change in Earnings[5]	Mean $\bar{X}_c$	Coefficient β_c	Change in Earnings[5]
Constant	1.000	8.1177	70,178	1.000	7.5422	59,644
Education[6]	11.813	−0.0135	412	10.580	0.0500	298
Education squared	153.060	0.0021		114.490	0.0002	
Experience[7]	23.319	0.0230	61	23.565	0.0416	69
Experience squared	712.550	−0.0005		727.690	−0.0006	
Education—Experience Interaction[8]	255.800	0.0005	4	219.860	−0.0007	−5
(Untrained) Trained[9]	0.2335	0.0138	119	0.2167	0.0315	249
(Single) Married	0.8466	0.1644	1,421	0.8471	0.1660	1,312
Other	0.0504	0.1515	1,310	0.0378	0.1549	1,225
(English) French	0.0571	−0.1047	−905	0.0921	−0.0987	−780
Bilingual	0.2587	−0.0135	−117	0.1969	0.0121	96
Neither	0.0006	−0.7627	−6,594	0.0086	−0.2671	−2,112
(Rural)[10] Town	0.1814	0.0685	592	0.1785	0.0689	544
City	0.7184	0.1014	877	0.7227	0.0935	740
(Maritimes)[11] Quebec	0.2156	0.1093	945	0.2669	0.1294	1,023
Ontario	0.4233	0.0941	814	0.5387	0.1571	1,242
Prairies	0.1725	−0.0081	−70	0.0741	0.0689	545
Br. Columbia	0.0890	0.0542	469	0.0821	0.2021	1,598

(Hours 35-39)[12]					
Hours 40-44	0.5627	-0.0405	-350	0.8207	0.0045	36
(Clerical)					
Manager	0.2256	0.2745	2,373	0.0674	0.3071	2,428
Science, Engineering, Mathematics	0.1321	0.2112	1,825	0.0905	0.1905	1,506
Social Science	0.0280	0.0888	768	0.0029	0.2837	2,243
Teaching	0.0123	0.0864	747	0.0004	-0.1358	-1,074
Health	0.0118	0.2893	2,501	0.0025	0.0655	518
Art, Recreation	0.0095	-0.0742	-642	0.0088	0.1793	1,418
Sales	0.0106	0.2192	1,895	0.0798	0.1508	1,193
Service	0.2895	0.2238	1,934	0.0268	-0.1155	-913
Processing	0.0028	-0.0418	-362	0.2024	0.0719	569
Assembly	0.0577	0.1415	1,224	0.3623	0.0409	324
Transportation Equipment	0.0470	0.1852	1,601	0.0302	0.0021	17

Source: Computed from data from the individual file of the Public Use Sample Tapes of the 1971 Census. Responsibility for the use and interpretation of these data rests solely with the author.

Notes:

[1] Sample size is 1,786 for the public sector and 4,897 for the private sector. R^2 is 0.50 for the public and 0.34 for the private sector. The dependent variable is the natural logarithm of annual earnings. The mean values in logarithmic form are 9.0647 for the public and 8.9756 for the private sector. The corresponding dollar values (antilogs) are $8,645 for the public and $7,908 for the private sector.

[2] The reference group for categorical variables is indicated in parenthesis.

[3] The public sector is the public administration and defence industry. However since only civilians working for pay or profit were included in the sample, then the only defence personnel would be civilians in the defence industry.

[4] Manufacturing industry.

[5] Marginal effect on average earnings of a unit change in the explanatory variable (i.e. $\partial y / \partial x = \beta y$ as explained earlier in footnote three). Here the regression coefficients are multiplied by the mean earnings of $8,645 in public and $7,908 in private sectors. Quadratic variables and interactions were evaluated at their means.

Notes to Table 1.1 continued on p. 8.

TABLE 1.1

EARNINGS EQUATION FOR PUBLIC-PRIVATE SECTORS FOR MALES, 1971

Notes — *continued*

6 Education in years of schooling. When the original data was coded in categorical form, this was converted to continuous form by assigning the midpoint of the category. For persons who attended the following university categories, the conversion to continuous years of education were: one to two years university = 14.5 years education (i.e. 1.5 years beyond grade 13, whether they had grade 13 or not); three to four years university without a degree = 15 years; three to four years university with degree = 16.5 years; five or more years university without a degree = 17 years; and five or more years university with a degree = 20 years.

7 Experience is defined as age minus education minus six, and it is restricted to nonnegative numbers.

8 Education multiplied by experience.

9 Completed a full-time vocational course.

10 Place of residence where rural was defined as rural non-farm (farm residence was excluded from the subsample), town was defined as urban under 30,000 population, and city was defined as over 30,000 population.

11 Maritimes does not include Prince Edward Island since sample data from here was unavailable to preserve confidentiality. Data from the Yukon and Northwest Territories were similarly excluded.

12 Number of hours per week usually worked in the reported job.

TABLE 1.2

t- AND F- STATISTICS FOR MALE EARNINGS EQUATIONS

Variable Name	Public		Private	
	t-Statistic	F-Statistic	t-Statistic	F-Statistic
Constant	57.61	—	85.64**	—
Education	−0.86	131**	4.72**	138**
Education squared	4.59**		0.62	
Experience	5.26**	80**	13.61**	157**
Experience squared	−9.65**		−15.98**	
Education-Experience				
Interaction	2.44*	—	−4.13**	—
(Untrained)				
Trained	0.86	—	2.61**	—
(Single)				
Married	7.01**	24**	9.97**	49**
Other	4.05**		5.28**	
(English)				
French	−2.74**	5**	−4.14**	17*
Bilingual	−0.63		0.75	
Neither	−2.75**		−5.05**	
(Rural)				
Town	2.62	10**	3.61**	16*
City	4.45**		5.59**	
(Maritimes)				
Quebec	3.44**	10**	4.39**	17**
Ontario	4.00**		6.09**	
Prairies	−0.31		2.25*	
Br. Columbia	1.77		6.78**	
(Hours 35-39)				
Hours 40-44	−2.42*	—	0.32	—
(Clerical)				
Manager	12.38**	17**	13.09**	23**
Science, Engineering,				
Mathematics	8.16**		8.63**	
Social Science	2.04*		3.13**	
Teaching	1.40		−0.57	
Health	4.45**		0.67	
Art, Recreation	−1.07		3.38**	
Sales	3.32**		6.91**	
Service	10.03**		−3.51**	
Processing	−0.33		3.98**	
Assembly	4.25**		2.48*	
Transportation Equipment	5.19**		0.07	

Note: **denotes significance at the 0.01 level and * at the 0.05 level.

comparability that is so often used as a criterion for public sector wage determination — then the earnings of public sector male workers would be only 9.0062 (i.e. $\Sigma \bar{X}_g \beta_c$) in logarithmic terms and $8,153 in dollar terms. Thus, if public sector workers were paid according to the pay structure of the private sector, their earnings would be reduced by $492 which is 6.2 per cent of private sector earnings. The remaining differential of $245 or 3.1 per cent in favour of public sector workers is due to their superior endowments of wage-determining characteristics.

In summary, the average earnings differential is approximately $737 or nine per cent in favour of public sector male workers. Approximately $245 or one-third of that may be attributed to their superior endowments of wage-determining characteristics, and $492, or two-thirds, may be attributed to their being paid higher wages for the same characteristics. Thus, the pure earnings advantage for males in the public sector, adjusted for differences in the wage-determining characteristics of the workers in the two sectors, is approximately $492 or six per cent.[6]

Relative Contribution of Variables to the Earnings Differential for Males

Table 1.3 gives the relative contribution of each of the variables in explaining the public-private earnings differential. Columns 1 and 2 express that contribution in units of the logarithm of earnings and columns 3 and 4 express the relative contributions as a per cent of the overall differential of 0.08907 in logarithmic terms. A positive entry indicates an advantage in favour of the public sector (and hence a positive contribution to the overall differential); a negative entry indicates an advantage in favour of the private sector. Obviously, the contribution of a variable can be larger than the overall differential itself, since the various factors can offset each other.

As the last row indicates, the overall differential in logarithmic terms is 0.08907 in favour of public sector workers. Of that differential, 0.03058 (column 1) or 34.3 per cent (column 3) can be attributed to the superior endowments — superior in the sense that they are associated with higher earnings — of public sector workers, and 0.05849 (column 2) or 65.7 per cent (column 4) can be attributed to a pure public sector wage advantage associated with the pay structure.

Of the superior endowments of public sector workers, clearly their higher education is the most important factor. When evaluated according to the private sector reward system for years of education, the higher education of public sector workers results in a 0.07 increase in their (log of) earnings relative to private sector employees. This is a very large proportion (79 per cent, as given in column 3) of the overall earnings differential of 0.089. A small portion of this is reduced

---

[6] These results are summarized in tabular form later in Table 1.4 which also gives the comparable figures for females.

TABLE 1.3

RELATIVE CONTRIBUTION OF VARIABLES TO THE EARNINGS DIFFERENTIAL[1] FOR MALES

Variable[2]	Contribution of Each Variable to (Log) Earnings Differential		Contribution as Per cent of Total Differential of 0.08907	
	Endowments $(\overline{X}_g - \overline{X}_c)\beta_c$	Pay Structure $(\beta_g - \beta_c)\overline{X}_g$	Endowments[3]	Pay Structure[4]
	(1)	(2)	(3)	(4)
Constant	0	0.57550	0	646.12
Education	0.07016	−0.45573	78.77	−511.65
Experience	−0.00184	−0.37464	−2.07	−420.61
Education-Experience Interaction	−0.02372	0.29750	−26.63	334.01
Training	0.00053	−0.00412	0.60	−4.63
Marital Status	0.00187	−0.00148	2.10	−1.66
Language	0.00634	−0.00726	7.12	−8.15
Residence	−0.00020	0.00559	−0.22	6.28
Province	−0.01660	−0.05744	−18.64	−64.49
Hours Worked	−0.00116	−0.02532	−1.30	−28.43
Occupation	−0.00480	−0.10589	−5.39	118.88
Total	0.03058	−0.05849	34.3	65.7
	0.08907		100.00	

Source: Calculated from regression coefficients (β's) and mean values of explanatory variables ($\overline{X}$'s) in Table 1.1. See text for a discussion of the decomposition technique.

Notes:

[1] As indicated at the bottom of the table, the overall differential in (log of) earnings is 0.08907 in favour of the public sector.

[2] See Table 1.1 for definition of the variable names.

[3] Column 1 divided by 0.08907.

[4] Column 2 divided by 0.08907.

by the negative education and experience interaction; nevertheless, the general conclusion remains that the greater education of public sector workers explains a large portion of their overall earnings advantage.

Most of the other endowment differences are small in comparison to the education factor, and, in fact, they are usually in favour of workers in the private sector. Thus, our earlier statement that approximately one-third of the overall public sector earnings advantage can be attributed to their superior endowments of wage determining characteristics, while still true, should be tempered with the caveat that this comes about largely because of the higher education of public sector workers.

With respect to differences in the pay structure between the two sectors (columns 2 and 4), the education variable, by itself, makes a large and negative contribution, indicating that the private sector tends to reward education much more than does the public sector. Although public sector male workers have a larger endowment of education, this is offset by a smaller premium for that education. Thus, the combined impact actually results in the education variable contributing negatively (0.07016 - 0.45573=−0.38557) to the overall public sector wage advantage. Alternatively stated, if both sectors had the same average education and the same returns to that education, the public sector earnings advantage would be considerably larger than it is: its small magnitude is due in large part to the fact that the public sector does not pay the private sector premium for education.

The experience variable also indicates that the private sector places a larger premium on experience and that the overall public sector earnings advantage would be considerably larger were this not the case. The exact impact of the experience variable — as with the education variable — is difficult to evaluate because of the education and experience interaction term. The large positive number for the interaction term illustrates that the public sector does pay a higher premium than does the private sector, for workers who have both high education *and* considerable experience, even though the public sector pays less for each of these components separately.

This may reflect the nature of the labour requirements of the two sectors, with education and experience being more complementary in the public sector and more in the nature of substitutes in the private sector; such would be the case, for example, if the public sector places a premium on personnel having both formal education *and* 'knowing the ropes and the in-and-outs' of the civil service. Alternatively, it may reflect the willingness of the public sector to pay for that rare combination of *both* high formal education and lengthy labour market experience, even if it is not valued so highly in the private sector.

Differences in the constant terms are also large indicating a large public sector earnings advantage not associated with differences in rewards for the possession of various endowments. While it is tempting to interpret differences in the constant terms as indicative of a public-private sector 'pure' wage differential — pure in the sense of being independent of the returns to education, experience, etc. — this interpretation is deceptive. As the decomposition of the overall earnings differential indicated, the pure wage advantage of the public sector is the result of *all* differences in the pay structure — that is, the differences in the regression coefficients, both slopes and intercepts. In terms of regression analysis, slopes and intercepts are interdependent, since the intercept is simply an adjustment factor to ensure that the mean of the dependent variable is equal to the mean of the explanatory variables plus the intercept. The actual magnitude of the constant term itself has little meaning, since the explanatory variables, with the exception of the categorical ones, do not have observations with zero values.

Differences in the intercept terms, of course, do have meaning since they indicate a constant earnings differential throughout the structure. Yet this constant earnings differential does not arise in a vacuum — independent of the wage determination process as indicated by the slope coefficients. The wage determination process is a complex interaction resulting in different premiums being paid for different factors, and adjustments being made to offset other anomalies.

For example, the larger constant term in the public sector may reflect an adjustment factor to compensate for the lower premium it pays for higher education or experience. Thus, highly educated or experienced workers in the two sectors may receive comparable earnings, even though the public sector compensation policy is blunter or more egalitarian in the sense that it does not differentiate its payments as much for differences in wage-determining characteristics. This may occur because of political pressure to follow an egalitarian wage policy — as for example in a national pay scale or a social minimum wage — or it may occur because of less market pressure to follow a compensation policy that pays according to productivity-related characteristics.

Whatever the reason, it appears that the government follows a more egalitarian compensation policy, not matching the private sector with respect to its rewards for *each* wage determining characteristic, but matching (and in fact surpassing) the private sector overall with respect to the combination of *all* wage-determining factors. It does match the private sector, however, by the payment of the constant wage premium irrespective of the wage-determining characteristics of its employees.

This has implications for the quality of public recruitment; it suggests that workers with low wage-determining characteristics will be especially interested in vying for public sector jobs to receive the constant wage premium. The more skilled workers, on the other hand, will be less interested in public sector employment since this constant wage premium may be offset by the fact that the public sector does not pay much of a premium for their high level of wage-determining characteristics. This potential problem in efficiency of recruitment must be recognized by any public sector employer that follows an egalitarian wage policy. Simply stated, the impression is that the public sector wage structure — which may be a desirable element of social policy — may create recruitment problems at the upper end of the earnings structure and job-rationing problems at the lower end.

Further Inferences from the Empirical Results for Males

The separate entries of Table 1.1 give a more detailed picture of the wage determination process in each sector. For example, marginal returns[7] to an

---

[7] As Appendix 1.1 illustrates, the marginal return to education is calculated as $RE = (\partial y/\partial E)/y = \beta_1 + 2\beta_2 E + \beta_5 X$ where β_1 is the regression coefficient for education, β_2 for education squared and β_5 for the education and experience interaction term. Evaluating this for the regression coefficients and mean values of education and experience as given in Table 1.1 yields: $RE_g = -0.01374 + 2(0.0021395)11.813 + 0.000503(23.319) = 0.0488$ in the public sector and $RE_c = 0.049957 + 2(0.00022244)10.58 - 0.00066011(23.565) - 0.0391$ in the private sector. When the interaction terms are omitted, for those with no experience (i.e. X equals zero), then the returns are 0.03707 in the public and 0.05447 in the private sector.

additional year of education are 4.88 per cent in the public sector and 3.91 per cent in the private sector. This implies an annual return of $422 (i.e. 0.04880 multiplied by $8,645) for the average public sector worker and $308 (i.e. 0.0391 multiplied by $7,908) for the average private sector worker.[8] However, much of this larger impact for public sector workers comes about because of the public sector premium for persons having *both* high education and experience. The marginal returns to education by itself, for persons with no labour market experience, (i.e. with the interaction term equal to zero, since X equals zero) are 3.7 per cent in the public sector and 5.4 per cent in the private sector. This is why, as illustrated in Table 1.3, the greater endowment of education of public sector workers contributes positively to the overall public sector earnings advantage, but then lower returns to education by itself contribute negatively. It also illustrates the operation of the more egalitarian compensation policy followed in the public sector: increments to education generally are not rewarded as much in the public sector as in the private sector. The fact that a public sector earnings advantage still prevails, on average, is a result of a public-sector wage premium that is not associated with rewards for the possession of wage-determining characteristics.

This is confirmed by the fact that the public sector also does not pay as high a premium for labour market experience as does the private sector. Evaluated at the average level of experience in the two sectors, the marginal returns[9] to a year of experience in the public sector are 0.0069 or $60 for the average public sector worker, and 0.0087 or $69 for the average private sector worker. Cumulated over a number of years, these differences in returns to experience can be a substantial amount, as illustrated by the large and negative impact of the differences in returns to experience in Table 1.3. As with the education variable, the public sector does not pay as large a premium for labour market experience as does the private sector. However, the overall earnings advantage of the public sector persists in spite of the failure of the public sector to match private sector returns to education or experience. The public sector earnings advantage is the result of a premium not explicitly associated with rewards for the possession of wage-determining characteristics.

While the education and labour market experience variables illustrate this phenomenon most dramatically, it is also prevalent for other wage-determining variables. Having completed a full-time training course yields a 3.15 per cent increase in earnings or $249 in the private sector, but only a 1.38 per cent increase in earnings or $119 in the public sector. Being bilingual as opposed to

---

[8] The calculations given in the text differ slightly from those displayed in the 'Change in Earnings' columns of Table 1.1, because of rounding (in the table).

[9] This is calculated in the same fashion as the marginal return to education as given in Appendix 1.1. That is, the return to experience is $RX = (\partial y/\partial x)/y = \beta_3 + 2\beta_4 X + \beta_5 E$, where β_3 is the regression coefficient for experience, β_4 for experience squared and β_5 for the education and experience interaction term. Evaluating this for the regression coefficients and mean values of education and experience as given in Table 1.1 yields for the public and private sector, respectively: $RX_g = 0.023022 - 2(0.0004724)23.319 + 0.000503(11.83) = 0.006931$ and $RX_c = 0.041624 + 2(-0.00055542)23.565 - 0.0006601(10.158) = 0.008743$.

knowing only English yields a 1.21 per cent or $96 increase in earnings in the private sector, but a *decrease* of 1.35 per cent or $117 in the public sector. The fact that bilingual workers in the public sector earn less than those who speak only English, even when other wage-determining factors are controlled for, is particularly surprising given the government policy of encouraging bilingualism.[10] Certainly in the private sector it is regarded as a positive attribute and rewarded accordingly; however, the return is not high — less than one half the return for completing a full-time vocational training program, and less than one-third the return from acquiring an additional year of formal education.

The observation that the public sector tends to pay its earnings premium by a constant earnings mark-up rather than by granting greater-than-competitive returns to the acquisition of positive wage-generating characteristics, is further illustrated by the calculation of earnings for hypothetical skilled and unskilled males in both the private and public sectors.[11] An unskilled male worker with eight years of education and ten years of experience and no training, and who is single, speaks English only, lives in a rural community in the Maritimes, and works 30 to 35 hours per week in a clerical job would have earned $4,290 (i.e. antilog 8.3641) in the public sector and $3,847 (i.e. antilog 8.255) in the private sector; the public sector worker has an earnings advantage of $443 or 11.5 per cent over his private sector counterpart with the same characteristics. Conversely, a skilled worker with 17 years of education, 30 years of experience, and who is trained, married, bilingual, lives in a city in Ontario, and works 40 to 44 hours per week as a manager would have earned $14,535 (i.e. antilog 9.5843) in the public sector and $14,369 (i.e. antilog 9.5728) in the private sector; the public sector worker has an earnings advantage of only $166 or one per cent over his private sector counterpart with the same skilled characteristics.

Clearly the public sector earnings advantage is greatest at low skill levels for persons with low wage-generating characteristics. In our calculations the public sector pure wage advantage for males of the same characteristics ranged from approximately 12 per cent for unskilled workers, to six per cent for average workers[12], to one per cent for skilled workers.

EMPIRICAL RESULTS FOR FEMALES

Decomposition of Public-Private Earnings Differential for Females

For females, based on the earnings equation presented later in Table 1.6, average earnings in logarithmic terms are 8.5987 (i.e. $\Sigma \, \beta_g \overline{X}_g$) in the public

---

[10] The (weak) negative impact of bilingual facility on public sector earnings may reflect a failure to control for the nature of education of bilingual workers, who may have received a 'classical' education that is not labour-market oriented. In addition, since our data groups the three levels of government, the impact of a *federal* policy to reward bilingual facility may be offset by the pay structures of the other governments.

[11] Calculated earnings are simply the sum of the regression coefficients of Table 1.1 times the value of the explanatory variables corresponding to the hypothetical worker.

[12] This is the pure earnings advantage for males in the public sector as calculated in the section on the decomposition of public-private earnings differentials for males.

sector and 8.3974 (i.e. $\Sigma \beta_c \overline{X}_c$) in the private sector, for a difference of 0.2013 in favour of the public sector. In dollar terms, this translates into an average earnings figure of $5,425 in the public sector and $4,436 in the private sector for a difference of $989 or 22.3 per cent in favour of the public sector. This unadjusted public sector earnings advantage for females reflects differences in both the endowments of workers and the pay structure between the public and private sectors.

If females in the public sector were paid according to the same pay structure as females in the private sector, their earnings would be only 8.5255 (i.e. $\Sigma \beta_c \overline{X}_g$) in logarithmic terms, which translate into $5,042 in dollar terms. This is $383 less than their actual average earnings of $5,425, and it represents a surplus payment of 8.6 per cent over the earnings of private sector workers. The remaining differential of $606, or 13.7 per cent, in favour of public sector females is due to their superior endowments of wage-determining characteristics.

In summary, for females, the average earnings differential is approximately $989 or 22.3 per cent in favour of public sector workers. Approximately $606 or almost two-thirds of that differential may be attributed to their superior endowments of wage-determining characteristics, and $383, or slightly over one-third, may be attributed to their being paid higher wages for the same characteristics. Thus, the pure earnings advantage for females in the public sector, adjusted for the wage-determining characteristics of the workers in the two sectors, is approximately $383, which is 8.6 per cent in excess of that of their private sector counterparts.

These results are summarized in Table 1.4 which also gives the comparable figures for males. In the public sector, both males and females have greater endowments of wage-determining characteristics than workers in the private sector. For males, these endowments account for approximately one-third of the overall earnings differential and differences in the pay structure account for approximately two-thirds of the overall differential of $737 or 9.3 per cent. For females, the weights are reversed, with superior endowments accounting for approximately two-thirds and differences in pay only one-third of the overall differential of $989 or 22.3 per cent. Thus while the overall public sector earnings advantage is larger for females, more of it is accounted for by their superior endowment of wage-determining characteristics. Both sexes in the public sector receive an economic rent or surplus payment relative to the private sector counterparts with the same wage-determining characteristics. For males, this surplus is $492 or 6.2 per cent in excess of their private sector counterparts; for females the surplus is $383 or 8.6 per cent in excess of their private sector counterparts.

The larger percentage surplus for females in the public sector is consistent with the hypothesis that the public sector engages in less wage discrimination than do private sector employers. The substantially lower earnings of females relative to males in either the private or public sectors, however, suggests that substantial discrimination prevails in all sectors.

TABLE 1.4

PUBLIC SECTOR EARNINGS ADVANTAGE AND ITS DECOMPOSITION

	Overall Differential	Amount Attributed To Endowments	Surplus
Males			
Dollar Advantage	737	245	492
As per cent of private earnings	9.3	3.1	6.2
As per cent of overall differential	100.0	33.4	66.6
Females			
Dollar Advantage	989	606	383
As per cent of private earnings	22.3	13.7	8.6
As per cent of overall differential	100.0	61.3	38.7

Source: Calculated from regression results reported in Tales 1.1 and 1.6.

Relative Contribution of Variables to the Earnings Differential for Females

As Table 1.5 indicates, the relative contributions of the different variables follows a pattern for females that tends to be similar to that of males. Females in the public sector have a larger endowment of education than females in the private sector, and this accounts for a large portion of the impact of their superior endowments of wage-determining characteristics. The only other endowment factor that accounts for a substantial portion of their earnings advantage is their occupational distribution: females in the public sector (unlike males) have an occupational distribution that yields higher earnings than the occupational distribution of females in the private sector.

To a certain extent this more favourable occupational dsitribution could reflect a rent or surplus just as do higher wages for the same characteristics. That is, the public sector may pay higher earnings by placing their employees into higher occupational groups than these same employees would be placed into if they were in the private sector. These employees would thereby receive a surplus payment by virtue of their excessively-high occupational classification, even if they received the same earnings as workers in the private sector in that same occupational classification.

While the more favourable occupational distribution of females in the public sector creates the *possibility* that some of this is an economic surplus, in reality the magnitude of this additional rent is probably small or nonexistent. An examination of the proportion of public and private sector females in each

TABLE 1.5

RELATIVE CONTRIBUTION OF VARIABLES TO THE EARNINGS DIFFERENTIAL[1] FOR FEMALES

Variable[2]	Contribution of Each Variable to (Log) Earnings Differential		Contribution as Per cent of Total Differential of 0.20119	
	Endowments $(\overline{X}_g - \overline{X}_c)\beta_c$ (1)	Pay Structure $(\beta_g - \beta_c)\overline{X}_g$ (2)	Endowments[3] (3)	Pay Structure[4] (4)
Constant	0	0.73980	0	367.71
Education	0.09635	−0.64537	47.89	−320.78
Experience	−0.01481	−0.20918	−7.36	−103.47
Education-Experience Interaction	−0.02588	0.25223	−12.86	125.37
Training	0.00731	−0.01784	3.63	−8.87
Marital Status	0.00209	−0.00389	1.04	−1.93
Language	0.01987	−0.00020	9.88	−0.10
Residence	0.00111	−0.02091	0.55	−10.39
Province	−0.02945	0.00054	−14.64	0.27
Hours Worked	0.01074	−0.03335	5.34	−16.58
Occupation	0.06063	0.01140	30.13	5.67
Total	0.12796	0.07323	63.60	36.40
	0.20119		100.0	

Source: Calculated from regression coefficients (β's) and mean values of explanatory variables ($\overline{X}$'s) in Table 1.6. See text for a discussion of the decomposition technique.

Notes:

[1] As indicated at the bottom of the table, the overall differential in (log of) earnings is 0.20119 in favour of the public sector.
[2] See Table 1.1 for definition of the variable names.
[3] Column 1 divided by 0.20119.
[4] Column 2 divided by 0.20119.

category (the mean X's for the occupation variable) indicates that the occupational distributions reflect the nature of the work done in the two sectors. Thus, the private sector has a large proportion of females in the low-wage assembly and processing occupations, and this accounts for a large portion of their less favourable occupational distribution.[13] In addition, the occupational groupings that are utilized in the census data are so broad that it is unlikely that people would be categorized into higher groupings, as opposed to being given an

---

[13] Conversely, the public sector has proportionately more females in the managerial, science-engineering-mathematics, and social science groups. Some part of this may reflect deliberate over-classification; more likely it reflects the true nature of labour demands in the public sector. It may also reflect the possibility that the public sector does not engage in as much occupational discrimination against women as does the private sector.

excessively high grade (and hence wage) within a broad category: this latter type of economic surplus is already captured by the earnings premium or excessive pay structure associated with public sector employment, since excessive occupational ranking *within* the broad occupational categories is not controlled for. For these reasons, it is unlikely that much — if any — of the more favourable occupational distribution of females in the public sector reflects a classification surplus additional to the earnings premium associated with the public sector pay-structure itself.[14]

As was the case for males, the pure pay advantage associated with being in the public sector for females (column 2 of Table 1.5) is dominated by the large impact of the differences in the constant terms. This offsets the negative impact of the lower return in the public sector for such factors as education or training. In other words, the pure pay advantage in the public sector occurs because of the payment of a constant premium rather than the payment of excessive returns for the acquisition of positive wage-generating characteristics.

Earnings Equations for Public and Private Sectors for Females

A Chow test on the equality of the slope coefficients resulted in a calculated F-statistic of a statistically significant 12.40 for females, indicating that the underlying wage determination process, as given by the slope coefficients, is different in the public and private sectors. The fact that the Chow statistic is larger for females than for males (5.17 for males) also illustrates that the difference in the underlying wage determination process between the private and public sectors is greater for females than for males — an observation that is consistent with the larger 'surplus' in female public sector wages, noted above.

The tendency of the public sector to pay its wage premium through a constant wage advantage rather than through excessive returns for the acquisition of human capital is further illustrated in the data of Table 1.6. As the column of mean values indicates, relative to females in the private sector, females in the public sector have considerably more education, almost as much labour market experience, and they have a much higher proportion who are trained and bilingual. However, their returns for these human capital characteristics tend to be lower than in the private sector.

For example, for the average female worker, marginal returns to education[15] are 3.5 per cent in the public sector and 3.3 per cent in the private sector. Much of this high return in the public sector, however, comes about because of the positive interaction effect of education and experience. When this

---

[14] An additional consideration that reinforces this conclusion is that census occupational slots are derived from the response of the enumerated individuals, rather than from objective classification schemes of employers.

[15] As illustrated in Appendix 1.1, marginal returns to education are: $RE_g = 0.06056 + 2(0.003656)11.819 + 0.000475(20.237) = 0.0353$ in the public sector, and $RE_c = 0.0272 + 2(0.00096)9.75 - 0.00062(20.865) = 0.0329$ in the private sector. When the interaction terms are omitted, for those with no experience (i.e. X equals zero), the returns are 0.02586 in the public and 0.04592 in the private sector.

TABLE 1.6

EARNINGS EQUATION FOR PUBLIC-PRIVATE SECTORS FOR FEMALES, 1971[1]

Variable Name[2]	Public[3]			Private[4]		
	Mean $\overline{X}_g$	Coefficient β_g	Change in Earnings[5]	Mean $\overline{X}_c$	Coefficient β_c	Change in Earnings[5]
Constant	1.000	8.3984	45,561	1.000	7.6586	33,974
Education[6]	11.819	-0.0606	191	9.750	0.0272	146
Education squared	145.230	0.0037	54	103.440	0.0010	35
Experience[7]	20.237	0.0169		20.865	0.0285	
Experience squared	614.020	-0.0003		622.820	-0.0004	
Education-Experience Interaction[8]	230.140	0.0005	3	188.460	-0.0006	-3
(Untrained)						
Trained[9]	0.2319	-0.0101	-55	0.1224	0.0668	296
(Single)						
Married	0.5212	-0.0473	-256	0.5724	-0.0401	-178
Other	0.1337	-0.0483	-262	0.1345	-0.0471	-209
(English)						
French	0.0300	-0.1660	-901	0.1295	-0.1306	-579
Bilingual	0.2101	-0.0048	-26	0.1677	-0.0088	-39
Neither	0.0000	0.0000	—	0.0318	-0.2281	-1,012
(Rural)[10]						
Town	0.1201	0.0142	77	0.1479	0.0159	70
City	0.8049	0.0340	217	0.7813	0.0657	291
(Maritimes)[11]						
Quebec	0.1282	0.2169	1,177	0.3072	0.1533	680
Ontario	0.5102	0.1772	961	0.5556	0.1797	797
Prairies	0.1965	0.0109	59	0.0644	0.0041	18
Br. Columbia	0.0791	0.0802	435	0.0474	0.1770	785

(Hours 35-39)[12]					
Hours 40-44	0.3342	-0.1388	-753	0.6093	-0.0390	-173
(Clerical)					
Manager	0.0723	0.2698	1,463	0.0269	0.2556	1,134
Science, Engineering, Mathematics	0.0246	0.3045	1,652	0.0142	0.1632	724
Social Science	0.0355	0.2217	1,203	0.0021	0.1439	638
Teaching	0.0191	0.1509	819	0.0014	0.3695	1,639
Health	0.0546	0.1870	1,015	0.0078	0.1202	533
Art, Recreation	0.0068	0.3550	1,926	0.0134	0.2648	1,175
Sales	0.0041	-0.2298	-1,247	0.0212	-0.0136	-60
Service	0.0559	0.0304	165	0.0156	-0.0756	-335
Processing	0.0014	-0.2689	-1,459	0.1118	0.0220	98
Assembly	0.0014	-0.5286	-2,867	0.3156	-0.1201	-533
Transportation Equipment	0.0000	0.0000	—	0.0007	0.5442	2,414

Source: Computed from data from the individual file of the Public Use Sample Tapes of the 1971 Census. Responsibility for the use and interpretation of these data rests solely with the author.

Notes:

[1] Sample size is 733 for the public sector and 1,413 for the private sector. R^2 is 0.35 for the public and 0.25 for the private sector. The dependent variable is the natural logarithm of hourly earnings. The mean values in logarithmic form are 8.4987 for the public and 8.3974 for the private sector. The corresponding dollar values (antilogs) are $5,425 and $4,436.

[2] The reference group for categorical variables is indicated in parenthesis.

[3] to [12] As the equivalently numbered notes to Table 1.1. With respect to note five, in these columns the regression coefficients are multiplied by the mean earnings, for females, of $5,425 in the public and $4,436 in the private sector.

TABLE 1.7

t- AND F-STATISTICS FOR FEMALE EARNINGS EQUATIONS

Variable Name	Public		Private	
	t-Statistic	F-Statistic	t-Statistic	F-Statistic
Constant	27.69**	—	49.93**	—
Education	−1.53	14**	1.35	20**
Education squared	2.72**		1.20	
Experience	0.27*	28**	5.81**	31**
Experience squared	−3.92**		−6.20**	
Education-Experience Interaction	1.05	—	−2.15*	—
(Untrained)				
Trained	−0.33	—	2.44*	—
(Single)				
Married	−1.59	1.35	−1.87	2
Other	−1.08		−1.55	
(English)				
French	−1.76	1.16	−3.31**	9**
Bilingual	−0.12		−0.28	
Neither	—		−4.19**	
(Rural)				
Town	0.23	0.45	0.40	3.34**
City	0.79		1.91	
(Maritimes)				
Quebec	3.14**	7.74**	2.54	8.01**
Ontario	3.65**		3.21**	
Prairies	0.21		0.06	
Br. Columbia	1.24		2.61**	
(Hours 35-39)				
Hours 40-44	−4.68**	—	−2.00	—
(Clerical)				
Manager	5.06**	4.30**	4.72**	7.41**
Science, Engineering, Mathematics	3.49**		2.20*	
Social Science	2.97**		0.77	
Teaching	1.54		1.62	
Health	3.14**		1.21	
Art, Recreation	2.22**		3.45**	
Sales	−1.14		−0.22	
Service	0.50		−1.04	
Processing	−0.75		0.67	
Assembly	−1.49		−4.80**	
Transportation Equipment	—		1.68	

Note: ** denotes significance at the 0.01 level and * at the 0.05 level.

interaction effect is omitted, and the returns are calculated for education alone, for those with no labour market experience, the returns drop to 2.6 per cent in the public sector and rise to 4.6 per cent in the private sector. In addition, the returns in the public sector would be even lower if they were calculated on the basis of the same average education of 9.75 years that was used in calculating the private sector returns: specifically, the public sector return to education would be two per cent when the education-experience interaction was included, and only 1.1 per cent without the interaction term. The returns to education, as such, for females are greater in the private than in the public sector.

This is not contradicted by the large dollar return of $191 (i.e. 0.0353 multiplied by $5,425) associated with an additional year of education for the average public sector worker, compared to $146 (i.e. 0.0329 multiplied by $4,436) for the average private sector worker. The large dollar return for the public sector worker occurs because of the larger base of $5,425 from which it was calculated, and because of the positive interaction effect of education and experience as well as the higher average level of education in the public sector from which the return was evaluated. When the public and private sector returns, respectively, are evaluated at the mean level of education and mean income of private sector workers they amount to $90 (i.e. 0.02033 multiplied by $4,436) and $146 (i.e. 0.0329 miltiplied by $4,436) with the interaction term, and $115 (i.e. 0.02586 multiplied by $4,436) and $204 (i.e. 0.04592 multiplied by $4,436) with no interaction term, that is for education alone. When evaluated on a common basis the dollar returns to education are greater in the private than public sector.

The failure of the public sector to match the private sector with respect to the rewards given for the acquisition of human capital is further illustrated by the negative return to training in the public sector (compared to the 6.6 per cent in the private sector), and by the negative effect for being bilingual. The impact of being bilingual is negative in both sectors; however, the negative impact is larger in the public sector.

For females, the only area where the public sector tends to match the private sector in its payment for human capital is with respect to payments for experience. For the average female, marginal returns to experience[16] are approximately one per cent in the public sector and 0.8 per cent in the private sector. Again, however, much of this higher return to experience in the public sector comes about because of the interaction effect of having both high education and experience.

The calculation of earnings for hypothetical skilled and unskilled females, in both sectors[17], illustrates that the public sector earnings advantage is greatest

---

[16] From Appendix 1.1, marginal returns to experience are: $RX_g = 0.016936 - 2(0.00031235)20.37 + 0.00047532(11.819) = 0.0099$ and $RX_c = 0.028547 - 2(0.00035372)20.865 - 0.00062093(9.7523) = 0.0077$.
[17] Calculated earnings are simply the sum of the regression coefficients of Table 1.6 times the value of the explanatory variables corresponding to the hypothetical worker.

at low skill levels. An unskilled female worker with eight years of education, ten years of experience and no training, and who is single, speaks English only, lives in a rural community in the Maritimes and works 30 to 35 hours per week in a clerical job would earn $4,144 (i.e. antilog 8.3294) in the public sector and $3,419 (i.e. antilog 8.1372) in the private sector; the public sector worker has an earnings advantage of $725 or 21.2 per cent over her private sector counterpart with the same characteristics. Conversely, a skilled female worker with 17 years of education, 30 years of experience, and who is trained, married, bilingual, lives in a city in Ontario and works 40 to 44 hours per week as a manager would have earned $10,032 (i.e. antilog 9.2135) in the public sector and $8,768 (i.e. antilog 9.0789) in the private sector; the public sector worker has an earnings advantage of $1,264 or 14.4 per cent over her private sector counterpart with the same characteristics. For the average public sector female worker, the earnings advantage[18] is $383 or 8.6 per cent over a private sector counterpart with the same characteristics.

Thus, in the case of females, the public sector percentage earnings advantage is greatest at low skill levels. However, it is also slightly higher at high skill levels than it is at the average skill level. This is in contrast to the pattern for males where the advantage declined continuously as the skill level increased. In the case of females, the large advantage at high skill levels occurs because of the higher returns to education and experience at very high levels of education and experience. If, for example, the hypothetical skilled female were to have 15 years of education and 20 years of experience, along with the other skilled characteristics defined earlier, the public sector would actually pay $221 or 2.7 per cent *less* than would the private sector.

In general, for both males and females the public sector percentage earnings advantage is greatest at the low skill levels, and it declines as the skill level increases. In the case of females, there is some evidence to suggest that the differential begins to widen slightly for persons with very high levels of education and experience.

SUMMARY AND POLICY ISSUES

Summary

A summary, by nature, glosses over the variety of problems that plague empirical work, including the estimation of earnings equations. The data are often imperfect, being too aggregative (e.g. the public sector and occupation variables), failing to control for quality (e.g. human capital variables), and at times simply not being available (e.g. non-wage aspects of employment including fringe benefits and working conditions). Alternative functional forms

---

[18] This is the pure earnings advantage for females in the public sector as calculated in the section on the decomposition of public-private earnings differentials for females.

of the estimating equation may give somewhat different results. In addition, the resulting estimates are simply 'point estimates' and are subject to the usual possibility of error that accompanies any statistical procedure. These qualifications should be kept in mind in interpreting the results now summarized.

Based on data from the 1971 Canadian census, average earnings for full-time full year male workers was $8,645 in the public (government) sector and $7,908 in the private (manufacturing) sector for a gross, or unadjusted, earnings difference of $737 or 9.3 per cent in favour of the public sector. Approximately $245 or one-third of that difference can be attributed to the superior wage-determining characteristics of public sector males, and $492 or two-thirds can be labelled an economic rent or surplus payment that arises because of the more generous pay structure given to public sector workers. If public sector workers were paid according to the same pay structures as private sector workers their average pay would be reduced by $492 to $8,153. Thus, for males in the public sector, the pure earnings advantage over their private sector counterparts of the same characteristics averages $492 or 6.2 per cent.

For females, average earnings were $5,425 in the public sector and $4,436 in the private sector for a difference of $989 or 22.3 per cent in favour of the public sector. Approximately $606 or slightly less than two-thirds of the difference can be attributed to the superior wage-generating endowments of females in the public sector, and $383 or slightly over one-third can be labelled a pure surplus arising because they are paid more for the same characteristics as their private sector counterparts. If females in the public sector were paid the same as their private sector counterparts the average earnings would fall by $383 to $5,042. Thus, the pure earnings advantage for females in the public sector is $383 or 8.6 per cent in excess of their private sector counterparts with the same characteristics.

In essence, while the overall unadjusted earnings differential in favour of public sector workers is substantial, especially in the case of females, much of it is accounted for by the superior endowments of wage-determining characteristics on the part of public sector workers. This is especially the case for females. Even after these wage-determining characteristics are controlled for, however, a substantial pure earnings advantage exists for public sector workers, over comparable workers in the private sector. While the absolute magnitude of this advantage is greatest for males, the proportionate advantage is slightly greater for females, because of their overall lower earnings. Given that the government sector employs approximately twice as many males as females, the average earnings advantage for public sector workers, over their private sector counterparts with the same characteristics, would be about seven per cent, slightly less for males and slightly more for females.

In the case of females, there is the possibility that their surplus earnings are even slightly larger than the estimated 8.6 per cent. This possibility occurs because they have a more favourable occupational distribution — favourable in the sense of being associated with higher earnings — than do females in the private sector. To the extent that they are 'overclassified' in the public sector and they could not achieve the same high occupational classification in the private sector, some part of the earnings associated with their superior occupational distribution should be reclassified as an economic surplus. For reasons indicated, however, the magnitude of this bias is likely to be small, if it exists at all.

The pure pay advantage of the public sector occurs because of the payment of a relatively constant premium rather than through the payment of excessive returns for the acquisition of positive wage-generating characteristics. In fact, the public sector tends to pay lower returns for education, experience, training and even for being bilingual. It does pay a premium for persons who have very high levels of education *and* experience, perhaps because they are regarded as complementary attributes in the public sector but more in the nature of substitutes in the private sector.

Because the public sector tends to pay a relatively constant premium rather than excessive returns for the acquisition of positive wage-generating characteristics, the public sector earnings advantage tends to be largest for the least skilled workers, at the lowest level of earnings. Based on some hypothetical calculations, for example, the pure earnings advantage for unskilled workers was 12 per cent for males and 21 per cent for females, compared to their respective average advantage of 6.2 and 8.6 per cent. With some notable exceptions discussed in the text, the earnings advantage often disappeared, and even became negative at the more skilled levels.

These results generally confirm those of earlier studies that utilized alternative data sets and methodologies. Based on occupational wage rate survey data, as well as data from the 1971 census, an earlier study concluded that "even after controlling for the impact of a variety of wage-determining variables . . . the government wage advantage is five to ten per cent when public employees include only those in government. The wage advantage of the government sector tends to be larger in the junior levels within an occupation, and smaller (or even negative) at the more senior levels." (Gunderson, 1977) In addition, from calculations based on various other data sets — Taxation Statistics, the Highly Qualified Manpower Survey, contract data from collective agreements, occupational wage rate surveys of municipal governments and Pay Research Bureau data — the following conclusion was reached: "In recent years the wages of public sector employees in Canada have exceeded those of their private sector counterparts by about five to 15 per cent. This wage advantage has been larger for females than males and for low-level as opposed to high-level occupations. In fact for high-level occupations the public sector may not even pay the competitive wage." (Gunderson, 1978a)

Clearly, the average advantage of approximately seven per cent, found in the present study, is well within the ranges found in the earlier studies. Based on the various empirical studies, the generalization that appears to be emerging is that wages of public sector workers tend to exceed those of their private sector counterparts by approximately five to 15 per cent, with seven per cent perhaps being a 'best guess'. The advantage is larger for females than males and it is largest at low skill levels.

Policy Issues

Given that the public sector does tend to pay a wage that is in excess of that paid in the private sector for comparable labour, there does appear to be room for the policy of applying more constraining influences to wages in the public sector. There are good grounds, however, for opposing the wholesale application of such constraining influences.

First, the excess is not large. Much of it may, in fact, be temporary, associated with a catch-up on the part of public sector workers, or with the new surge of unionism in the public sector — a phenomenon that is usually associated with unusually high wage gains in the early years. Also, the excess is only an excess relative to private sector workers, and, as many have suggested, what is so virtuous about private sector earnings to the extent that they are influenced by discrimination, unequal bargaining power, reserves of unemployed workers, and segmented labour markets?

This highlights a basic dilemma that would be associated with the strenuous application of constraining influences on public sector earnings. Since the excesses are greatest for females and for low-wage workers in general, constraining these excesses would have the most adverse impact on those who are already in a disadvantageous position in the labour market. This could clearly conflict with the government objectives of equal pay for females and of raising the wages of the working poor in general. On the other hand, if public sector earnings at the more skilled levels were constrained further, severe recruitment problems could occur, given that these earnings tend to be roughly comparable to those in the private sector.

Clearly, as in most elements of public policy, trade-offs amongst legitimate objectives are involved. As a personal reflection, the public sector earnings advantage is not so seriously out-of-line as to merit an alarmist policy that could have more severe adverse consequences. Rather, a more appropriate policy would be to monitor carefully public sector settlements and the public-private earnings differential, so that public debate can determine when the earnings differential should be curbed, even if this may have other adverse consequences. The policy of monitoring public sector earnings may also go a long way towards curbing excessive settlements, given the importance of the political process in public sector wage determination.

APPENDIX 1.1 THE CALCULATION OF MARGINAL RETURNS TO EDUCATION

An earnings equation of the form

$$\ln y = \beta_0 + \beta_1 E + \beta_2 E^2 + \beta_3 X + \beta_4 X^2 + \beta_5 E \cdot X + \ldots$$

where y is earnings, E education, X experience, and the β's are the parameters to be estimated, can be expressed as

$$y = \exp(\ln y) = \exp(\beta_0 + \beta_1 E + \beta_2 E^2 + \beta_3 X + \beta_4 X^2 + \beta_5 E \cdot X + \ldots).$$

The additional earnings that result from an additional year of education is

$$\partial y / \partial E = (\beta_1 + 2\beta_2 E + \beta_5 X) y.$$

Dividing through by y to express the additional earnings as a percent of actual earnings — that is, as a marginal return to the forgone income associated with acquiring education — yields

$$RE = (\partial y / \partial E)/y = \beta_1 + 2\beta_2 E + \beta_5 X.$$

This marginal return can be calculated for various values of E and X, for example their mean values. For workers with no experience ($X = 0$), the marginal returns to education are simply $\beta_1 + 2\beta_2 E$.

Similarly, marginal returns to experience are:

$$RX = (\partial y / \partial X)/y = \beta_3 + 2\beta_4 X + \beta_5 E.$$

REFERENCES

Gunderson, M. (1977) "Empirical Evidence of Public-Private Sector Wage Differentials in Canada" (Ottawa: Anti-Inflation Board).

Gunderson, M. (1978a) "Public-Private Wage and Non-Wage Differentials in Canada: Some Calculations from Published Tabulations", Chapter Seven in David K. Foot (ed.) *Public Employment and Compensation in Canada: Myths and Realities* (Toronto: Butterworth & Co. for The Institute for Research on Public Policy).

Gunderson, M. (1978b) "Public Sector Wage Determination: A Review of the Literature", Chapter Eight in David K. Foot (ed.) *Public Employment and Compensation in Canada: Myths and Realities* (Toronto: Butterworth & Co. for The Institute for Research on Public Policy.)

Smith, S. (1975) "Government Wage Differentials" *Working Paper 65* (Princeton: Princeton University, Industrial Relations Section).

Smith, S. (1976) "Pay Differentials Between Federal Government and Private Sector Workers" *Industrial and Labour Relations Review* 29, January, 179-97.

Chapter Two

Government as Indirect Employer

by
Meyer W. Bucovetsky*

INTRODUCTION

This investigation of Canadian public sector employment issues would be incomplete without recognizing that governments utilize manpower indirectly as well as directly. Private sector jobs that depend on government purchases of goods and services are impelled by public sector policies no less than are the jobs defrayed by the government payroll. This chapter is concerned with the number of employed Canadians whose jobs depend on government purchases and with the incomes generated by government expenditures: both of them in comparison with the size and cost of direct public employment. It also analyzes the shifting size and composition of the purchases that give rise to the indirect government payroll. Government often has latitude either to undertake its own production or to contract its requirements to outside producers; it may also have the capability of altering its own production processes so as to use more purchased materials and less labour, or the converse. We examine these issues in the light of the quantitative evidence.

The main research tool and quantitative source used was Statistics Canada's 'Open Input-Output Model', covering each of the years from 1961 to 1971, and in the most disaggregated detail available. The model and our use of it are described in the next section.

The bulk of the chapter is concerned with detailing three sets of numbers derived from the model and with analyzing trends and interactions within and among the number-series. The three time series that are of interest are: 'direct' government employment (numbers of jobs represented by the government payroll), 'real' government purchases (goods and services bought by government from the private sector, expressed in dollars of constant purchasing power), and

Editor's Note; **Meyer Bucovetsky** is Associate Professor in the Department of Political Economy and Scarborough College, and Associate of the Institute for Policy Analysis, all at the University of Toronto.
* The author bears a considerable debt to the Structural Analysis Division of Statistics Canada especially to R. B. Hoffman and Nugent Miller, for providing the data required for the study. Richard Bird and David Foot made useful comments on earlier versions and gave other procedural help. Morley Gunderson also provided valuable comments. None of them, however, is implicated in the presentation and conclusions.

'indirect' government employment (the number of jobs generated by those purchases). It turns out that the relationships among the three time series are very different in respect to the separate sectors of government we are able to isolate.

Our last set of calculations concerns the larger role of government as income distributor. We estimate the proportion of Canadian personal income that resulted from government's spending choices. The final section of the chapter summarizes our procedure and conclusions, and indicates some limitations of our approach.

THE DATA BASE

The Open Canadian Input-Output Model

The basis of this study is the Input-Output system described by its authors as an 'Open Output Determination Model' (Statistics Canada, 1977a, p. 31).[1] The underlying Canadian Input-Output accounts are 'rectangular', in contrast with the more usual 'square' or strictly inter-industry system. In the rectangular system, commodities and industries are treated as separate, non-identical categories. The accounts are based on two empirically-derived and complementary sets of tables that give a condensed portrait of the values of production flows through the business sector of the Canadian economy over a given year. A 'make' (or output) table shows the values of each commodity produced by each industry during the year. A 'use' (or input) table shows how the commodity values were disposed of, either as operating inputs to specified industries for further processing, or as elements of 'final demand' for personal consumption, government requirements, business investment or exports (net of imports). As well as commodity disposals, this table shows, for each industry segment and each source of 'final demand', the amount of direct value added in the form of factor payments (labour income, earnings of the self-employed, and 'surplus' or gross returns to capital), and commodity and other indirect taxes (net of subsidies).

Use of the Input-Output accounts for prediction or analysis depends on assuming proportionality with respect to all flows described by the two tables. For example, it is assumed that the proportion of each commodity supplied by each of the relevant industries in a year is invariant to the specific originating source of the demand.[2] Again, it is assumed that, in a given industry in a given year, each commodity output embodies a proportion of all materials, labour and capital used by the industry, determined by the share of the commodity in the value of industry output.

---

[1] Much of the following description is based on Bucovetsky (1973). For a more complete description of the model see Statistics Canada (1977a).

[2] The proportion of each commodity demand filled from imports is also assumed not to vary with the specific source of the commodity demand.

The two tables, in combination, can be used to trace the propagation of any actual or hypothetical set of final-user commodity demands through the structural linkages of the industrial sector. Each quantum of any commodity bought by a final user requires that the supplying industry buy material inputs from other industries. With due allowance for import leakages, ultimately a gross value of Canadian industrial output is produced that exceeds the net market value of the postulated final demand, to the extent that intermediate goods and services are used up in meeting that net demand. Factor incomes are thus generated all the way up the production-pipeline.

The Input-Output accounts, then, can be used to track the ultimate value of Total Domestic Output, by industry, that emanates from any commodity-composition of final demand. The exercise yields a distribution of the resultant factor earnings (wages, salaries and supplementary labour income, net income of unincorporated business, and corporate 'profit' inclusive of depreciation). The accounts themselves do not directly yield a count of the number of industrial jobs generated by the final demand. Nor is that number easily extracted from dollars of labour income generated, because net income of unincorporated business also represents rewards from employment (the income of proprietors and independent professionals, an amalgam of labour and capital earnings). However, Statistics Canada has separately estimated a set of empirical 'job coefficients' relating man-years of work (for both the employed and the self-employed) to dollars of output in each industry in each year. Consequently, once Total Domestic Output by industry is calculated for any set of commodity demands, an employment count can also be derived. [3]

Another capability that Statistics Canada has developed (although it is not shown in the published Input-Output tables) is that of extracting the amount of 'Interest and Dividend Income Paid to Persons' from the corporate 'surplus' total implied by a specified final demand. When this is added to the income of labour and the self-employed, we have the total dollar amount of personal income generated.

One important element of the present study does not itself require 'running' the Input-Output model: this is the empirical final demand expenditure tabulation included in the accounts. This gives a convenient portrayal of commodity purchases and direct factor costs by each demand-originating sector. If the

---

[3] At the time of writing, industry 'job coefficients' exist only for the years 1961 to 1970 inclusive. In the present study, employment generated by government purchases in 1971 had to be estimated indirectly. It was assumed that the ratio of numbers of self-employed in each industry to numbers of hired employees held constant between 1970 and 1971. The rate at which average wages in each industry changed between 1970 and 1971 was obtained from *Employment, Earnings and Hours*, Statistics Canada, #72-002 (monthly). Wage income, in each industry, due to government demand in 1971, was divided by the corresponding magnitude for 1970. The quotients were deflated by the appropriate wage change between the two years and multiplied by the total number of jobs (employed and self-employed) in 1970. Given our assumption of the constant ratio of self-employment to paid-employment, this gave us an estimate of total jobs generated in 1971. The 'indirect government employment' estimates for 1971, in the tables of this chapter, are, therefore, less precise than are those for the other years. The method used, however, is superior to other alternatives, for example, simply using the 1970 job coefficients. (The latter alternative is certain to result in an overestimate of 1971 indirect employment, because it ignores both output price increases and productivity gains in the processing sector.)

current dollar amounts of these expenditures are deflated by an appropriate unit-cost index, direct final demand spending in 'quantity' units can be compared across years. Magnitudes of direct spending can also be linked to the propagated effects indicated by the model, so that relative direct and indirect consequences of the expenditure may be compared.

DIMENSIONS AND SECTORS

The published Input-Output tables (Statistics Canada, 1977a) are restricted to two levels of aggregation that describe condensed versions of the full accounts. The dimensions of the complete model (which was used in the present calculations) permit a finer targeting of demand sources and a more accurate depiction of resultant detail. The processing sector, in the full ('worksheet' level) model, consists of 191 industries and 595 commodities.[4] 136 separate sources of final demand are identified among the broad categories of consumption, capital investment, government, export and import.

The interest of the present study lies in the effects of historical government expenditures, for which calculations were made separately for the eight government segments that are identified. Recorded expenditures on goods and services for all eight categories, for the years 1961 to 1971 inclusive, were traced to their ultimate effect on employment and personal income. Direct effects (i.e. government employment and payroll) were distinguished from indirect effects (i.e. employment and income that ultimately resulted from government purchase of 'commodities' from the private sector).

STATICS AND TIME

Perhaps the most distinctive feature of the Input-Output system developed by Statistics Canada is that its tables are re-calculated for each year's transactions, and integrated with the National Income Accounts for that year.[5] In this way a consistent time series of final demands and processing sector coefficients is maintained. The 'Open Output Determination Model' is now operational for the years 1961 to 1971 inclusive.

Despite its annual re-calculation, the Input-Output system remains a static predictor because the structural relationships imbedded in the tables do not allow for varying the fixed capital and inventory coefficients.[6] However, our purpose now is not to predict but, rather, to reconstruct past history, and in that sense the

---

[4] Eight of the industries and eight of the commodities are 'dummies', artificial catch-alls used as a convenient device for routing heterogeneous groupings (like office supplies) to their ultimate industry source.

[5] In contrast, the United States compiles new tables only at three to four year intervals, which is a handicap to users. For example, Stern (1975) estimates industrial output effects of government expenditures for 1972 by extrapolating the inter-industry coefficients for a single year, 1963.

[6] For forecasting purposes, a fully operational dynamic Input-Output model requires a complete description of the capital structure of the processing sector to supplement the flow of current transactions (Miernyk, 1965, pp. 113–14).

model is a dynamic instrument. It is able to transcend the fixed 'commodity to labour' proportions that are inherent in a single set of tables. While it cannot extricate substitutions involving capital goods, it does illuminate the changing flow coefficients of all industries and changing commodity demands of governments.

The Government Sector

The aggregate government sector, in the Input-Output model, conforms with the definitions of the National Income and Expenditure Accounts. Hence, government is rather narrowly identified with activities that are "non-commercial in nature. . . . (that are) undertaken by the society on a collective basis and financed for the most part out of taxation or government borrowing". (Statistics Canada, 1975, p. 165)

In this framework, government business enterprises, including the federal Post Office Department, are not part of the government sector but, rather, are treated as falling within the business (processing) sector. In the education field, publicly-administered primary and secondary schools and provincially operated community colleges are part of the government sector, but universities are regarded as private non-profit institutions falling within the personal sector.

It should also be noted that Input-Output government outlays exclude 'non-exhaustive' government expenditure (cash transfer payments, including subsidies to industry and universities, and interest on the public debt) since these outlays do not themselves absorb real economic resources when they are acquired by private-sector decision-makers.

Two of the eight sources of government expenditure that are detailed in the Input-Output model comprise gross investment in capital goods: i.e. Machinery and Equipment, and Construction. There is no further breakdown as to the level of government making the investment. Current (operating) expenditures of Canadian governments are distinguished among six sources:

- Hospitals
- Education
- Defence
- Other Municipal
- Other Provincial
- Other Federal

Current expenditures are detailed gross of any offsetting government revenues raised by way of user charges and fees. In conformity with the conventions of the National Income and Expenditure Accounts, all outlays for defence purposes are treated as current expenditures.

All eight government segments, then, originate demands for the goods and services (commodities) produced by the processing sector. However, only the six 'current' sources are assigned an expenditure for direct labour usage. The five non-defence 'current' sources are also assessed a 'surplus' charge that (unlike 'surplus' in the processing sector) is confined to the depreciation of fixed assets.[7]

HOSPITALS AND MEDICAL CARE

The way in which the costs of medical and hospital treatment are handled in the National Accounts, and, therefore, in the Input-Output model, requires some elaboration. Since 1961 (following introduction of universal hospital care under the federal *Hospital Insurance and Diagnostic Services Act* of that year) hospitals have been considered a branch of the government sector. Thus, in the Input-Output accounts (for all the years in the present analysis) hospital employees are covered by the direct government payroll. Non-payroll operating expenditures and capital expenditures of hospitals give rise to indirect government employment just as do the analogous outlays of government departments.

With respect to medical care services, all of the provinces introduced public medical care insurance plans at different times between 1962 and 1971. By 1971 all of them had qualified for federal assistance under the *Medical Care Act* of 1968. Thus, over the period of the present survey, expenditures for medical care services, in the Input-Output accounts, were progressively transferred from personal expenditure to provincial government expenditure. The notable increase in government purchases of the Health Services 'commodity' — and therefore in indirect government employment — does not necessarily imply an increase in real total national outlays on medical care. Rather, it represents mainly a progressive substitution of public for private spending. This qualitative change in the menu of goods and services provided by government, over the period considered, was unique. In much of the analysis of this chapter Health Service expenditures have been segregated in order that they not distort our measurement of the effects of quantitative changes in the traditional government-provided goods and services.

It should also be emphasized that, in this analysis, government payments to medical care personnel are handled differently from the payroll of hospitals. People rendering medical services (other than those employed in hospitals or government departments) are not considered direct government employees. Payments made by the provincial medical care funds are 'government current expenditure on goods and services' for the Health Services 'commodity'; therefore, they give rise only to indirect employment within the private sector. The largest part of these payments, the income of independent doctors, is carried ultimately to 'Net Income of Unincorporated Business' in the Health Service industry.

---

[7] It may be noted that, while government gross capital formation by the five non-defence sectors is bulked, depreciation charges on existing capital are separated among the sectors.

Qualifications

One caution bears emphasis before we report our findings. The Input-Output accounts portray the operation of an economy in a particular equilibrium setting. Users of the model ascribe a set of propagated effects to a particular self-starting demand impulse. It is easy to take the next step and conclude that if the impulse did not take place the effects would totally vanish. This can become a foolish numbers game in which the parts become greater than the whole; e.g. it might be shown that an overwhelming proportion of manufacturing jobs depend on the service sector, but also that an overwhelming proportion of service sector jobs depend on manufacturing demand. Like the fable of 'The Blind Men and the Elephant' it all depends on which part of the beast the investigator is clutching.

In the present study, the government is in the 'open' or exogenous sector. Its demands are unexplained; we simply trace their effect through the 'closed' portion of the model. What this implies is that while our estimates of the indirect employment and factor earnings generated by government demand are as accurate as we can make them, they are so only with respect to the state of the economy at the time to which the observations refer (which, of course, included the given government expenditure). If part of that demand had not eventuated, relative prices would have been different (so also tax collections might have been different), other demand and supply decisions would have altered, and the net reduction in employment would probably have been less than what our exercise might predict.

A related point is that, in this study, we have chosen not to measure 'induced' effects: those outputs and earnings that result from spending by the recipients of direct and indirect factor income. It is, indeed, possible further to 'close' an Input-Output model so that, for example, households are moved to the processing sector; i.e. households become an 'industry' whose 'inputs' include consumer expenditures and whose 'outputs' include labour services. In that case, as in our study, government purchases generate direct and indirect labour income, but, then, when that is spent, the earnings 'induced' by the household spending are attributed to the original government outlay. In that case, too, the re-spending effects of personal cash transfer receipts from government may also be traced to government.[8] In general, the smaller one makes the 'open' or exogenous fraction of the economy, the larger the proportion of total economic activity that any postulated exogenous demand must necessarily explain.[9] For the present study, our decision was that, to determine the effects of government expenditure decisions, we should confine our interest to effects that are governed

---

[8] The 'Open Output Determination Model' is only one of a number of versions of the Input-Output accounts prepared by Statistics Canada; one variant is an output determination model that is 'closed' with respect to the household sector (Statistics Canada, 1977a, p. 31).

[9] In the limit, if an Input-Output model were totally 'closed', in the sense that all final spending activities are induced within the system, only an aggregate level of final demand could be chosen; the relative composition of output could not be varied (Yan, 1969, pp. 42–3).

by the technological structure of the economy; we omitted those effects that depend on further choices by individual consumers.

INTERPRETING THE RESULTS

Direct Government Employment

A problem arises in relating the indirect employment due to government expenditure to numbers directly employed in the public service. One conclusion that emerges from the broad current investigation of public sector employment is the very profusion of quantity measures of the public service: all 'accurate' on some criterion, but all different (Bird, 1978), and none entirely appropriate to the Input-Output framework. Since government is outside the processing sector, for which Input-Output 'job coefficients' exist, it is not possible to infer the precise number of man-years associated with the tabulated cost of government 'Wages, Salaries and Supplementary Labour Income'.

However, as supplementary information to the Input-Output model, cost deflators do exist for the unit labour-costs of the six government sectors. Hence, if an estimate is made of the dollar value of average labour costs in each government sector in a single year, a consistent 'wage' series may be derived for the 11-year span. When annual Input-Output government payrolls are divided by the average 'wage', a consistent direct-job-number series also emerges. Such a series was constructed, based on estimated average payroll-cost per employee in 1971; the 1971 unit costs were themselves derived, for each of the six government sectors, from the most appropriate auxiliary data source.[10] The constructed series covering Direct Government Employment is given in Table 2.1. Note that, since the sources from which the 'wage cost' information was obtained in the main ignore casual and part-time government employment, Table 2.1 is best interpreted as portraying the number of 'full-time equivalent' man-years of employment in a particular sector in a given year.[11]

---

[10] For hospitals, the 'auxiliary source' was data supplied by the Health Division of Statistics Canada (See Bird, 1978, Table A 2.3). For education, it was data from the Labour Division of Statistics Canada, for 1973 (Bird, 1978, Table A 2.2). The estimate of 1973 average education earnings was then deflated to 1971 levels using relative wage-income values from *Taxation Statistics*, Revenue Canada (annual). Armed forces employment was estimated by interpolation from Department of National Defence data for 31 March; military pay and allowances came from the National Accounts. Civilian defence employment and payroll came from *Federal Government Employment*, Statistics Canada, #72-004 (quarterly). Average payroll costs for 'other municipal' employees came from *Local Government Employment*, Statistics Canada, #72-009 (quarterly). For 'other provincial' employees, information from *Provincial Government Employment*, Statistics Canada, #72-007 (quarterly) was adjusted to exclude provincial hospital and education employees. Finally, average earnings for 'other federal' employees were calculated from *Federal Government Employment*, Statistics Canada, #72-004 (quarterly), adjusted to exclude the defence and Post Office components.

[11] The precision of our direct man-years series is open to question; this, in turn, casts some doubt on the precision of the indirect to direct ratios we derive later. For time trend analysis this is of little consequence so long as the unit-wage-cost deflators are correct. For example, if our estimated 1971 average wage were too low, our 1971 direct employment number would be too high; but the derived job numbers for 1961 to 1970 would be overstated by the same proportion. Hence, the time trends of direct employment and the indirect to direct ratio would not be affected.

TABLE 2.1

ESTIMATED DIRECT GOVERNMENT EMPLOYMENT IN INPUT-OUTPUT FRAMEWORK, CANADA, 1961 TO 1971

(man-years)

Government Sector

Year	Hospitals	Education	Defence	Other Municipal	Other Provincial	Other Federal	Total Government
1961	204,006	267,008	165,981	126,416	102,193	127,307	992,911
1962	218,225	284,386	172,063	132,171	110,253	131,232	1,048,330
1963	231,567	301,879	169,374	138,195	112,805	127,586	1,081,406
1964	249,049	319,525	162,844	146,112	121,774	136,229	1,135,533
1965	264,156	337,332	154,043	150,758	121,926	140,703	1,168,918
1966	288,327	364,858	145,310	161,084	124,805	157,630	1,242,014
1967	325,142	412,435	139,434	172,723	139,937	170,260	1,359,931
1968	350,779	436,675	137,507	175,145	162,137	187,187	1,449,430
1969	363,630	462,567	135,583	197,747	178,645	199,774	1,537,946
1970	370,007	481,820	122,362	199,317	204,671	200,708	1,578,885
1971	380,000	489,036	127,980	209,954	207,787	213,737	1,628,494
Rate of Growth, per cent per annum	7.0	6.8	−3.4	5.4	7.7	6.1	5.4

Note: This is a synthetic series that was constructed from three elements:

(1) Input-Output series on Government Direct Expenditure for Wages, Salaries and Supplementary Labour Income.

(2) Input-Output payroll-cost deflators for each government sector.

(3) Estimates that were made, for 1971, of average employee remuneration in each government sector (from other information sources, see footnote ten in text).

DIRECT EMPLOYMENT GROWTH

Over the period 1961 to 1971, direct employment grew in all five non-defence sectors; the most rapid rate of growth was in 'other provincial' employment, but the dispersion of growth rates among the five sectors was relatively small. Defence employment shrunk more or less steadily throughout the period. Total direct government employment, excluding defence, grew at a compound annual rate of almost 6⅔ percent.[12]

Government Real Commodity Purchases

Statistics Canada has computed price-deflators for each of the 595 Input-Output commodities. When current dollar values of government expenditure on goods and services are deflated by these indexes, and the deflated expenditures are aggregated by government sector, we get what is, in effect, a currently-weighted combination of base-weighted commodity quantities. The resultant series approximates a 'real quantity' measure of annual government purchases; it expresses the value of those purchases, for each year, in terms of constant 1961 prices. A summary of these 'real' values is presented in Table 2.2.[13]

GROWTH OF REAL PURCHASES

In the period analyzed, government absorption of real goods and services, in the aggregate, grew at a somewhat more rapid rate than did its direct absorption of labour (6.4 per cent a year for total government purchases versus 5.4 per cent a year for employment). But the growth rates of real purchases vary across sectors, rather more so than do the growth rates of direct employment. Total gross capital investment — analytically distinct from purchases that are dissipated currently — increased more slowly than did government employment and much more slowly than did total current-account purchases.

Among individual current demand sources and commodities (not tabulated), the most spectacular relative increase occurred in 'other federal' demand for commodity number 561, Education Services. From uniform zero entries before 1967, federal purchases of Education Services rose to a 1971 level of $159 million, expressed in 1971 dollars, or $97 million in constant 1961 dollars. But

---

[12] In every instance that an annual growth rate is cited in this chapter, it was calculated by regression of the logarithms of the 11 relevant observations on the time variable.

[13] For the years 1962 to 1971, Total Current Purchases (in constant 1961 dollars), displayed in the tenth row of Table 2.2, are slightly lower than the equivalent aggregates published in Statistics Canada (1977b), and the discrepancy widens somewhat over time. The numbers used here were obtained by deflating each disaggregated commodity purchase by each government sector using price deflators provided by Statistics Canada, and the accuracy of calculations was checked. The source of the discrepancy cannot be traced, given the aggregative character of the published tables. One possible explanation is a revision of some of the price series. In any event, the discrepancy does not materially alter the conclusions reached in this study. For example, the growth rate of Total Current Purchases is shown in Table 2.2 as 8.0 per cent per year; if the published aggregate values are substituted, the growth rate becomes 8.1 per cent per year.

TABLE 2.2

REAL 'COMMODITY' PURCHASES BY GOVERNMENT, CANADA, 1961 TO 1971[1]
(millions of constant 1961 dollars)

Source of Government Demand	1961	1962	1963	1964	1965	1966	1967	1968	1969	1970	1971	Growth Rate per cent per annum
Capital Investment												
Machinery and Equipment	174	195	203	224	251	314	298	314	271	264	330	5.7
Construction	1,488	1,677	1,695	1,658	1,903	2,058	2,086	2,080	2,062	2,050	2,270	3.7
Current Purchases for												
Hospitals	270	283	320	339	364	401	393	417	448	477	519	6.4
Education	206	216	239	282	355	395	383	496	509	599	630	12.7
Defence	744	757	612	620	560	599	629	578	531	525	529	−3.2
Other Municipal	452	506	517	535	621	637	651	667	664	704	705	4.4
Other Provincial	366	318	369	378	437	603	789	938	941	1,307	1,428	17.4
Other Provincial exclusive of 'Health Service' commodity	359	310	353	355	407	547	707	808	667	749	696	10.5
Other Federal	256	260	261	308	338	425	472	616	671	768	825	14.3
Total Current Purchases[2]	2,295	2,340	2,318	2,464	2,676	3,060	3,317	3,714	3,763	4,380	4,637	8.0
Total Current Purchases exclusive of 'Health Service' commodity	2,278	2,318	2,284	2,419	2,620	2,979	3,208	3,554	3,461	3,793	3,875	6.4
Total Government Purchases[2]	3,957	4,212	4,216	4,345	4,830	5,432	5,701	6,107	6,096	6,695	7,237	6.4
Total Government Purchases exclusive of 'Health Service' commodity	3,939	4,190	4,181	4,301	4,774	5,351	5,592	5,948	5,794	6,108	6,475	5.4

Notes:

[1] For the years 1962 to 1971, current dollar government purchases of each of the 595 Input-Output commodities were deflated by the appropriate 'producer price' index. The totals here are net of commodity indirect taxes.

[2] Columns may not add exactly, because of rounding.

in terms of absolutes, as may be expected, these magnitudes are dwarfed by rising provincial purchases of Health Services. The latter grew in real terms at a compound rate of 62 per cent a year; for the reasons noted earlier, a comparison of the growth of government 'commodity' demand with that of government employment is best done with Health Services omitted.

But, even when Health Services are exluded from the reckoning, the growth rate of total real purchased non-capital inputs exceeded that of directly-employed labour. The public service was growing, as was the real magnitude of public sector consumption, but government in the aggregate was apparently shifting its input-mix in the direction of greater emphasis on purchased goods and services. A suggestive comparison is that, excluding defence spending, aggregate government real non-capital purchases grew at the annual rate of 11.2 per cent, inclusive of Health Services, and 9.3 per cent, when Health Service costs are also excluded. (Non-defence direct employment was meanwhile growing by 6.6 per cent.) The relative shift to purchases is especially notable in the 'other federal' and 'education' sectors. Contrary to the general tendency, however, direct employment in both the 'hospital' and 'other municipal' sectors grew more rapidly than did real outside purchases. In the defence sector, both direct employment and real commodity purchases declined, but direct employment fell somewhat more rapidly (defence 'labour' declined at a 3.4 per cent annual rate compared with 3.2 per cent for real defence purchases).

INPUT SUBSTITUTION

From the evidence, one might conclude that, in choosing their input-mix, government decision-makers are not insensitive to relative price movements; i.e. to cost minimizing considerations. Over the 11-year span, unit-labour costs did rise more swiftly than did the composite unit-cost of purchased goods and services. The weighted average of the six public sector wage indexes grew at the rate of 7.4 per cent a year; the implicit price deflator for total current-use 'commodities' grew at less than half that rate: 3.4 per cent overall or 3¼ per cent when Health Services are excluded.[14]

Too much of a case, however, should not be made for the price-conscious nature of the purchases-for-labour substitution. At least five kinds of substitution may have been involved in public sector decision-making over the period.

- Substitution within the mix of the traditional government-provided outputs. The absolute (and relative) decline in National Defence is an example; in this case one

---

[14] Since the wage-cost deflator grew more rapidly than did the purchase-cost deflator, government payroll showed a more rapid rate of growth relative to expenditure on purchased current inputs, when both are expressed in *current* dollars (rather than as real magnitudes). For example, excluding defence, current dollar government wages, salaries and supplementary labour income grew at an average rate of 14.5 per cent a year. Non-defence, non-capital commodity purchases, in current dollars, grew by 15.1 per cent a year, inclusive of provincial spending on Health Services, and by 12.8 per cent when the latter are excluded. In the case of defence, the difference in relative annualized rates of change, as between real and current dollar measures, is even more dramatic. Current dollar defence payroll costs rose by 4.0 per cent a year, while current dollar non-labour defence expenditure fell by 0.4 per cent a year. (As noted above, in 'real' dollars both fell, but defence 'labour' fell rather more rapidly.)

which, other things equal, should have increased the overall ratio of direct employment to real purchases (defence being relatively 'materials intensive'). Other changes in output emphasis, however, may well have worked in the opposite direction.

- The substitution of public for market provision of consumer goods and services. Medical care, we know, is the prime exhibit, and that change necessarily implied an overall increase in purchases relative to direct government labour.
- The substitution of government production for government subsidization (via transfer payments). An example, here is the growth of Community Colleges relative to Universities. Government direct employment and 'commodity' purchases would both increase, but in indeterminate proportions.[15]
- The substitution of private production (and public purchase) for public production of outputs that are, in either case, provided by government outside the market system. This is often termed the decision to 'buy not make'; an example would be a shift to private contracting of municipal garbage removal.
- Factor substitution in the sense of the microeconomic theory of the firm, where a given quantum of output is viewed as producible with varying input proportions. If input coefficients are variable, 'materials' might be substituted in government production, for labour and/or capital.

Over any period of time there are doubtless many instances of all five kinds of substitution taking place within the compass of public sector decision-making. Only the last two might connote a deliberate change of factor mix in response to changing relative market prices. Our data are, unfortunately, too gross for testing the sensitivity of governments to price signals.

Experimental time series regressions were, in fact, estimated on the 11 observations for each of the six government sectors and their aggregate. The dependent variable was constant dollar current-account purchases divided by real employment; the explanatory variable was the relevant government wage-cost price deflator divided by the appropriate purchases' unit-cost implicit deflator (both variables in logarithmic form). If the composition of government output were relatively constant, if the underlying production function permitted the substitution of one input for the other, and if the decision-maker reacted to price signals, the calculated regression slope would be an estimate of the elasticity of substitution of 'purchases' for labour. The results, on the whole, were inconclusive (which is not surprising, given the heterogeneous forces at work). The aggregate government regressions yielded estimates in a plausible range (0.36 including health, and 0.72 excluding health), and within acceptable confidence limits.[16] But the result is clearly an accident of aggregation, because,

---

[15] The example cited — a relative increase in government direct production of education — would itself likely have impelled an increase in total growth of direct government employment relative to real purchases, since education is labout-intensive in comparison with all other sectors of current demand. But, again, other compositional changes may have worked in the opposite direction.

[16] Taken literally, the result indicates that for each percentage point increase in the unit-cost of labour relative to the unit-cost of 'purchases' government is able — and willing — to increase the quantity ratio of its 'purchases' to its labour by about ⅔ (or ⅓ with Health included) of a percentage point. The t statistics on the regression slopes were 3.69 when Health was excluded and 6.38 with Health included, indicating that, at the 99 per cent confidence level, we could accept both that the coefficients are greater than zero and that they are less than positive unity.

with the single exception of 'Education', none of the sectoral regressions was satisfactory. The 'Hospitals' and 'Other Municipal' regressions (as might be expected by comparing the growth rates of direct employment to those of purchases) showed a negative reaction to factor price relatives. In the case of 'Hospitals', an implied likely value of zero for the 'elasticity of substitution' was strongly indicated. This might suggest that in the case of hospital outputs, the underlying production function is of the truly 'fixed coefficient' variety: i.e. that there is little scope for factor substitution of the fifth type that was listed above. Alternatively, it may indicate that, while hospital administrators could have substituted relatively cheaper 'materials' for relatively more expensive labour, they had no incentive to do so. In any event, since our regressions totally omitted consideration of the 'third' factor, capital, they do little to elucidate the true production function for government outputs.

THE SHIFT TO SERVICE DEMAND

In a more impressionistic vein, perusal of the time-trend of all real commodities purchases indicates a strong relative tendency by all government sectors toward emphasizing the purchase of services and away from the purchase of tangible goods. In the case of education, the commodity purchases with the greatest rate of increase over time were transportation, communications and utility services. In the other five sectors—and especially 'other provincial' (even with Health excluded) and 'other federal'—the progressively greater emphasis was toward the more 'personal' services: Business Management Services, Education, Advertising and Promotion, and the like. It is presumably in the last categories that the greatest opportunity lies for switching from 'make' to 'buy'.

Especially notable is the growth in demand for commodity 566, Business Management Services, by 'other provincial' governments (and to a lesser extent by 'other federal'). The real amount purchased was relatively flat until 1965, and then started a rapid rise that made for an overall 11-year average annual growth rate of 25.2 per cent in the 'other provincial' sector, and 14.5 per cent in the 'other federal'. This category embraces indirect employment of contract labour, quite probably for many functions that might have been performed by departmental employees (i.e. the substitution of private for public production).

CONTRACT LABOUR

More generally, the tendency of governments increasingly to use 'contract labour' for services they might themselves have produced has been blamed by some for the 'employment insecurity' that has allegedly recently gripped the public service. (In this connection, see Chapter Four of the present volume.) The decision to 'buy not make' certain services may, indeed, be a response to relative prices. The unit cost deflator for Business Management Services, for example, rose only at the rate of 4.4 per cent a year between 1961 and 1971 (as compared with the 7.4 per cent rate we noted for aggregate public sector wage costs).[17] On the other hand, in an era of apparent increasing hostility toward 'bureaucratic government' the growth of contracting may have little to do with cost efficiency; rather, it may be a politically expedient defence against the accusatory job numbers that are so often hurled by the critics.

Some observers have inferred a recent tendency for governments to try to retain only the best of their own personnel by generally encouraging early retirement, coupled with the practice of 'hiring back' wanted employees on a consulting basis. In this sense, contracting may be an innovative personnel policy used to by-pass rigid civil service rules and practices.

The data on government real commodity purchases over time suggest a number of areas for study or speculation. Over the period under review, the trend was unmistakably upward, more so than was the trend of government employment. A less certain proposition is whether or not these trends illustrate a conscious effort by government decision-makers to minimize cost. The number of jobs that were impelled by these commodity purchases is discussed in the next section.

Indirect Government Employment

In this section, we present the main results of manipulating the Input-Output model to estimate the number of jobs in industry that are propagated by government's purchases. The raw results covered 11 years, eight originating government sectors and 183 affected industries. Condensed versions appear in the following tables.

Tables 2.3 and 2.4 give, in considerable detail, the breakdown of indirect government employment for the terminal years, 1961 and 1971.[18] Total indirect employment in all industries rose by a total 43 per cent between the two years, but the increase was by no means spread evenly across industries or in terms of the originating government sector.

The changed industrial emphasis in the ten-year interval is what might be expected from the commodity-demand shifts discussed in the previous section.[19] That is, there was an actual decline in indirect government employment in Agriculture, Other Primary Industries and Durable Goods Manufacturing. There

---

[17] The empirical literature, meagre though it is, indicates that for the majority of activities examined, private producers on contract can better the unit-cost levels of public sector producers. For a review of United States studies, see Spann (1977). A recent Canadian study (Krashinsky, 1978) concludes that day care for children is more expensive in publicly run centers than in publicly-supported, privately-operated centers.

[18] It should be recalled that the estimates for 1971 were not made directly from the year's 'job coefficients' as was done for the other years. See footnote three above.

[19] Input-Output takes account of all indirect employment in the industrial pipeline behind the final supply of a purchased commodity. But the models generally confirm the presumption that most indirect employment is stimulated at the front end of the pipeline. Service-type commodities are most stimulative of service industry employment.

TABLE 2.3

INDUSTRIAL EMPLOYMENT GENERATED BY GOVERNMENT PURCHASES, CANADA, 1961

(man-years)

	Source of Government Demand								
	Capital Investment		Current Purchases for						Total Government Demand
Industrial Grouping	Machinery and Equipment	Construction	Hospitals	Education	Defence	Other Municipal	Other Provincial	Other Federal	
Agriculture	184	1,624	5,608	777	1,315	1,473	1,558	1,152	13,691
Other Primary Industries	211	5,761	710	436	1,085	1,473	896	224	10,796
Durable Goods Manufacturing	6,889	38,753	1,882	1,913	26,447	4,788	3,887	1,659	86,218
Non-Durable Goods Manufacturing	2,175	8,633	8,144	4,311	6,634	5,175	3,880	3,294	42,246
Construction	194	82,879	2,531	3,767	11,383	14,105	17,115	3,800	135,774
Transportation and Storage	946	9,659	1,773	2,781	5,005	4,319	3,283	1,940	29,706
Communications	238	1,925	1,236	712	1,879	2,034	1,809	2,782	12,615
Utilities	61	841	548	293	729	1,460	341	535	4,808
Wholesale Trade	1,805	13,499	2,676	2,018	5,558	4,311	2,864	1,518	34,249
Retail Trade	1,040	5,885	2,000	1,430	2,908	3,392	2,322	1,561	20,538
Finance, Insurance, Real Estate	213	2,552	593	780	1,121	1,420	1,948	2,831	11,458
Health Services	—		169	6	319	117	471	362	1,444
Business and Professional Services	298	9,100	1,745	2,083	3,609	7,121	3,395	4,533	31,884
Other Services	159	1,301	1,204	1,227	3,217	2,217	2,105	2,021	13,451
TOTAL: All Industries	14,413	182,412	30,819	22,534	71,208	53,406	45,874	28,212	448,878

Note: In this and all subsequent tables (unless another source is specified) the results reported follow from tracing the impact of government demand through Statistics Canada's 'Open Output Determination Model'. Man-years of employment follow from Total Domestic Output by industry, when the appropriate 'job coefficients' are applied.

TABLE 2.4

INDUSTRIAL EMPLOYMENT GENERATED BY GOVERNMENT PURCHASES, CANADA, 1971

(man-years)

Industrial Grouping	Capital Investment		Current Purchases for						Total Government Demand
	Machinery and Equipment	Construction	Hospitals	Education	Defence	Other Municipal	Other Provincial	Other Federal	
Agriculture	126	869	4,802	984	1,037	1,679	2,290	1,560	13,347
Other Primary Industries	172	4,345	543	628	483	1,303	1,245	748	9,467
Durable Goods Manufacturing	6,126	37,647	2,569	3,407	9,905	4,712	4,889	4,136	73,391
Non-Durable Goods Manufacturing	2,132	8,028	10,338	8,316	3,540	5,528	7,736	7,775	53,393
Construction	126	121,670	2,150	3,518	5,127	10,314	13,329	3,970	160,204
Transportation and Storage	951	8,031	1,959	10,665	2,810	5,681	5,304	4,057	39,458
Communications	276	2,361	1,945	2,270	2,187	2,814	6,654	5,140	23,647
Utilities	43	577	698	1,190	451	1,599	774	882	6,214
Wholesale Trade	2,431	12,407	3,932	4,509	2,928	5,060	5,694	5,153	42,114
Retail Trade	1,692	7,795	2,670	3,730	2,042	4,692	5,593	5,503	33,717
Finance, Insurance, Real Estate	251	3,570	1,057	1,886	843	2,410	5,236	5,299	20,552
Health Services	—	2	1,143	24	182	307	40,470	241	42,369
Business and Professional Services	814	22,855	4,229	9,750	5,154	13,352	19,101	25,708	100,963
Other Services	196	1,836	2,269	2,633	2,536	3,503	6,172	5,662	24,807
TOTAL: All Industries	15,336	231,993	40,304	53,510	39,225	62,954	124,487	75,834	643,643

Source of Government Demand

was a below average increase in Non-Durable Goods Manufacturing and Construction. In the last case, the Construction industry, a total increase of some 24,000 man-years is more than accounted for by the 39,000 additional Construction industry jobs due to government capital investment; in this industry, too, government non-capital purchases, in 1971, evoked fewer indirect jobs than they did in 1961.

Service industry indirect government employment stands in contrast to the goods-producing industries: all of the service industry groupings show increases between the two years. Among the summary groupings tabulated here, the largest absolute increase, 69,000 jobs, is shown in the group of 'Business and Professional Service' industries.[20]

Table 2.5 shows the 'all industry' totals of indirect government employment for all 11 years and all originating government sectors. The trend of total indirect employment was generally upward throughout the period for all government-demand sources, with the notable exception of defence. Indirect employment due to government investment in machinery and equipment (the smallest single source of indirect employment) also did not grow steadily, but peaked in 1966 and followed an irregular trend afterward.

GROWTH OF INDIRECT EMPLOYMENT

Growth trends of indirect employment are made explicit in Table 2.6, which gives the average annual percentage change for each of the industry/originating-sector cells that were distinguished in Tables 2.3 and 2.4. Health Services (now viewed not as a commodity but as an employing industry) again shows up as the outstanding growth exhibit. Second place belongs to the Business and Professional Services Industry, particularly that portion accounted for by 'other provincial' and 'other federal' purchases. The overall growth rate of indirect employment, when capital investment is included, was 3.9 per cent, which compares with the growth rate for direct government employment (Table 2.1) of 5.4 per cent. A better basis for comparison, however, would be to ignore the indirect employment generated by investment in fixed assets, since capital investment does not include any direct government employment. The rate of growth of the aggregate indirect employment due to all government non-capital purchases (not tabulated) was the same as that of direct employment, 5.4 per cent a year; but that rate is reduced to 4.4 per cent when effects on the Health Service industry are excluded. What is apparent is that indirect government jobs failed to grow as quickly as did the real commodity purchases responsible for them. This is a subject to which we will return.

---

[20] In our summary tables, the industry group we call 'Business and Professional Services' comprises four 'worksheet level' Input-Output industries: #171, Education and Related Services; #176, Professional Services to Business; #177, Advertising Services; #183, Miscellaneous Services to Business and Persons.

TABLE 2.5

EMPLOYMENT INDIRECTLY GENERATED BY GOVERNMENT PURCHASES, CANADA, 1961 TO 1971

(man-years)

Source of Government Demand	1961	1962	1963	1964	1965	1966	1967	1968	1969	1970	1971
Capital Investment											
Machinery and Equipment	14,413	15,892	16,371	16,533	17,446	20,719	18,629	17,337	13,629	12,933	15,336
Construction	182,412	201,288	200,393	186,890	211,344	224,394	234,679	217,832	216,317	214,914	231,993
Current Purchases for											
Hospitals	30,819	29,992	33,166	33,777	34,237	35,090	36,329	37,013	37,132	38,866	40,304
Education	22,534	22,748	24,215	26,617	31,764	33,689	34,552	41,945	43,798	50,513	53,510
Defence	71,208	67,822	53,392	51,946	45,083	49,045	49,049	41,536	36,918	35,720	39,225
Other Municipal	53,406	58,267	57,338	56,523	61,709	61,391	66,118	65,259	61,249	63,342	62,954
Other Provincial	45,874	39,923	43,927	42,424	48,244	64,307	83,510	92,822	92,094	119,928	124,487
Other Provincial exclusive of Health Service Industry	45,403	39,345	42,810	40,839	46,153	60,599	77,740	84,150	74,776	86,520	84,017
Other Federal	28,212	27,597	28,105	31,799	33,641	39,827	47,005	55,727	61,937	71,558	75,834
Total Current Purchases	252,053	246,349	240,143	242,986	254,678	283,349	316,563	334,302	333,128	379,927	396,314
Total Current Purchases exclusive of Health Service Industry	250,609	244,537	237,501	239,707	250,649	277,775	308,596	323,386	313,655	344,473	353,947
Total Government Purchases	448,878	463,523	456,907	446,409	483,468	528,462	569,871	569,471	563,074	607,774	643,643
Total Government Purchases exclusive of Health Service Industry	447,434	461,710	454,264	443,130	479,438	522,887	561,899	558,552	543,598	572,317	601,274

TABLE 2.6

GROWTH RATES OF INDUSTRIAL EMPLOYMENT GENERATED BY GOVERNMENT PURCHASES, CANADA, 1961 TO 1971
(average growth rate, per cent per annum)

Industrial Grouping	Capital Investment		Source of Government Demand — Current Purchases for						Total Government Demand
	Machinery and Equipment	Construction	Hospitals	Education	Defence	Other Municipal	Other Provincial	Other Federal	
Agriculture	-3.9	-6.2	-1.1	3.9	1.1	2.2	9.9	5.6	1.3
Other Primary Industries	-3.8	-3.6	-3.6	3.8	-9.1	-2.5	-5.9	2.6	-2.1
Durable Goods Manufacturing	-3.1	-0.9	2.4	6.0	-10.4	0.4	6.6	10.9	-1.8
Non-Durable Goods Manufacturing	-0.8	-1.2	2.4	7.4	-5.4	1.0	10.4	10.9	3.0
Construction	-5.3	3.4	-1.5	0.3	-7.4	-3.3	-0.3	1.1	1.6
Transportation and Storage	-1.1	-2.5	0.8	16.2	-5.6	3.2	9.4	9.6	3.7
Communications	—	1.5	4.7	13.3	-1.1	2.9	18.2	7.4	6.7
Utilities	-2.2	-2.2	3.8	21.0	-4.7	2.0	14.5	8.3	4.6
Wholesale Trade	2.0	-1.5	3.0	8.3	-7.2	1.6	10.7	15.1	2.1
Retail Trade	4.4	2.1	2.6	10.6	-3.1	3.5	13.1	15.7	5.6
Finance, Insurance, Real Estate	0.8	3.2	7.2	10.0	-3.5	5.6	12.5	7.1	6.7
Health Services	—	—	18.6	18.2	-7.5	9.1	59.2	-2.2	41.1
Business and Professional Services	9.3	10.3	9.8	17.0	3.7	5.8	24.4	22.2	13.5
Other Services	-0.3	2.1	6.7	7.4	-2.9	4.1	14.1	12.8	6.7
TOTAL: All Industries	-0.8	1.9	2.7	9.8	-6.2	1.6	13.3	12.1	3.9
TOTAL: All industries excluding Health Services	-0.8	1.9	2.3	9.8	-6.2	1.5	9.4	12.2	3.2

INDIRECT TO DIRECT EMPLOYMENT RATIOS

Trends in the connection between indirect and direct government employment are exhibited in Table 2.7. In the top half of the table, the numbers shown, by demand-sector and year, are percentage ratios of indirect employment due to non-capital expenditure only, to direct government employment.[21] In the bottom half of the table, indirect employment due to government investment in Machinery and Equipment, and Construction, has been added to the indirect employment credited to the five non-defence current demand sectors, in estimated proportions.[22]

Table 2.7 indicates that, overall, for every 1,000 direct government employees in 1971, there were 395 jobs created outside the public service by the requirements of government; 243 of those jobs were due to non-capital demands and 152 to capital investment. Among individual government sectors, the largest number of 'outside' jobs in relation to direct employment was in the 'other provincial' category: and the statement holds true whether or not capital investment and Health Services are included.

In the first year of the time series, 1961, the overall ratio of indirect to direct employment was higher, at 452 'outside' jobs for every 1,000 jobs inside government; 252 were due to non-capital demands and 200 to capital investment. The aggregate ratio of indirect to direct, in the bottom half of Table 2.7 (effects of capital investment included) declines more or less regularly over the 11-year period. The aggregate ratios are more nearly constant when investment effects are omitted.

Over the 11-year span, the indirect to direct employment ratios decline with respect to hospitals, defence and 'other municipal' government; this holds true with or without considering fixed asset purchases, although in an across-sector sense, heavy investment in capital goods by the municipal sector makes it the second largest contributor to the overall ratio. There is a mildly upward trend in the ratios applicable to education and 'other provincial' (exclusive of Health Services), on account of current purchases only, but these trends are broadly downward if capital investment is reckoned. Only 'other federal' and 'other provincial' including Health Services display consistent appreciation of the ratios with or without capital investment.

---

[21] In analyses based on Input-Output, the quantitative relationship of 'effect' to 'cause' is often expressed as a 'multiplier': how much total employment, income, or whatever, direct and indirect, is ultimately generated for each direct unit. (See, for example, Bucovetsky, 1973.) In the present study we judged that percentage ratios of indirect to direct employment were simpler to portray and less likely to be interpreted as implying a causal relationship. The ratios we use are easily translated into multipliers. An indirect/direct employment ratio of 39.5 per cent, for example, as was the case for aggregate government expenditure in 1971, translates into a multiplier of 1.395.

[22] As was mentioned above, the Input-Output accounts do not distinguish among originating sources of government investment. The proportions we applied here were derived from *Private and Public Investment in Canada*, Statistics Canada and Department of Industry Trade and Commerce, #61-205 (annual). Aggregate annual government sector investment demands, detailed in that publication, are not quite identical to the Input-Output aggregates, but they are close.

TABLE 2.7

RATIOS OF 'INDIRECT' TO DIRECT GOVERNMENT EMPLOYMENT, CANADA, 1961 TO 1971
(per cent)

Government Sector	YEAR										
	1961	1962	1963	1964	1965	1966	1967	1968	1969	1970	1971
'INDIRECT' EFFECT OF CURRENT EXPENDITURE ONLY											
Hospitals	15.1	13.7	14.3	13.6	13.0	12.2	11.2	10.6	10.2	10.5	10.6
Education	8.4	8.0	8.0	8.3	9.4	9.2	8.4	9.6	9.5	10.5	10.9
Defence	42.9	39.4	31.5	31.8	29.3	33.8	35.2	30.2	27.2	29.2	30.6
Other Municipal	42.2	44.1	41.5	38.7	40.9	38.1	38.3	37.3	31.0	31.8	30.0
Other Provincial	44.9	36.2	38.9	34.8	39.6	51.5	59.7	57.2	51.6	58.6	59.9
Other Provincial exclusive of effect on Health Services	44.4	35.7	38.0	33.5	37.9	48.6	55.6	51.9	41.9	42.3	40.4
Other Federal	22.2	21.0	22.0	23.3	23.9	25.3	27.6	29.8	31.0	35.7	35.5
TOTAL Government	25.4	23.5	22.2	21.4	21.8	22.8	23.3	23.1	21.7	24.1	24.3
TOTAL exclusive of effect on Health Services	25.2	23.3	22.0	21.1	21.4	22.4	22.7	22.3	20.4	21.8	21.7
'INDIRECT' EFFECT OF CURRENT EXPENDITURE PLUS PRORATED CAPITAL INVESTMENT											
Hospitals	25.0	23.8	23.0	20.8	19.8	19.0	17.3	16.1	15.0	15.1	15.4
Education	19.5	26.0	25.6	19.1	23.4	23.7	23.1	23.3	20.6	21.0	20.6
Defence	42.9	39.4	31.5	31.8	29.3	33.8	35.2	30.2	27.2	29.2	30.6
Other Municipal	78.2	80.5	78.7	73.1	76.4	72.5	68.7	65.6	59.1	59.6	61.1
Other Provincial	102.1	89.3	95.2	94.6	101.5	115.3	118.7	100.1	91.8	94.8	100.8
Other Provincial exclusive of effect on Health Services	101.6	88.8	94.2	93.3	99.8	112.3	114.5	94.8	82.1	78.5	81.3
Other Federal	56.2	49.5	44.5	43.8	48.5	49.1	49.9	49.3	48.0	51.0	50.4
TOTAL Government	45.2	44.2	42.3	39.3	41.4	42.5	41.9	39.3	36.6	38.5	39.5

RELATION TO THE EMPLOYED LABOUR FORCE

Table 2.8 shows the proportion of total Canadian employment accounted for by direct and indirect government jobs. For example, in 1971, 19.9 per cent of total Canadian employment was accounted for by our measure of direct government employment, and 7.4 per cent by indirect employment.[23]

But while there was a mild upward trend over the period in the proportion of total Canadian employment attributable to the direct government category (the percentage for 1961, for example, was 16.1), the proportion ascribed to indirect government employment was virtually stationary over the period, in a range from 6.6 per cent to 7.5 per cent (the former in 1964, the latter in 1967).[24] This evidence gives no ground for either celebration or alarm at the burgeoning relative role of government as source of employment. On the other hand, in terms of incremental employment, the government sector (direct and indirect) filled a more substantial role. If one compares the absolute increase in direct and indirect government employment between the two end-years, 1961 and 1971, with the increase in total Canadian employment, the view may be taken of the public sector having filled about 40 per cent of the new jobs added to the economy between those years.

SENSITIVITY OF INDIRECT TO DIRECT RATIOS

An interesting issue arises when one compares the Canadian ratios of indirect to direct government employment to those of the United States, inferred from the work of Ginzberg (1976) and Hiestand (1977).[25] The United States ratios appear to be considerably higher than the Canadian, although they fall over time. The following ratios for the United States are approximate, because the source (Hiestand, 1977, Tables 4 and 6, pp. 336-37) gives the data on indirect government employment only as percentages of the total employed labour force.

---

[23] It may be of interest to compare the Canadian proportions of direct and indirect government employment to total national employment, with the analogous proportions for the United States, cited in Hiestand (1977, pp. 336–37).

	Canada		United States	
	1970	1971	1970	1973
Direct	19.8%	19.9%	16.5%	15.8%
Indirect	7.2	7.4	9.1	8.4
	27.0	27.3	25.5	24.2

[24] The 11 annual percentage ratios of indirect government employment to total Canadian employed labour had a mean of 7.13 per cent and a standard deviation of 0.266. The coefficient of variation (standard deviation divided by mean) was 0.037, or under 5 per cent, implying that constancy is a reasonable interpretation of the time series of proportions.

[25] See also footnote 23 above.

United States Indirect to Direct Government Employment Ratios
(per cent)

1960	1970	1973
62	55	53

The explanation of higher United States ratios seems to follow mainly from the different treatment of publicly-financed health care in the two countries. In Canada the hospital 'industry' is itself a component of the government sector (contributing to the denominator of the indirect/direct ratio). The United States has no universal government health program. Nonetheless, an important part of health care costs (including hospitals) is government-financed under Medicare (for the elderly) and Medicaid (for the needy). To the extent that some hospital costs are paid in the U.S. as government 'purchases', some hospital employment

TABLE 2.8

DIRECT AND INDIRECT GOVERNMENT EMPLOYMENT IN PROPORTION TO THE EMPLOYED LABOUR FORCE, CANADA, 1961 TO 1971
(per cent)

	Direct	Indirect	Direct plus Indirect
1961	16.1	7.2	23.3
1962	16.5	7.3	23.8
1963	16.6	7.0	23.6
1964	16.9	6.6	23.5
1965	16.8	6.9	23.6
1966	17.1	7.2	24.3
1967	18.2	7.5	25.7
1968	19.0	7.3	26.3
1969	19.5	6.9	26.4
1970	19.8	7.2	27.0
1971	19.9	7.4	27.3

Sources: Direct Government Employment from Table 2.1.
Indirect Government Employment from Table 2.5.
Total Canadian Employed Labour Force from *Historical Labour Force Statistics*, Statistics Canada, #71-201 (annual). Data used were those from the former (pre-1975) Labour Force Survey, to ensure comparability across years. Numbers in the armed forces were added to the total employment data.

moves to the government-indirect category. There would, on the other hand, be relatively fewer medical practitioners on the United States government indirect payroll than is the case in Canada. Relative to Canada, the denominator of the United States ratio has a decrement and the numerator has both an increment and a decrement.

For illustrative purposes, we experimented with the Canadian data for 1971 to see if we might manipulate hospital and health care expenditure to yield the same overall ratios for Canada as those applicable to the United States. It turns out that if the entire Canadian health care industry, as it existed in 1971, were in the private sector, but if 27 per cent of all health and hospitalization demands were paid for as 'commodity purchases' by government, the overall ratio of indirect to direct government employment in Canada would have been 55 per cent (against the actual 39.5 per cent).

The foregoing exercise is not presented as a precise reconstruction of the Canadian economy on the United States model. It is propounded to illustrate the point that indirect to direct employment ratios (and the related 'multiplier' concept) are based on specific, if somewhat arbitrary assumptions. To make the point more general, all calculated Input-Output 'multipliers' are highly sensitive to the demarcation of the 'propellent' or 'causative' activity; in the present case to the defined boundaries of government.[26] If the compilers of the Canadian National Accounts had chosen to assign the hospital industry to the private sector, the overall ratio of indirect to direct government employment in 1971 would have been twice as large as it now appears. Similarly, if government enterprises and the universities were allotted to the government sector, direct public employment would increase, the ratio of indirect to direct government jobs would fall, and the proportion of indirect plus direct public employment to national job totals would rise.

INDIRECT EMPLOYMENT AND REAL PURCHASES

In Table 2.9, the sectoral totals of indirect government employment are examined with reference to a different standard, the quantity of real government commodity purchases. The table shows the number of jobs propagated each year by every one million constant 1961 dollars of government purchases from the processing sector. We may note a uniformly declining time-trend for these numbers, in all categories of government demand. The table confirms a judgment that was made previously: indirect employment failed to keep pace with the rising trend of real government demand.

On average, over the 11-year period, about 100 man-years of industrial employment were generated by every one million dollars worth of government purchases (in 1961 prices). But by 1971 the job count had fallen to about 89

---

[26] As we intimated earlier, the size of calculated multipliers is even more sensitive to the set of activities assigned to the processing or 'closed' sector of the model.

TABLE 2.9

RATIOS OF 'INDIRECT' EMPLOYMENT TO REAL DOLLARS OF GOVERNMENT PURCHASING, CANADA, 1961 TO 1971

(man-years of industrial employment generated by each one million constant 1961 dollars of government 'commodity' purchases)

Source of Government Demand	YEAR										
	1961	1962	1963	1964	1965	1966	1967	1968	1969	1970	1971
Capital Investment											
Machinery and Equipment	82.9	81.6	80.8	73.9	69.5	66.0	62.4	55.2	50.3	48.9	46.5
Construction	122.6	120.0	118.2	112.7	111.1	109.0	112.5	104.7	104.9	104.9	102.2
Current Purchases for											
Hospitals	114.3	106.1	103.5	99.6	94.1	87.6	92.5	88.7	82.9	81.4	77.6
Education	109.4	105.2	101.5	94.2	89.5	85.4	90.3	84.6	86.1	84.3	84.9
Defence	95.7	89.6	87.3	83.6	80.5	81.8	78.0	71.8	69.5	68.0	74.2
Other Municipal	118.1	115.1	110.9	105.6	99.3	96.3	101.5	97.8	92.3	90.0	89.3
Other Provincial	125.3	125.4	119.0	112.2	110.3	106.6	105.8	98.9	97.9	91.8	87.2
Other Provincial exclusive of Health Services	126.4	126.9	121.2	115.0	113.4	110.8	109.9	104.1	112.0	115.5	120.7
Other Federal	110.1	106.2	107.7	103.1	99.5	93.7	99.5	90.4	92.3	93.2	91.9
Total Current Purchases	109.8	105.3	103.6	98.6	95.2	92.6	95.4	90.0	88.5	86.7	85.5
Total Current Purchases exclusive of Health Services	110.0	105.5	104.0	99.1	95.7	93.3	96.2	91.0	90.6	90.8	91.3
Total Government Purchases	113.4	110.1	108.4	102.7	100.1	97.3	100.0	93.2	92.4	90.8	88.9
Total Government Purchases exclusive of Health Services	113.6	110.2	108.6	103.0	100.4	97.7	100.5	93.9	93.8	93.7	92.9

man-years (for government as a whole) from about 113 in 1961. In all years, the most job-stimulative purchases were those of the 'other provincial' sector (Health Services excluded). That sector's job-creativity also shows the least rate of decline over the time-span.[27] It seems plausible to ascribe the almost-divergent behaviour of the non-health provincial sector to a significant shift in the make-up of its purchases, in the late 1960s, toward goods and services of higher labour intensity.[28]

There are two reasons why, in general, indirect government jobs failed to grow as quickly as did the real commodity purchases responsible for them. One reason is a rise in import coefficients. That is, over the 11-year period, the Canadian economy was becoming more 'open'; the import content embodied in any final demand was growing with a concomitant decline in domestic content.[29]

The more significant reason, however, is productivity growth in terms of output per employed person in the domestic private sector. The counterpart of generally declining ratios of indirect employment to real government purchases is increasing labour productivity in industry. The reciprocals of the ratios in Table 2.9 are a rough measure of the trend in real government purchases produced by each private sector worker — and the trend was rising.

PATTERNS OF INPUT SUBSTITUTION

If one compares the operating (non-capital) inputs of the five non-defence sectors, two contrasting patterns emerge that tie together the different proportions and growth rates mentioned in this chapter, and that relate input substitution in the public economy to growing labour productivity in the private sector and a rising import content.

For example, in three sectors: hospitals, education and 'other federal', direct employment grew at almost identical rates (between six and seven per cent a year). The goods and services bought by all three embodied a progressively smaller domestic labour requirement for each unit purchased. In one pattern, exemplified by education and 'other federal', considerable factor substitution of purchased inputs for direct labour also took place within the governmental input-mix. In both cases, the rate, over time, at which the sector was able (and/or willing) to substitute purchases for direct labour exceeded the rate of

---

[27] The annual percentage rate of decrease in the indirect job to real purchase ratio was 2.4 for total government (with or without investment). For 'other provincial' exclusive of Health Service purchases, the rate of decline was 1.0 per cent a year; in this case—unlike the other ratios in the table—the coefficient of correlation with time was very weak.

[28] Examination of the disaggregated 'other provincial' commodity purchase series shows no single category to which could be attached full responsibility for the apparent mid-series shift toward higher labour intensity. However, as mentioned, growing provincial demand for Business Management Services was particularly evident in the later years' observations.

[29] It should, of course, be acknowledged that a more 'open' economy also implies a rising level of exports. But since foreign trade is not part of the Input-Output processing sector, the nature of the model is such that commodity imports cannot propagate domestic employment.

labour-productivity growth and import growth embodied in its purchases. That implies, as we have seen, that the growth of indirect employment exceeded the growth of direct employment in the education and 'other federal' sectors.

In the case of hospitals, on the other hand, the sector's absorption of direct labour and purchased inputs grew more or less in tandem, while its indirect labour became more productive and the import content of its purchases grew. Thus, indirect labour generated by hospital demand necessarily increased more slowly than did direct hospital employment. The 'other municipal' sector follows the hospital pattern; and 'other provincial', exclusive of health expenditure, somewhat irregularly reproduces the education and 'other federal' pattern.

Government as Income Distributor

This final interpretative section deals with the more general role of government as income distributor. We begin with the implications of the Input-Output model with respect to the personal income generated by both direct public employment and government purchases. Somewhat more conjecturally, we extend the discussion to include 'non-exhaustive' government spending, and relate all categories to total personal income.

PERSONAL INCOMES FROM GOVERNMENT PAYROLL AND PURCHASES

Table 2.10 summarizes government direct payrolls (wages, salaries and supplementary labour income) and the total private sector earnings due to government purchases of goods and services. The total of indirect earnings as a proportion of direct payroll is larger than is the ratio of the indirect to direct job numbers. This is not surprising because total indirect earnings include capital returns paid to persons.[30] Like the 'job ratios', however, the indirect to direct earnings ratios follow a downward trend over time. The downward trend is accentuated when the generated earnings of independent health professionals are excluded from the reckoning. Despite the declining ratios to direct payrolls, it is apparent that the absolute amount of indirect earnings that depend on government purchases has followed a rising trend.[31]

The numbers here are, of course, too gross to draw definitive conclusions about the wage rates of government employees relative to the wages of those on the indirect government payroll. It is suggestive, however, to note that, between

---

[30] One set of calculations made by Kubursi (1978, p. 78) using the Ontario inter-industry Input-Output model, is of 'income multipliers' (direct plus indirect income divided by direct) for nine provincial functional expenditure categories. The weighted average of the nine income multipliers is 1.53. This is remarkably close to the corresponding number for all Canadian governments as of 1965, in Table 2.10, where indirect to direct earnings are 56 per cent, implying a multiplier of 1.56.

[31] As shown in Table 2.10, the 11-year growth rate of all indirect earnings due to government purchases was 10.1 per cent, inclusive of earnings of independent health professionals, and 9.0 per cent when they are excluded. These rates may be compared to a 9.2 per cent average annual growth of GNP, and 9.6 per cent growth of personal income, over the same period.

TABLE 2.10

PERSONAL INCOME DUE TO DIRECT GOVERNMENT EMPLOYMENT AND GOVERNMENT PURCHASES, CANADA, 1961 TO 1971

(millions of current dollars)

Category of Personal Income	1961	1962	1963	1964	1965	1966	1967	1968	1969	1970	1971	Average Growth Rate per cent per annum
Direct Government Payroll (Wages, Salaries and Supplementary Labour Income)	3,826	4,170	4,497	4,941	5,364	6,188	7,366	8,432	9,696	10,861	12,024	12.8
Indirect Earnings generated by Government Purchases												
Labour Income	1,837	1,961	2,005	2,015	2,335	2,756	3,047	3,210	3,366	3,806	4,364	9.2
Net Income of Unincorporated Business	234	254	269	272	314	372	422	502	627	920	1,184	17.0
Interest and Dividends paid by Business to Persons	244	270	279	303	353	418	399	429	438	473	533	7.9
TOTAL Indirect Earnings[1]	2,315	2,485	2,554	2,589	3,002	3,546	3,868	4,141	4,431	5,199	6,081	10.1
Ratio (per cent) to Direct Payroll	60.5	59.6	56.8	52.4	56.0	57.3	52.5	49.1	45.7	47.9	50.6	
TOTAL Indirect Earnings, excluding Net Income of Unincorporated Business in Health Service industry that is due to Provincial Government Demand	2,311	2,481	2,544	2,575	2,982	3,508	3,808	4,041	4,213	4,725	5,382	9.0
Ratio (per cent) to Direct Payroll	60.4	59.5	56.6	52.1	55.6	56.7	51.7	47.9	43.5	43.5	44.8	

Note: [1]Columns may not add exactly because of rounding.

1961 and 1967, the ratio of indirect labour income (excluding proprietor and capital income) to the direct government payroll exceeded the ratio of indirect job numbers to direct job numbers. Beginning in 1968, the comparison is reversed: the indirect to direct number ratio (indirect excluding health personnel) is larger than the indirect to direct payroll ratio. This suggests that wage relatives between the private and public sectors moved in a direction favourable to public sector employees, over the period examined.[32]

PERSONAL INCOMES FROM ALL GOVERNMENT SPENDING

In Table 2.11 an attempt was made to determine the proportion of Canadian personal income for which all government spending activity was responsible. What is required is to add transfer payments, and other government payments to persons, to the amounts shown in Table 2.10, and to divide the totals by personal income, as computed in the National Accounts. The exercise, unfortunately, is not straightforward.

In the first place, the Input-Output tables are on a 'Domestic' basis whereas the denominator of the calculation, personal income, is on a 'National' basis.[33]

Secondly, interest on the public debt, in the third row of Table 2.11, is overstated in the sense that we want only amounts received by persons. The National Accounts route all domestic interest on the public debt through the business sector, regardless of whether the payee is a person, a business, or another government. The true amount received by persons cannot be determined; that portion is imbedded in the business outlay totals (Statistics Canada, 1975, p. 185).

The reader is also reminded that the role of government is understated in this table, as in all tables of the chapter, if we mean 'government' to include publicly owned enterprises and the universities.

Subject to these cautions, the table still suggests the rough magnitude and direction of government's role as income-source. What is indicated is that, in the early 1970s, something of the order of 40 per cent of personal income in Canada originated with decisions made by government. The table also indicates that the comparable proportion had been constant, at a 32 to 33 per cent level from 1961 through the mid-1960s.

The fact that so many Canadians are dependent on government for their sustenance does not mean that all those incomes would not have been received if a government had not done the spending. (An apt example is income from health service.) Moreover, the total impact of government must also comprehend the

---

[32] For example, in 1961 the ratio of indirect to direct job numbers (excluding health) was 45.1 per cent; indirect labour income divided by direct labour income was 48.0 per cent. In 1971, the two ratios, respectively, were 36.9 per cent and 36.3 per cent. The spread in 1970 was somewhat wider than in 1971. These crude calculations are consistent with trends in public-private wage differentials examined in Gunderson (1978).

[33] The 'Domestic' basis covers output and earnings generated by economic activity that takes place in Canada, without regard to the residence of factor owners. The 'National' basis is concerned with the earnings of Canadian-resident factor owners, regardless of where those earnings originate.

TABLE 2.11

PERCENTAGES OF PERSONAL INCOME ATTRIBUTABLE TO GOVERNMENT EXPENDITURE, CANADA, 1961 TO 1971

Category of Personal Income	YEAR										
	1961	1962	1963	1964	1965	1966	1967	1968	1969	1970	1971
Direct Payments by Government											
Wages, Salaries and Supplementary Labour Income	12.7	12.7	12.9	13.3	13.1	13.4	14.6	15.1	15.7	16.3	16.2
Transfer Payments and Capital Assistance to Persons	9.0	8.9	8.6	8.6	8.4	8.2	9.2	9.8	10.0	10.5	11.2
Interest on the Public Debt (to residents)	3.5	3.6	3.6	3.6	3.6	3.5	3.6	3.7	3.9	4.2	4.2
Indirect Earnings generated by Government Purchases	7.7	7.6	7.3	6.9	7.3	7.7	7.6	7.4	7.2	7.8	8.2
TOTAL Direct Payments and Indirect Earnings	32.9	32.8	32.4	32.4	32.3	32.8	35.1	36.2	36.7	38.8	39.8

Sources: Personal Income, Transfer Payments, Capital Assistance and Debt Interest from *National Income and Expenditure Accounts*, Statistics Canada, #13-201 (1977), and #13-531 (1976).
Government Payroll and Indirect Earnings from Table 2.9.

Note: Columns may not add exactly because of rounding.

effects of taxation on outputs and incomes. Nonetheless, Table 2.11 demonstrates that, apart from the ever-rising influence of government on the character of national output, its role as the determining agent of the income distribution has increased sharply in recent years.

SUMMARY AND CONCLUSIONS

SUMMARY

This chapter has tried to relate the indirect effects of government expenditure to the quantities of labour and real goods and services that were the original objects of its expenditure. The data source was Statistics Canada's 'Open Output Determination Model' for the years 1961 through 1971, supplemented by other statistical sources when necessary. Commodity purchase values were price-deflated to serve as an index of real quantities. Numbers of direct government jobs were also estimated for comparison with real commodity purchases and the numbers of indirect jobs generated by non-labour expenditure. These amounts were calculated, separately, for six sources of government current, or flow, demand, and two aggregated categories of government investment in fixed assets. Our final effort was a less precise assessment of the comprehensive totals of personal income for which government choices are responsible.

Close attention was given to the comparative time trends and rates of growth (or decline) of the tabulated amounts. In particular, evidence was sought as to shifts and substitutions in government's input-mix in response to rising direct labour costs and increasing private sector output per employed person.

In detailing the main results, the effects of government spending on health care service, apart from hospitalization, were often deducted. Over the period examined, Health Services represented a unique instance of a shift from private decision-making to public allocation.

LIMITATIONS

Apart from our possible errors of application and interpretation, limitations that are inherent in the methodology should be noted. Representing, as it does, a fixed equilibrium, the Input-Output model does not disclose whether the manpower and other resource inputs here attributed to government might have been otherwise employed. The open model does not reckon the further stimulation of employment and income that results from re-spent wages and other personal incomes.[34] Since it is a static (although annual) model it makes no

---

[34] Given the availability of a more 'closed' model, this does not represent a 'limitation' inherent in the Input-Output method, but rather a decision — in the author's opinion the correct one — to confine the study to those effects that stem from government's own spending choices.

allowance for the labour and other inputs required to reproduce the capital assets consumed in production; nor can it be used directly to illustrate factor substitutions involving capital resources.

Direct government activity is defined so as to exclude government business enterprises, and even the activities of a 'commercial' government department: the Post Office. Also absent are the spending effects of the government-supported universities.

Despite these restrictions the Input-Output model provides a wealth of information on government activities that the present study has scarcely begun to exhaust. Only the most cursory attention, for example, was given to the commodity composition of government's fixed asset and defence purchases. It might be instructive to analyze the shifting mixture of inputs in the beleaguered defence department as it responded to shrinking real budgets and altered responsibilities.[35]

CONCLUSIONS

The study confirms (if it needed confirmation) that absolute numbers of direct government employees, in Canada, increased through the 1960s into the 1970s. It conveys the additional information that total indirect government employment, the number of jobs that depend on government purchases, also increased, although not as rapidly, in the aggregate. Real purchases themselves (in one sense a substitute for direct labour, in another sense a complement), in general, rose more quickly than did either class of employment. In two sectors, however, hospitals and 'other municipal', direct jobs increased more rapidly than did real commodity purchases. The most aberrant category, defence, experienced a decline in respect to all three measures: direct employment at a slightly more rapid pace than real purchases, and indirect employment the most rapidly. Contrary to the aggregates, indirect employment dependent on the education, 'other federal' and 'other provincial' sectors rose more quickly than did direct employment.

In 1971, our calculations show that the 'full-time equivalent' total direct government labour force amount to 1.6 million persons (up from one million in 1961). In 1971, government demand generated a further 644 thousand jobs in industry (up from 449 thousand in 1961).

To put the employment growth in perspective, however, we noted that in relation to total national employment, the relative growth of the direct government labour force was comparatively small (rising from 16.1 per cent of employed labour in 1961 to 19.9 per cent in 1971), and that, in relative terms, indirect employment remained constant around an average of 7.1 per cent of employed labour.

---

[35] In the defence sector, there is another kind of flow-input substitution possible, one that we did not pursue here: that is, substitution between military and civilian personnel.

Throughout the period, there was a marked shift with respect to both the character of government purchases and the industrial composition of indirect employment away from goods and toward services (or from primary and secondary to tertiary industry).

Among the government sectors, the one with the most pronounced stimulative effect on indirect labour (in both absolute and relative terms) was the provincial sector (omitting its Health Service expenditure). The provincial sector, and to a lesser extent the federal government, stepped up their purchase of Business Management Services to a notable degree in the late 1960s; this might be construed as a shift to contract labour from direct labour.

We used an array of growth rates and a simple regression to test for more general evidence of substitution between purchased inputs and direct labour among government's current flow inputs. Our conclusion is that the response of the five non-defence sectors to changing relative input prices is highly variable. The education, 'other provincial' and 'other federal' sectors do illustrate a progressive increase in the use of real purchases relative to labour. In all three cases, the substitution was more rapid than was the concurrent increase in labour productivity and import content embodied in the purchased goods and services. That would account for a rise in the ratio of indirect to direct labour.

Hospitals show evidence of stricter complementarity between direct labour and purchased inputs. Given rising imports and rising output per worker in the private sector, that implies a falling ratio of indirect to direct labour. 'Other municipal' government shows a similar trend.

With respect to the proportion of total personal income that can be traced to the decisions of government, we estimated that close to 40 per cent would be the rough measure for 1971, an increase of about seven percentage points from the proportions that held before 1967. These estimates are imprecise, but they indicate that government is an important and growing income re-distributor, apart from its role as resource allocator.

REFERENCES

Bird, R.M. (1978) "The Growth of the Public Service in Canada", Chapter Two in David K. Foot (ed.) *Public Employment and Compensation in Canada: Myths and Realities* (Toronto: Butterworth & Co. for The Institute for Research on Public Policy).

Bucovetsky, M.W. (1973) "A Study of the Role of the Resource Industries in the Canadian Economy" *Working Paper 7301* (Toronto: University of Toronto, Institute for Policy Analysis).

Ginzberg, E. (1976) "The Pluralistic Economy of the U.S." *Scientific American 235: 6,* December, 25-29.

Gunderson, M. (1978) "Public-Private Wage and Non-Wage Differentials in Canada: Some Calculations from Published Tabulations", Chapter Seven in David K. Foot (ed.) *Public Employment and Compensation in Canada: Myths and Realities* (Toronto: Butterworth & Co. for The Institute for Research on Public Policy).

Hiestand, D.L. (1977) "Recent Trends in the Not-for-Profit Sector" in *Research Papers Sponsored by the Commission on Private Philanthropy and Public Needs,* Vol. I (Washington: U.S. Department of Treasury).

Krashinsky, M. (1978) "The Cost of Day Care in Public Programs" *National Tax Journal* 31: 4, December (forthcoming).

Kubursi, A.A. (1978) "Differential Income and Employment Multipliers of Ontario Government Expenditures", Chapter Six in John Bossons (ed.) *Input-Output Analysis of Fiscal Policy in Ontario* (Toronto: Ontario Economic Council).

Miernyk, W.H. (1965) *The Elements of Input-Output Analysis* (New York: Random House).

Spann, R.M. (1977) "Public versus Private Provision of Government Services", Chapter Four in Thomas E. Borcherding (ed.) *Budgets and Bureaucrats: The Sources of Government Growth* (Durham: Duke University Press).

Statistics Canada (1975) *National Income and Expenditure Accounts,* Vol. 3, #13-549E (Ottawa: Information Canada).

Statistics Canada (1977a) *The Input-Output Structure of the Canadian Economy, 1961-71,* #15-506E (Ottawa: Supply and Services, Canada).

Statistics Canada (1977b) *The Input-Output Structure of the Canadian Economy in Constant 1961 Prices, 1961-71,* #15-507E (Ottawa: Supply and Services, Canada).

Stern, I. (1975) "Industry Effects of Government Expenditures: An Input-Output Analysis" *Survey of Current Business* 55: 5, 9-23.

Yan, C.-S. (1969) *Introduction to Input-Output Economics* (New York: Holt, Rinehart and Winston).

Chapter Three

Political Cycles, Economic Cycles and the Trend in Public Employment in Canada

by
David K. Foot*

INTRODUCTION

A number of general hypotheses have been proposed concerning the growth of the public sector relative to that of the private sector over time. These hypotheses are most often formulated in terms of expenditure growth, but it is not unusual to find this used as a proxy for employment growth because often adequate data on the latter are not available. Recently this subject has received renewed attention as a possible explanation for some of the trends in modern society (e.g., Bacon and Eltis (1976) in the U.K., Ginzberg (1976) in the U.S.).

A different group of hypotheses have been concerned with the systematic cyclical deviations of relative public sector growth around the long-run trend. Investigators have focussed attention on two types of deviation from the trend: those that may be related to an economic cycle (e.g., Rafuse (1965)) and those that may reflect vote-conscious behaviour on the part of political incumbents (e.g., Nordhaus (1975)).

This chapter examines the postwar evidence on these phenomena in Canada and tests some of the hypotheses which have been proposed to account for this evidence.

THEORY

Much of the theoretical work concerning this subject has been based on a simple two-sector model of the macro-economy. Different authors have used different names for these sectors, with the most common distinction being between the 'public' and the 'private' sectors of the economy. These sectors are defined to cover a broad spectrum of economic activity, with all activity being

Editor's Note: **David K. Foot** is Associate Professor in the Department of Political Economy and Research Associate of the Institute for Policy Analysis at the University of Toronto. Some of the material contained in this chapter was presented, under the same title, to the Twelfth Annual Meeting of the Canadian Economics Association in London, Ontario, May 28, 1978.

*This chapter has benefited considerably from the valuable advice of my colleagues, especially R. M. Bird and M. W. Bucovetsky, although responsibility for the final result rests with the author.

allocated to one sector or the other based on a 'sold or not sold-in-the-market place' criterion (e.g., Johnston, 1975) or, alternatively, on a 'profit making or not-for-profit' criterion (e.g., Ginzberg, 1976). Factors determining the relative growth of the two sectors are then usually presented and analyzed.

Perhaps the best known of these hypotheses can be traced to Baumol (1967) who showed that the relative size of the two sectors depended on the price elasticity of the demand for their output and the relative rate of increase in their productivity. By distinguishing between a 'technologically progressive' sector and a sector with only 'sporadic increases in productivity'.[1] Baumol argued that increasing unit costs over time in both sectors will be reflected in relatively higher prices for the output of the less 'progressive' sector and, with a negative price elasticity of demand, a declining relative output.[2] Alternatively, if for some reason the less 'progressive' sector output is to be maintained at a constant level (and quality) or at a fixed ratio to the output of the 'technologically progressive' sector, then a rising proportion of national resources must be devoted to the less 'progressive' sector over time. *If* the less progressive sector can be identified with the public sector and the technologically progressive sector with the private sector, this likely will be accompanied by an increasing ratio of public sector employment to total employment and, given existing national income accounting conventions of measuring the value of government outputs by their input cost, an increasing share of national income devoted to the public sector over time.

If different rates of productivity increase do not exist, then an increasing share can be explained by a relatively less elastic demand for public sector output or a shift in the income distribution (see Lynch and Redman, 1968). Note, however, that if the activity allocation is based on a 'sold or not sold-in-the-market place' criterion it may be very difficult to measure the relevant price elasticity of demand, although the same measurement problem also exists with respect to public sector productivity. Consequently, it appears to be almost impossible to isolate these effects empirically and instead broad trends are observed and theoretical models outlined in the literature—though there has been little work successfully linking theory and observation.

A number of hypotheses have also been advanced concerning systematic deviations of the relative public sector ratio around the long-run trend line. For expositional convenience these can be classified broadly as 'economic' and 'political' explanations. Rafuse (1965), building on the earlier work of Hansen and Perloff (1944), examined the fiscal behaviour of junior governments in the context of fiscal stabilization policy. Noting that national governments can follow the Keynesian tradition of anticyclical behaviour with respect to output and employment, but that sub-national governments are much less capable of

---

[1] It appears to be quite common for these to be loosely identified with the 'private' and 'public' sectors, respectively.

[2] More accurately, those 'nonprogressive' goods for which the absolute value of the elasticity of demand with respect to price is greater than the absolute value of the elasticity of demand with respect to income, or those for which the income effect is negative, will tend to vanish.

such stabilizing behaviour because they possess less fiscal flexibility and considerably less monetary flexibility (e.g., they cannot borrow from the central bank), Rafuse concluded that their behaviour can often be procyclical and, consequently, fiscally perverse. In a later Canadian study which examined the fiscal behaviour of both federal and provincial-municipal governments, Robinson and Courchene (1969) found very little evidence to confirm the fiscal perversity hypothesis[3] and recent evidence for the U.S. (see Ebanks (1976) and Borcherding (1977)) suggests that exactly the opposite may be true.

Recently, Nordhaus (1975) has explored the effects of a 'political cycle' on government behaviour. Using a carefully developed theoretical model he concludes that governments are motivated to attempt to make the unemployment rate follow a 'sawtooth' pattern, increasing it right after an election and then gradually reducing it to the lowest level immediately preceding the next election. This model is apparently well suited to political systems with fixed periods between the elections (such as in the U.S.). In a parliamentary system, although the government cannot forecast the exact time of the next election with complete certainty, it does have considerable control over the timing which is likely to reflect vote-conscious behaviour on behalf of the incumbents. Consequently, the model, which suggests the possible impact of a political cycle on the unemployment rate and (to the extent that government employment is one of the policy variables as suggested in the Robinson-Courchene study) on the ratio of public to total employment, would appear to be an hypothesis worthy of investigation in both types of political system.

It should be pointed out that these three hypotheses — the Baumol trend hypothesis, the Hansen and Perloff fiscal perversity hypothesis and the Nordhaus political cycle hypothesis — are independent hypotheses and can *all* be simultaneous explanations of the variations in the ratio of public sector output or employment to total output or employment over time.

DATA

Tables 3.1 and 3.2 present the ratio of public sector employment to total employment for Canada over the postwar period. In Table 3.1, this ratio is derived from *Taxation Statistics* data.[4] Five sub-sectors of the public sector can be identified in this publication. These include not only the usual three 'government' categories of federal, provincial and municipal, but also include a separate category for all educational institutions operated on a nonprofit basis and one for all other nonprofit institutions, such as hospitals, charitable and religious

---

[3] Of particular interest for this paper is the Robinson-Courchene finding that government expenditure on wages and salaries shows a definite countercyclical behaviour at all levels of government, especially the federal, which, on their interpretation ". . .suggests the use of government employment as a direct weapon for federal stabilization measures" (1969, p. 183).

[4] 'Employment' in these data is interpreted as total taxable plus nontaxable returns. For definitions and a detailed review of these data see Foot and Thadaney (1978).

TABLE 3.1

**PUBLIC EMPLOYMENT AS A PERCENTAGE OF
TOTAL EMPLOYMENT IN CANADA, 1946-1975[1]**

Year	Federal	Provincial	Municipal	Total Government	Educational	Institutional	Total Public
1946	4.63	2.06	2.12	8.80	2.24	1.88	12.93
1947	3.68	1.97	1.98	7.63	2.26	1.97	11.86
1948	3.53	2.35	2.09	7.96	2.24	1.99	12.18
1949	3.87	2.69	2.16	8.72	1.72	1.87	12.31
1950	3.72	2.63	2.14	8.49	1.84	1.89	12.23
1951	3.48	2.49	2.12	8.09	1.80	1.91	11.80
1952	3.49	2.58	2.13	8.20	1.77	2.06	12.03
1953	3.62	2.65	2.24	8.52	1.76	2.21	12.48
1954	3.84	2.74	2.35	8.94	1.92	2.54	13.41
1955	3.70	2.76	2.43	8.89	1.92	2.59	13.40
1956	3.58	2.66	2.28	8.52	1.98	2.78	13.28
1957	3.65	2.88	2.35	8.88	1.99	2.70	13.57
1958	3.81	3.07	2.56	9.43	2.30	3.15	14.89
1959	3.76	3.25	2.60	9.61	3.01	3.29	15.91
1960	3.76	3.23	2.87	9.86	2.53	3.81	16.20
1961	3.88	3.36	3.04	10.28	2.70	4.02	17.00
1962	3.75	3.60	3.10	10.45	2.96	4.29	17.71
1963	3.65	3.69	3.33	10.68	2.98	4.73	18.38
1964	3.57	3.85	3.36	10.78	3.13	5.18	19.09
1965	3.45	3.91	3.24	10.60	3.21	5.39	19.20
1966	3.34	3.87	3.32	10.53	3.33	5.37	19.23

1967	3.35	3.94	3.47	10.76	3.39	5.76	19.90
1968	3.22	3.94	3.53	10.69	3.61	5.97	20.26
1969	3.13	3.95	3.49	10.57	3.65	6.25	20.47
1970	3.18	4.01	3.62	10.80	3.78	6.33	20.92
1971	3.37	4.14	3.79	11.30	3.58	6.24	21.13
1972	3.28	3.90	3.86	11.03	3.03	6.05	20.12
1973	3.03	3.86	3.43	10.32	3.08	5.72	19.12
1974	3.01	3.88	3.33	10.22	3.06	5.72	19.00
1975	2.99	3.99	3.78	10.76	2.70	5.85	19.31

Source: *Taxation Statistics* (Ottawa: Revenue Canada, Taxation) annual issues.

Note:

[1] Figures in the table show total taxable plus nontaxable returns in each category expressed as a percentage of total taxable plus nontaxable returns in Canada for each year.

TABLE 3.2

GOVERNMENT EMPLOYMENT AS A PERCENTAGE OF TOTAL EMPLOYMENT IN CANADA, 1961-1976[1]

Year	Federal	Provincial	Local	Total Government
1961	5.92	2.56	2.34	10.82
1962	5.72	2.51	2.31	10.54
1963	5.53	2.56	2.35	10.43
1964	5.38	2.53	2.33	10.25
1965	5.26	2.57	2.33	10.16
1966	5.23	2.59	2.33	10.15
1967	5.30	2.67	2.40	10.37
1968	5.07	2.83	2.44	10.34
1969	5.00	2.82	2.47	10.29
1970	4.88	2.95	2.59	10.41
1971	4.93	3.14	2.58	10.65
1972	4.99	3.19	2.59	10.77
1973	4.96	3.09	2.65	10.70
1974	4.93	3.09	2.62	10.64
1975	4.98	3.25	2.70	10.93
1976	5.06	3.21	2.69	10.95

Sources: *Federal Government Employment, Provincial Government Employment* and *Local Government Employment* (Ottawa: Statistics Canada) quarterly issues.

Note:
[1] Annual averages of quarterly observations. See footnote 7 to text for further details.

organizations, etc. Consequently, the total of these five sub-sectors corresponds more closely to the public sector concept discussed above than would just the total of the three 'government' categories. Note, however, that the figures exclude the armed forces,[5] government business enterprises and any imputation for other persons *indirectly* employed by the government sector (as is done, for example, in Ginzberg (1976) and Bucovetsky (see Chapter Two)). In addition, they include some activity which might be considered part of the 'private' sector, such as the employment of charitable organizations. However, it is likely that these inclusions and exclusions are relatively minor when compared with the broad concept of the public sector as is suggested by the theory outlined above.

---

[5] These would add another 0.8 per cent to the total in 1975. Data on the armed forces are not available from *Taxation Statistics* for the period 1952 to 1973.

The ratios presented in Table 3.1 are *not* based on employment data; rather they represent tax-filers who are classified by type of employer based on their *reported, main* source of income. Such a classification may include (or even exclude) a number of persons not usually considered part of public sector employment. As an alternative, therefore, Table 3.2 presents a comparable ratio derived from government employment data.[6] Unfortunately, it is not possible to obtain such data for as long a period or for as broad a concept of the public sector from these sources, although it is possible to obtain them on a quarterly, or even monthly, basis. As a result of these considerations, the ratios presented in Table 3.2, which are annual averages of quarterly observations, include only the three 'government' categories and cover the period 1961 to 1976.[7]

The two data sets are remarkably consistent, each showing that total government approximately accounted for between 10 and 11 per cent of total employment in Canada in the 1960s and 1970s. Both suggest that the 1975 ratio was not very different from the 1961 ratio, a finding reported by Bird (1978). The taxation data (Table 3.1) suggest that this ratio has risen approximately two percentage points since the 1940s and 1950s. The composition of the total differs somewhat between the two sources. The greater importance of the federal ratio in Table 3.2 apparently arises because of the inclusion of government business enterprise employment which is excluded from the government data in *Taxation Statistics*. Both tables show a downward trend in the federal percentage and an upward trend in the provincial and municipal percentages. The taxation data (Table 3.1), which also include information on educational and institutional employees over the period, indicate that total public employment in Canada rose from 11.9 per cent of total Canadian employment in 1947 to 21.1 per cent in 1971.[8] It has since declined to a level around 19 per cent.[9] From the figures it is also apparent that the 'government' share of this total has been gradually declining over the postwar period.

Each of the hypotheses outlined above was tested using the information presented in Tables 3.1 and 3.2. The Baumol trend hypothesis was examined using a linear time trend and two alternative nonlinear trend variables. The Hansen and Perloff fiscal perversity hypothesis was tested by considering the deviation of the per cent growth in Canadian real GNP from the average over the

---

[6] These data are obtained from the various governmental bodies using either administrative record or survey format based on payroll data. They are published quarterly by Statistics Canada in *Federal Government Employment* (Catalogue No. 72-004), *Provincial Government Employment* (Catalogue No. 72-007) and *Local Government Employment* (Catalogue No. 72-009).

[7] A description and extensive review of these data can be found in Foot, Scicluna and Thadaney (1978a, see especially Tables 4.1 and 4.2). The denominator, total employment in Canada, was obtained from Statistics Canada's *Canadian Statistical Review* (Catalogue No. 11-003E) with the data for 1976 being estimated to conform with the pre-1976 data obtained from the previous Labour Force Survey. Neither the numerator nor the denominator were seasonally adjusted.

[8] A similar figure is reported by Perry (1975) and Bird (1978).

[9] A similar decline for the U.S. is reported by Ginzberg (1976).

period under consideration. The existence of fiscal perversity would require a positive relationship with this variable.

The Nordhaus political cycle hypothesis was tested with a number of different variables.[10] First, a federal election dummy variable was employed, which implies a change in the employment ratio only in the years when a federal election took place. This is represented by the vertical lines in Figure 3.1. Second, a Nordhaus 'sawtooth' effect was approximated by connecting the top of one election dummy to the bottom of the next (as shown by the solid line in Figure 3.1). Third, a 'cyclical' political variable was generated by noting that employees cannot be instantaneously fired after an election (as implicitly assumed by Nordhaus) but are gradually released until the government 'senses' an approaching election after which employment is gradually increased. To construct this variable the government's 'sense' was assumed to be based on a four-year election cycle so that it runs down employment for the first two years after which gradual increases occur. Where the time between elections is of a shorter duration it is assumed that the government acts as if it 'senses' the next election at the mid-point between the elections. The resulting variable is also presented in Figure 3.1 (by the broken line). A fourth political variable was designed to represent a special feature of the parliamentary system — the minority government — under which any of the above alternative political behaviours might be modified. The months of minority federal government in each year was employed as the relevant variable in this context. Finally, a 'political popularity' variable was constructed from Gallup Poll hypothetical (and actual) election standings data.[11] This variable, constructed to measure the per cent of the electorate which would vote for the party in power if a federal election were held, provides a well-publicized, reasonably objective measure of the cyclical popularity of the federal government. This is probably the most relevant political cycle variable in a parliamentary system, where the timing of an election is not known with certainty. The Nordhaus model would predict an increase in employment prior to an election and a decrease in employment following an election. Presumably the same motivation to stay in power would induce the government to increase employment during periods of minority government and low political popularity.

However, in a somewhat different context, Fisher (1964) found that political competition was inversely related to spending (and hence employment). Since times of election and periods of minority government and low popularity

---

[10] Only the effects of federal elections are considered here. This provides a type of 'controlled experiment' since only federal employment would be expected to be sensitive to the federal political cycle variables. In this sense, significant sensitivity recorded by other categories of public employment to these variables would be considered 'spurious'. The effects of provincial and municipal elections could be handled in the same way.

[11] I am indebted to R. Johnston for making this data available to me. Annual and quarterly averages were obtained from the frequent but irregular Gallup Poll results by interpolating to obtain a monthly series and then averaging to obtain the quarterly and annual figures.

FIGURE 3.1
FEDERAL POLITICAL CYCLE VARIABLES, 1945-1976[1]

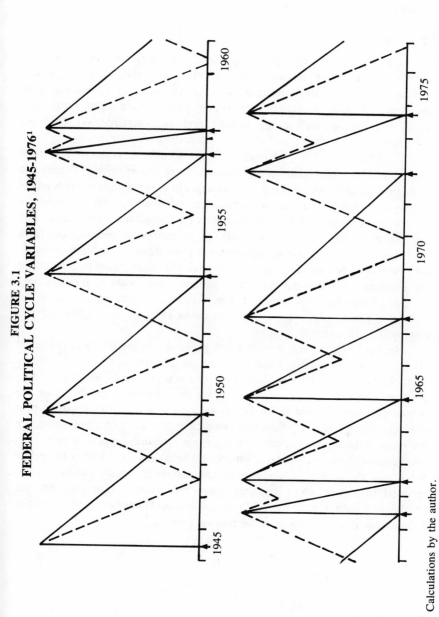

Source: Calculations by the author.

Note:

[1] A vertical arrow indicates an election quarter. See the text for an identification and description of the variables constructed from this information.

could be interpreted as periods of increased political competition, the Fisher model would predict the opposite behaviour to the Nordhaus model. Consequently, the sign of the relationship with the political cycle variables cannot be determined *a priori*.

RESULTS

Tests of the Baumol trend hypothesis are presented in Table 3.3. Significantly negative trends are obtained for the federal ratio, while significantly positive trends are obtained for all other categories, including the two aggregate categories.[12] Generally, there is little difference between the results for the two sets of data, but the trends for the shorter periods are generally lower, verifying that the increases in the ratios have been moderating in recent years.

Since the Baumol trend hypothesis is not specific as to the form that the trend should take, two nonlinear specifications were also examined. The inverse of the time variable, which implies that an upper or lower asymptote exists on the employment ratio, and the logarithmic transformation, which implies a decreasing or increasing rate of growth, were considered. The results (not included) are ambiguous as to the choice of an appropriate specification. Over the longer period the linear trend variable is unambiguously superior, whereas over the shorter periods the inverse trend variable is superior (and both nonlinear specifications are somewhat better than the linear specification) thus reflecting the gradual slowing in the rate of change of these ratios towards the end of the estimation period. However, to facilitate easier comparison, a linear trend is employed in all remaining results.

Next the Hansen and Perloff fiscal perversity hypothesis was examined using the economic cyclical variable outlined in the previous section. A positive coefficient reflects procyclical behaviour (or fiscal perversity) while a negative coefficient reflects anticyclical behaviour (or fiscal stability). On this basis, the federal government could be labelled as anticyclical and provincial government procyclical (see Table 3.4). Results for municipal government are ambiguous. On the basis of taxation data, the two aggregate categories appear to reflect an overall move from anticyclical to procyclical behaviour on behalf of the public sector over the period. However, these conclusions are hardly justified by the reported t-statistics which certainly leave the distinct impression that the employment behaviour of the public sector in Canada has been neither fiscally perverse not fiscally stable over the postwar period.[13]

---

[12] These results are broadly consistent with the findings of Hodgetts and Dwivedi (1969).

[13] These results suggest that the somewhat different conclusions reached by Robinson and Courchene (1969) based on revenue-expenditure data over the 1952 to 1965 period warrant further investigation.

TABLE 3.3

TESTS OF THE TREND HYPOTHESIS[1]

Employer	Taxation Statistics[2]		Employment Statistics[3]
	1946-1975	1961-1975	1961-1976
Federal	−0.029	−0.055	−0.014
	(−6.4)	(−8.3)	(−10.0)
Provincial	0.072	0.030	0.014
	(17.1)	(3.8)	(17.1)
Municipal	0.069	0.042	0.007
	(17.5)	(4.3)	(9.7)
Total Government	0.112	0.017	0.007
	(11.2)	(1.0)	(2.9)
Educational	0.062	0.012	n.a.
	(7.5)	(0.6)	
Institutional	0.186	0.127	n.a.
	(18.9)	(4.8)	
Total Public	0.359	0.156	n.a.
	(14.4)	(2.8)	

Notes:

[1] Figures in parentheses are t-statistics.

[2] Figures show the average annual change in the trend of taxable plus nontaxable returns in each category expressed as a percentage of total returns.

[3] Figures show the average quarterly change in the trend of government employment in each category expressed as a percentage of total employment.

n.a.—Not available.

TABLE 3.4

TESTS OF THE FISCAL PERVERSITY HYPOTHESIS[1]

Employer	Taxation Statistics		Employment Statistics
	1946-1975	1961-1975	1961-1976
Federal	−0.030	−0.004	−0.025
	(−2.2)	(−0.2)	(−1.1)
Provincial	0.014	0.025	0.004
	(1.1)	(1.4)	(0.3)
Municipal	−0.005	0.005	−0.006
	(−0.4)	(0.2)	(−0.5)
Total Government	−0.021	0.027	−0.027
	(−0.7)	(0.7)	(−0.7)
Educational	−0.008	0.049	n.a.
	(−0.3)	(1.0)	n.a.
Institutional	−0.01)	(0.9)	
	(−0.1)	(0.9)	
Total Public	−0.030	0.134	n.a.
	(−0.4)	(1.0)	

Note:

[1] Figures in the table show the estimated coefficient (with t-statistics in parentheses) on a variable measuring the per cent change in real GNP. A positive sign reflects 'fiscal perversity'. A linear time trend variable and intercept were also included in the specification.

n.a.—Not available.

Table 3.5 presents the results of hypothesis testing with the political cycle variables. Since only federal variables are considered, the reported results are confined to the federal, total government and total public categories. The signs included at the top of each column indicate the sign required for agreement with the Nordhaus model — the opposite sign would be required for agreement with the Fisher model. The distinct impression from these results is that the timing of federal elections and the state of the federal parliament (minority/nonminority)

TABLE 3.5

TESTS OF THE POLITICAL CYCLE HYPOTHESES
(t-statistics)

Data, Period and Employer	VARIABLE[1]				
	Dummy (+)	Sawtooth (−)	Cycle (+)	Minority (+)	Popularity (−)
Taxation Statistics:					
_1946-1975_					
Federal	0.7	−0.1	0.9	1.0	−0.6
Government	0.6	−0.5	0.7	0.7	−1.4
Public	−0.3	−0.2	−0.4	0.5	−1.9
_1961-1975_					
Federal	0.4	−1.5	−0.2	0.2	−1.3
Government	−0.3	−0.4	−1.7	−0.7	0.3
Public	−0.7	−0.3	−2.6	−1.4	1.5
Employment Statistics:					
_1961-1976_					
Federal	0.1	−1.3	0.7	−0.6	−3.7
Government	0.1	−1.6	0.1	−0.7	−2.1

Note:

[1] See text for a description of each of the variables. These variables were introduced in addition to a linear time trend and an economic cycle variable. The minority variable was introduced in addition to the trend, economic and political cycle variable. The signs at the top of each column represent the signs appropriate for the Nordhaus model. Opposite signs would be predicted by the Fisher model.

have not had a significant impact on the ratio of public to total employment in Canada over the postwar period.[14] The popularity variable is probably a more important political determinant in a parliamentary system, where the period between elections is not known with certainty. The signs obtained for this variable generally confirm the Nordhaus model and the results with the employment statistics do suggest that there has been a *significant* impact of the popularity of the ruling party on federal employment behaviour since 1961.[15] Moreover, although generally not significant, it is interesting to note that in almost all cases the signs for the federal category, where the most noticeable impact of federal political cycles should be felt, confirm the Nordhaus model — namely, that federal government employment increases in the period of a federal election, during periods of minority government, or during periods of low political popularity.

The impact of the economic cycle and political popularity variables were retested with a one year delay between the reporting of the state of the economy and/or the popularity of the ruling party on the assumption that it takes time for the government to react and implement its decision in employment policy.[16] The general conclusion from these results (not included) is that the lagged economic cycle variable performed marginally better than the unlagged variable, but the lagged political popularity variable generally performed marginally worse than its unlagged counterpart. However, the above conclusions remain unaltered.[17]

Each of the above hypotheses was retested using total population as the denominator since total population grew less rapidly than either total taxation returns or total employment. This is reflected, for example, in an increase in the ratio of total taxation returns to total population from approximately one quarter in the mid-1940s to approximately one half in the mid-1970s.[18] The relatively slower growth in total population results in *all* ratios having significantly positive secular trends and the downturn of the 1970s not being quite as pronounced.

---

[14] This confirms the finding by Nordhaus (1975) for Canada.

[15] This finding was retested with the *number* of employees (rather than the ratio) as the dependent variable and the same conclusion was obtained. The t-statistics were -3.9 for federal, and -1.8 for total government.

[16] It is implicitly assumed that the government can react more quickly when it does not have to rely on an outside agency, such as Statistics Canada or the Gallup organization, for its information.

[17] It is interesting to note that the introduction of seasonal dummy variables did have a significant impact on the equation, although not on the sign or significance of the variables discussed above. The relevant $F(3,57)$ test statistics for seasonality for the two periods were 14.8 and 25.8 respectively. This *suggests* that the seasonal pattern in government employment (see Foot, Scicluna and Thadaney, 1978b) is significantly different from that of total employment in Canada.

[18] The correlation between these two variables was 0.958 for the 1946-1975 period and 0.988 for the 1961-1975 period. Total employment rose from a 1961 average of 33.2 per cent of total population to a 1976 average of 41.4 per cent. The correlation over this period, based on quarterly data, was 0.972.

However, all other conclusions are unchanged. The general impression is that the economic and political factors examined here have not been significant determinants of the ratio of public employment to total population in postwar Canada, with the possible exception being the impact of the popularity of the federal ruling party on federal employment behaviour.[19]

CONCLUSIONS

The evidence presented in this paper indicates that Canada is no exception to an apparent worldwide postwar trend of an increasing amount of employment being located in the 'public' sector. The evidence suggests that about 20 per cent of total employment is *directly* located in the public sector, while a little over half of this is located in the three levels of government. There is little difference between the ratios in 1961 and in 1975. The postwar trend has not been the same for all categories with the federal percentage declining and the provincial and municipal shares increasing. It appears that the share of total government in total public has decreased over this period. Whether these trends can be attributed to differing price (and income) elasticities of demand and/or different rates of productivity growth cannot be determined until certain conceptual and measurement innovations result in better data for the public sector. However, what does seem to be clear from these results is that, generally, the cyclical economic and political factors at the national level examined in this chapter do not appear to have had a significant impact on the variation in the ratio of 'public' employment to total employment (or to total population) around their trend values over the postwar period in Canada. However, results with employment statistics do suggest that there has been a significant impact of the popularity of the federal ruling party on federal government employment since 1961, and that the relationship follows the Nordhaus model — namely, that federal government employment rises during periods of low political popularity.

---

[19] The t-statistics were -4.0 for federal, and -2.4 for total government.

REFERENCES

Bacon, R. and W. Eltis (1976) *Britain's Economic Problem: Too Few Producers* (London: Macmillan).

Baumol, W. (1967) "Macroeconomics of Unbalanced Growth: The Anatomy of Urban Crisis" *American Economic Review* 57, 415-26.

Bird, R.M. (1978) "The Growth of the Public Service in Canada" in David K. Foot (ed.) *Public Employment and Compensation in Canada: Myths and Realities* (Toronto: Butterworth & Co. for The Institute for Research on Public Policy).

Borcherding, T.E. (1977) "One Hundred Years of Public Spending, 1870-1970" in T.E. Borcherding (ed.) *Budgets and Bureaucrats: The Sources of Government Growth* (Durham: Duke University Press).

Bucovetsky, M.W. (1978) "Government as Indirect Employer", Chapter Two in *This Volume*.

Ebanks, W. (1976) "The Stablizing Effects of Government Employment" *Exploration in Economic Research* 3, 564-83.

Fisher, G.W. (1964) "Interstate Variation in State and Local Government Expenditure" *National Tax Journal* 17, 57-74.

Foot, D.K. and P. Thadaney (1978) "The Growth of Public Employment in Canada: The Evidence from Taxation Statistics, 1946-1975" in David K. Foot (ed.) *Public Employment and Compensation in Canada: Myths and Realities* (Toronto: Butterworth & Co. for The Institute for Research on Public Policy).

Foot, D.K., E. Scicluna and P. Thadaney (1978a) "The Growth and Distribution of Federal, Provincial and Local Government Employment in Canada" in David K. Foot (ed.) *Public Employment and Compensation in Canada: Myths and Realities* (Toronto: Butterworth & Co. for The Institute for Research on Public Policy).

Foot, D.K., E. Scicluna and P. Thadaney (1978b) "The Seasonality of Government Employment in Canada" in David K. Foot (ed.) *Public Employment and Compensation in Canada: Myths and Realities* (Toronto: Butterworth & Co. for The Institute for Research on Public Policy).

Ginzberg, E. (1976) "The Pluralistic Economy of the U.S." *Scientific American* 235, 25-29.

Hansen, A. and H. Perloff (1944) *State and Local Finance in the National Economy* (New York, Norton).

Hodgetts, J.E. and O.P. Dwivedi (1969) "The Growth of Government Employment in Canada" *Canadian Public Administration* 12, 224-38.

Johnston, J. (1975) "A Macro-Model of Inflation" *Economic Journal* 85, 288-308.

Lynch, L.K. and E.L. Redman (1968) "Macroeconomics of Unbalanced Growth: Comment" *American Economic Review* 58, 884-86.

Nordhaus, W.D. (1975) "The Political Business Cycle" *Review of Economic Studies* 42, 169-90.

Perry, D.B. (1975) "Public Sector Employment" *Canadian Tax Journal* 23, 560-62.

Rafuse, R.W. (1965) "Cyclical Behaviour of State Local Finances" in R.A. Musgrave (ed.) *Essays in Fiscal Federalism* (Washington, Brookings), 63-121.

Robinson, T.R. and T.J. Courchene (1969) "Fiscal Federalism and Economic Stability: An Examination of Multi-Level Public Finances in Canada, 1952-1965" *Canadian Journal of Economics* 2, 165-89.

Chapter Four

Professionalization of the Canadian Public Sector

by
*Morley Gunderson**

INTRODUCTION AND SUMMARY

The rapid and sustained growth of professionals in the Canadian public sector has been such that the problems of salaried professionals and of public employment are now inextricably mixed: salaried professionals are predominantly employed in the public sector, and public sector employment is predominantly professional. It is not possible to understand either phenomenon — salaried professionalism, or public sector employment — without an understanding of the other.

If the public sector is broadly interpreted to include health and education personnel, that sector employs over two-thirds of all professionals. Most of the remaining one-third, in the private sector, are heavily dependent upon public funds for their employment. Approximately five to ten per cent of all professionals are directly employed by the government, that is in civil service jobs at various levels of government. The importance of the public sector as a source of employment for professionals has been growing steadily in Canada at least since the 1930s.

Professionals have a variety of defining characteristics that often conflict with the bureaucratic demands of public sector employers, especially with respect to such matters as job assignments, supervision, special privileges, and the use of non-professionals. These defining characteristics of professionals include a high degree of specialized education and training, an identity with their profession, a high degree of self-government and autonomy over their internal

Editor's Note: **Morley Gunderson** is Associate Professor in the Faculty of Management Studies and Scarborough College and Associate of the Centre for Industrial Relations, all at the University of Toronto. The present chapter is an abridgement of a longer study, with the same name, that received restricted circulation in August 1977.

*The author's acknowledgements include the staff at the Centre for Industrial Relations, University of Toronto, especially Marcelle Elhadad for research assistance, Dorothy and Jean Newman for library assistance, and Deborah Campbell for typing. Without implicating them for the contents of the study, he is grateful for discussion and helpful suggestions from Dave Beatty, Richard Bird, Meyer Bucovetsky, John Crispo, John Kervin and Noah Meltz, of the University of Toronto, Jack Barbash and Everett Kassalow, of the University of Wisconsin, and Edith Epstein, Alan Gladstone, Gerald Starr and Ralph Turvey of the International Labour Organization in Geneva.

affairs, and ethical codes that are associated with community responsibility. In addition, their labour market is often characterized as segmented from other markets, and, in the public sector, subject to certain peculiarities such as the absence of a profit constraint and the prevalence of more egalitarian wage policies.

Professional labour in the public sector has been subjected to increasing strain. Demand for its services appears to be waning for a number of reasons. These include reduced overall growth of the public sector, and an altered age structure of the population whose effect is to reduce the demand for teaching and health personnel. Competitive pressure arises from the growing numbers of paraprofessionals, new professions and technically-skilled labour in general. Under recent circumstances, the public sector professional labour market has been characterized by soaring expectations followed by unfulfilled aspirations.

In response to many of the tensions that have arisen from the conflict between professional aspirations, on the one hand, and the requirements of bureaucratic organizations and the dictates of the marketplace on the other hand, salaried professionals have increasingly turned toward collective bargaining in a variety of forms. They may form separate bargaining units or be subsumed in the bargaining unit of white-collar or even production unions. Their bargaining agent may be a professional association, a union, or both. To the extent that professional associations have engaged in collective bargaining they have taken on many of the characteristics of a trade union, and they have added to the tension when they try to represent the interests of both their salaried and self-employed members.

It is difficult to make generalizations about the expected impact of professional unions. They do have the power to put forth a united front because of their professional solidarity and because they may influence entry into their profession. However, this may be offset by a variety of forces including an identification with management and an aversion toward engaging in union-like tactics. Internal dissensions may also occur with self-employed members of the association, non-professionals in the bargaining unit, and even with the different age, sex or skill groups of the professional union itself. In addition, the demand elasticity conditions facing professionals are not uniform. Consequently, it is not possible to generalize unequivocally on the expected impact of professional unions, although it is unlikely that they would have only a weak effect.

Unionization gives rise to a variety of legal questions regarding the appropriate bargaining unit, bargaining agent and scope of collective bargaining. One response to these issues is to treat professionals like other workers and accommodate them under existing labour relations laws. In such circumstances, legal precedents already exist on many issues; others can be determined by labour boards or arbitration decisions, and others can be solved by the give-and-take of collective bargaining and internal union trade-offs.

This paper first summarizes the evidence as to the quantity, the growth and the characteristics of professional labour in the Canadian public sector. It then elaborates on the inherent conflicts, tensions and policy issues that were outlined above. It concludes with some speculative observations that are rather in the nature of personal reflections.

I. NUMERICAL DESCRIPTION OF PROFESSIONALS IN PUBLIC SECTOR

Growth of Professionals in Government Sector

Table 4.1 illustrates the rapid and sustained growth of professionals in various levels of government in Canada since 1931. The government sector is taken here to mean public administration and defence, and therefore excludes the large group of teaching and health care professionals who do not work directly for government, but who would be considered part of the larger public sector.

Not only have professionals in government grown dramatically in absolute magnitude, from less than 8,000 in 1931 to over 86,000 in 1971, but also they have grown faster than the rapidly expanding government sector itself: as the second row illustrates, professionals have increased their representation in the government labour force from approximately seven per cent in 1931 to over 13 per cent in 1971.

This representation in the government labour force is only slightly higher than the overall representation of professionals in the total labour force, which increased from 6.1 per cent in 1931 to 12.7 per cent in 1971. However, when one considers that the total labour force includes the large and rapidly growing number of teaching and health care professionals (as well as government professionals) then the fact that professionalization of the government sector has slightly exceeded that of the total labour force is remarkable indeed.

Because the professionalization of the government sector has slightly exceeded that of the non-government sector, and because of the rapid growth of the government sector between 1931 and 1971, professionals in the government sector have constituted a growing portion of all professionals. This is illustrated in row five where professionals in the government sector have grown from 3.2 per cent of all professionals in 1931 to 7.9 per cent in 1971.

Although professionals in government are still mainly males, male predominance has steadily decreased, over time, from 91 per cent in 1931 to 79 per cent in 1971. As the last panel of Table 4.1 illustrates, however, this reflects a general pattern whereby the total government labour force is becoming less male-dominated. The decline of male dominance is even greater in the total labour force. In essence, females have made fewer inroads into the prestigious and remunerative professional category of government employment than into other occupational groups within the government sector or into the labour force as a whole. Professional employment in the government sector remains

TABLE 4.1

PROFESSIONAL LABOUR FORCE IN THE GOVERNMENT AND ALL INDUSTRIES, CANADA, 1931-1971

	1931	1941	1951	1961	1971
(Both Males and Females)					
Professionals in government	7,657	12,543	20,133	45,730	86,100
As per cent of government labour force	6.99	9.14	8.65	11.31	13.46
Professionals in all industries	238,077	282,242	385,676	634,271	1,093,115
As per cent of total labour force	6.08	7.20	7.40	10.00	12.67
Government professionals as per cent of all professionals	3.22	4.45	5.22	7.21	7.88
(Males only)					
Professionals in government	6,932	11,193	17,365	38,078	68,010
As per cent of government labour force	7.36	10.25	9.69	12.24	14.28
Professionals in all industries	120,293	152,166	217,902	360,478	567,010
As per cent of total labour force	3.70	4.52	5.38	7.87	10.01
Government professionals as per cent of all professionals	5.76	7.36	7.97	10.56	11.99

(Proportion males)

Professionals in government	90.6	89.2	86.3	83.3	79.0
Government labour force	85.2	79.6	77.0	76.9	74.5
Professionals in all industries	50.5	53.9	56.5	56.8	52.7
Total labour force	83.0	80.2	77.7	72.2	65.7

Source: 1931 to 1961 figures are computed from Meltz, N. (1969) *Manpower in Canada 1931-1961* (Ottawa: Manpower and Immigration) pp. 82, 84. Figures for 1971 are computed from 1971 Census, *Economic Characteristics: Occupation by Industry*, Special Bulletin 94-792, Table 2.

Note: The 1971 census does not use the 'professional' occupation title, as do the earlier censuses. It is taken here to mean those in the following six major occupational groups: natural science, engineering, and mathematics; social sciences; religion; teaching; medicine and health; and artistic, literary and recreation. Because of changes in the 1971 occupational classification, the 1971 figures may not be directly comparable with those of earlier years.

male-dominated, even more so than government employment in general, and certainly more so than employment in all other industries combined.[1]

Current Picture of Professionals in Public Sector

For the census year 1971, Table 4.2 gives the professional labour force in the various levels of government. Government employment is taken to mean the census industry classification of public administration and defence: it does not include the public sectors of education, health and welfare, or transportation, communications and utilities.

As the last column of Table 4.2 indicates, in 1971 approximately 86,100 or 13.5 per cent of the total government labour force were in the six major occupational groups designated as professional. In descending order of magnitude, the major occupational groups were science, engineering and mathematics (employing 6.7 per cent of the government labour force or one-half of all government professionals), social sciences (three per cent), medicine and health, teaching, and art-literature-recreation. The teaching and medicine and health groups are small because most are not employed directly by government but rather are in the larger public sector which includes the teaching and health industries.

The separate figures for each level of government indicate that provincial governments employ a disproportionately large number of professionals: 21.5 per cent or over one-fifth of all provincial employees are professional compared to 11.1 per cent for the federal government, 10.1 per cent for local governments, and 12.7 per cent for all industries combined. However, the federal government is still a larger employer of professionals, employing slightly more than the provincial government, which in turn employs over twice as many as the local levels of government.[2]

Table 4.3 gives an alternative picture of professionals in the public sector by extending the definition of the public sector to include education, health, and social work as well as direct government employment. Clearly the public sector, in this broader context, is the dominant employer of the professional labour force, employing close to 70 per cent of all professionals. Direct government employment for the three levels of government (excluding direct government employment in teaching and health) accounts for about 5.2 per cent of the

---

[1] The small proportion of professionals who are males in the all industry category (second last row), to a large extent reflects the dominance of female professionals in teaching and health care. Since males have increasingly entered these professions, however, the proportion of males in the all industry category has been roughly constant between 1931 and 1971: male inroads into these professions have been approximately offset by female inroads into the other professional categories.

[2] The larger percentage of professionals among provincial employees, as compared with those of the federal government, occurs here because the census data set attributes to provincial governments only half the total labour force that it does to the federal government. Using different criteria, other data sources enhance the relative contribution of provincial governments to total public sector employment. For a comparison of all the data sources relating to total government employment, see Bird (1978).

employment of professionals, with teaching and health accounting for 31.9 and 29.9 per cent respectively. If teaching and health are included in the provincial public sector, on the grounds that most of their budgets are determined there, then the provincial sector accounts for 63.7 per cent of the employment of all professionals. Obviously, in considering the professionalization of the public sector, both our definition of professional and of the public sector matter. However, broadly interpreted to include teachers and medicine and health personnel, the public sector employs over two-thirds of all professionals.

In fact, for most of the occupations listed in Table 4.2, public funds or regulation play a large role in influencing salaries and employment. This would be true for many scientists in the private sector, for architects and engineers working on government contracts, for engineers in the regulated utilities, transportation and communication sector, and for many in the art, literature and recreation sectors. If public sector employment is interpreted very broadly to include not only direct government employment, but also employment in not-for-profit religious, teaching and health institutions, as well as in the often-publicly-regulated sector of transportation-communications and utilities, and in sectors heavily dependent upon government contracts or subsidy, then the vast majority of professionals are employed in the public sector. The problems of the professional — especially the salaried professional but even the self-employed professional dependent upon the public sector — are inextricably tied to the issues of public sector employment in general. Conversely, the fact that professionals also constitute such a large portion of the public sector itself means that understanding the behaviour of the public sector labour market requires an understanding of the issues of professionalism, especially of the salaried professional.

Detailed Picture of Professionals in Federal Government

At the federal level, the Pay Research Bureau collects considerable data on federal government employees, including professionals, for whom the Treasury Board is the employer. Most professional employees in the federal civil service fall into the scientific and professional occupational category — one of the six major occupational categories established to define bargaining units for collective bargaining under the Public Service Staff Relations Act. As Table 4.4 indicates, in 1977 there were 24,125 employees in the scientific and professional group, constituting 8.6 per cent of the 282,197 federal government employees who bargain with the Treasury Board.[3]

---

[3] These numbers are smaller than the 36,400 professionals (representing 11.1 per cent of the federal labour force of 328,775), based on 1971 census figures, as given in Table 4.2. Presumably the census figures include casual and part-time persons, as well as federal employees who do not bargain with the Treasury Board. In addition, some professional occupation groups, mainly in the art, literary and recreation field, listed in Table 4.4, do not fall into the scientific and professional category as used by the Pay Research Bureau.

TABLE 4.2

PROFESSIONAL[1] LABOUR FORCE IN VARIOUS LEVELS OF GOVERNMENT, CANADA, 1971

Occupation[2]	All Industries	Public Administration and Defence			
		Federal[3]	Provincial	Local	All Government[4]
Science, engineering, mathematics	234,135	21,435	14,800	6,380	42,695
Science	53,420	8,655	5,180	400	14,255
Architects and Engineers	80,920	4,290	3,300	2,705	10,335
Other occupations in					
Architecture and Engineering	73,550	5,605	4,930	2,945	13,490
Mathematics, Statistics	26,245	2,880	1,390	335	4,615
Social sciences and related	79,055	5,375	9,695	3,995	19,105
Social science	11,500	1,470	1,485	110	3,080
Social work	30,535	2,085	5,275	3,270	10,640
Law	20,815	1,000	1,795	355	3,160
Library, museum	10,420	500	375	235	1,115
Religion	23,595	80	75	135	290
Teaching	349,290	3,810	2,730	340	6,900
University	26,480	—	—	—	—
Elementary and Secondary	271,760	2,105	765	—	2,875
Medicine and Health	326,560	3,075	5,870	1,910	10,870
Diagnosing and treating	39,110	810	790	145	1,740
Nursing and therapy	233,140	1,565	4,020	1,490	7,085

Artistic, literary, recreation	80,480	2,625	1,475	2,115	6,240
Art	30,000	610	380	245	1,240
Performing arts	18,400	350	115	75	545
Writing	17,045	1,305	465	45	1,835
Recreation	15,040	355	510	1,750	2,620
All professional[5]	1,093,115	36,400	34,645	14,875	86,100
All occupations	8,626,925	328,775	161,465	147,025	639,585

Source: 1971 Census, *Economic Characteristics: Occupation by Industry*. Special Bulletin 94-792, Ottawa: Information Canada, 1976. Table 2.

Notes:

[1] The 1971 Census does not use the 'professional' occupation title, as do earlier censuses. It is taken here to mean those in the following six major occupational groups: natural science, engineering, and mathematics; social sciences; religion; teaching; medicine and health; and artistic, literary and recreation.

[2] The six major professional occupation groups also include those sub-occupations classified as 'other' within the major occupation group.

[3] Federal government includes defence services.

[4] 'All government' includes other government offices, as well as the federal, provincial and local levels of government.

[5] 'All professional' is the sum of those in the six major professional occupation groups.

TABLE 4.3

PROFESSIONAL LABOUR FORCE IN PUBLIC SECTOR, CANADA, 1971

Sector	Number of Professionals[1]	Per Cent of Professional Labour Force
Teaching	349,290	31.9
Medicine and Health	326,560	29.9
Social Work	30,535	2.8
Federal Government[2]	27,430	2.5
Provincial Government[2]	20,770	1.9
Local Government[2]	9,355	0.9
All public[3]	763,940	69.9
Private[4]	329,175	30.1
Total	1,093,115	100.0

Source: Table 4.2.
Note:
[1] As in note 1 of Table 4.2.
[2] Excluding those in teaching, medicine and health, and social work.
[3] Sum of above groups.
[4] Difference between total and public figures. In this case the private sector would include those in the transportation-communication-utilities sector as well as library and museum workers and those in religion who are not employed directly by the government.

Table 4.5 gives a more detailed breakdown of the distribution of federal employees *within* the scientific and professional category. In descending order of numerical importance, the largest groups are education (16.0%), auditing (12.6%), economics, sociology and statistics (11.2%), engineering (10.7%), scientific research (9.4%), and nursing (9.0%). These six groups constitute almost 70 per cent of federal employees in the scientific and professional category, with the remaining 23 groups each constituting less than three per cent.

TABLE 4.4
DISTRIBUTION OF EMPLOYEE CATEGORIES, FEDERAL GOVERNMENT, MARCH 31, 1977

Occupational Category	Number of Employees	Per cent of Total
Executive	1,217	0.4
Scientific and professional	24,125	8.6
Administrative and foreign service	50,071	17.7
Technical	26,316	9.3
Administrative support	72,764	25.8
Operational	107,704	38.2
All categories	282,197	100.0

Source: Pay Research Bureau, correspondence from N. Allen, Manager, Public Service Data, June 29, 1977.

Although not tabulated here, the detailed age distribution of federal 'scientific and professional' employees is of some interest.[4] There are relatively fewer very young or very senior employees in the scientific and professional category than there are amongst federal employees in general, i.e., proportionately, more professionals are in the 25-50 age group. One explanation is that, prior to age 25, professional training is still being acquired, and, after age 50, many professionals have moved into executive or management positions, or professional obsolescence has compelled them to leave their former category. In addition (or alternatively), the age distribution of professional employees may reflect the expansion path followed by the public sector over time, with public service employment of professionals having grown most rapidly in the 1960s and early 1970s.

---

[4] Age distribution was calculated from a restricted data source, *The Composition of the Public Service of Canada* (Ottawa: Pay Research Bureau), Table 12.

TABLE 4.5

DISTRIBUTION OF FEDERAL GOVERNMENT EMPLOYEES BY OCCUPATIONAL GROUPS WITHIN THE SCIENTIFIC AND PROFESSIONAL CATEGORY, MARCH 31, 1977

Occupational Group	Number of Employees	Per cent of Total
Actuarial science	18	0.08
Agriculture	382	1.58
Architecture and town planning	428	1.77
Auditing	3,042	12.61
Biological sciences	820	3.40
Chemistry	435	1.80
Defence scientific	489	2.03
Dentistry	63	0.26
Economics, sociology and statistics	2,690	11.15
Education group	3,854	15.98
Engineering and land survey	2,572	10.66
Forestry	118	0.49
Historical research	267	1.11
Home economics	73	0.30
Law	522	2.16
Library science	447	1.85
Mathematics	128	0.53
Medicine	381	1.58
Meteorology	595	2.47
Nursing	2,182	9.04
Occupational and physical therapy	80	0.33
Pharmacy	89	0.37
Physical sciences	584	2.42
Psychology	91	0.38
Scientific regulation	536	2.22
Scientific research	2,260	9.37
Social work	176	0.73
University teaching	204	0.85
Veterinary science	599	2.48
All scientific and professional	24,125	100.00

Source: Pay Research Bureau, correspondence from N. Allen, Manager, Public Service Data, June 29, 1977.

Highly Qualified Manpower Data

By providing labour market information on workers with a university degree, the Highly Qualified Manpower Survey conducted by Statistics Canada in 1973 provides information on educated manpower, a group that is similar in many respects to professional workers. To be sure, not all university graduates work as professionals — although university graduation is increasingly used as a requirement for entering a profession — nor are all professionals university graduates. Nevertheless, university graduation is one of the more common, measurable, defining characteristics of a profession; consequently, information on university graduates may be useful in describing the labour market behaviour of professionals.

Table 4.6 gives the distribution of Highly Qualified Manpower — hereafter referred to as HQM professionals — for different age groups for various industries in the private and public sector. The public sector here is broadly defined to include workers in education, health, welfare, and the often publicly-regulated transportation-communications-utilities sector, as well as the various levels of government.

As the last row of Table 4.6 indicates, almost two-thirds of HQM professionals of all ages worked in the public sector with the remaining one-third in the private sector. In descending order of relative magnitude, the largest users of HQM professionals were education, health and welfare, manufacturing (durable and non-durable combined), business service, and then federal administration. The public sector proportion of total HQM professionals declines the older is the age group. Across the age groups, a falling share in education more than compensates for a mildly rising share among the other public sector components.

Table 4.7 compares the HQM and census figures on professionals in the private and public sectors. When a university degree or diploma is regarded as a condition of being a professional the number of professionals drops, as evidenced by the much smaller figure for the number of HQM professionals. This is especially important in areas of emerging professionalism, where new professions are constantly being established, as in the health care field: here the number of university degrees amongst 'census professionals' is small.

For the different levels of government an interesting pattern emerges. In the federal administration, there appear to be a large number of university graduates (HQM professionals) who are not employed in any of the six major professional occupations of the census. Conversely, at the local level, there are many who are grouped as professional, who do not have a university degree. Over-qualification appears to be more prominent at the senior levels of government, with under-qualification of the professional staff being a possibility at the junior levels.

Whichever set of data is used, the fact remains that the public sector is the predominant employer of professional labour. Direct government employment at

TABLE 4.6
INDUSTRIAL DISTRIBUTION OF HIGHLY QUALIFIED MANPOWER
IN PUBLIC AND PRIVATE SECTORS, BY AGE, CANADA, 1973
(per cent of 'all-industry' total)

Industry[1]	Age[2]							
	under 24	24 to 28	29 to 33	34 to 38	39 to 43	44 to 53	54 and over	All ages
	Private Sector							
Primary[3]	0.5	0.8	0.1	0.8	1.0	1.6	1.3	1.1
Mines, quarries, oil	1.1	1.1	1.5	1.9	1.6	1.9	1.5	1.5
Durable manufacturing	3.2	3.6	4.5	4.8	4.7	5.4	4.5	4.5
Non-durable manufacturing	5.2	4.6	5.1	5.4	5.6	6.2	5.3	5.3
Construction	0.7	1.2	0.9	1.4	1.6	1.4	1.0	1.2
Trade	5.0	4.3	4.1	4.1	4.4	5.3	5.6	4.6
Finance, insurance, realty	3.0	4.5	3.7	3.4	3.2	3.3	4.1	3.8
Personal service	6.7	2.9	1.9	1.5	1.8	1.7	2.4	2.2
Business service	5.8	9.7	9.4	9.3	9.6	9.2	8.2	9.2
Religious	1.1	0.4	1.2	2.1	3.1	3.9	7.3	2.6
Total Private	32.2	33.2	33.5	34.8	36.6	39.9	41.2	36.1
	Public Sector							
Transportation, communication utilities	3.7	3.4	3.7	3.5	3.3	3.5	3.5	3.5
Education	47.7	42.3	43.3	42.2	38.6	31.2	28.6	38.4

Health, welfare	7.0	9.0	9.2	10.1	11.2	13.2	14.2	10.8
Federal administration	3.9	6.7	6.0	5.2	5.6	7.2	6.6	6.3
Provincial administration	3.0	4.3	3.4	3.4	3.7	4.1	4.8	3.9
Local administration	2.6	1.0	0.8	0.9	0.1	0.9	1.2	1.0
Total Public	67.8	66.8	66.5	65.2	63.4	60.1	58.8	63.9
All industries[4]	100.0	100.0	100.0	100.0	100.0	100.0	100.0	100.0

Source: Highly Qualified Manpower Survey, Statistics Canada, 1973, Table 25 (microfilm).

Notes:

[1] Industry of job of longest duration held in last 12 months.

[2] Calculated by subtracting the year of birth from 1973.

[3] Agriculture, forestry, fishing and trapping.

[4] Does not include other government offices, unspecified or undefined, did not work, or no industry.

all three levels accounts for 5.3 per cent of all 'census professionals' and 11.2 per cent of all 'HQM professionals'. Public sector employment, here including education, health and welfare, as well as direct government employment, accounts for 70 per cent of all 'census professionals' and 60 per cent of all 'HQM professionals'. As a general statement, then, approximately two-thirds of all professionals are employed in the public sector, with about five to ten per cent in direct government employment.

TABLE 4.7

COMPARISON OF CENSUS AND HQM PROFESSIONALS

Sector	1971 Census		HQM Data	
	Number	Per Cent	Number	Per Cent
Education	349,290	31.9	211,395	38.4
Health, Welfare	357,095[1]	32.7	59,625	10.8
Federal administration	27,430	2.5	34,510	6.3
Provincial administration	20,770	1.9	21,710	3.9
Local administration	9,355	0.9	5,460	1.0
Public	763,940	69.9	332,700[2]	60.4
Private	329,175	30.1	217,745	39.6
Total	1,093,115	100.0	550,545	100.0

Source: 1971 Census data adapted from Table 4.3. HQM data computed from HQM Survey, Statistics Canada, Table 25 (microfilm).

Notes:

[1] Medicine, health and social work.

[2] Excludes 19,305 HQM professionals in the transportation-communications-utilities sector who have here been included in the private sector, to facilitate comparisons with the 1971 census data.

Table 4.8 gives the average income for HQM professionals in various private and public sectors. The separate tabulations by sex and type of last highest earned qualification, and the restriction to those persons working full-time and full-year, were made to make public/private sector salary comparisons for more homogeneous groups of people. Obviously, a variety of wage-determining factors are not controlled for, so that the numbers at best are only suggestive of public and private sector salary differentials for HQM professionals.

The unweighted average figures for all degrees (last column) indicates that male HQM professionals receive a slight earnings advantage in the public sector (about five per cent), and female graduates receive a larger advantage of about 17 per cent over those in the private sector. However, much of the higher average income in the public sector, for males at least, comes about because of the larger number of those with advanced degrees. When the average incomes are compared for the same type of degree, HQM earnings for males in the public sector very often fall short of those in the private sector, and for females their salary advantage is often reduced. The data are really too fragmentary, however, to make generalizations concerning public/private sector salary differentials for HQM professionals of similar qualifications.

TABLE 4.8

AVERAGE INCOME OF HIGHLY QUALIFIED MANPOWER IN VARIOUS PRIVATE AND PUBLIC SECTORS, BY SEX AND TYPE OF LAST HIGHEST EARNED QUALIFICATION, PERSONS WORKING FULL TIME AND 40 TO 52 WEEKS, CANADA, 1973

Industry	General Degree	Specialized Under-graduate	Post Bachelor Certificate	Medical	Graduate Diploma or Certificate	M.A.	Ph.D.	All Degrees
(Private)				(male)				
Agriculture	6,300	8,800	n.a.	20,600	n.a.	14,300	18,400	12,600
Mines, quarries, oil	16,400	19,700	20,800	28,000	22,600	19,400	22,800	19,000
Durable manufacturing	16,100	18,600	22,300	26,400	18,500	19,200	21,200	18,200
Nondurable manufacturing	15,700	18,200	21,000	23,200	21,100	19,500	21,400	17,800
Construction	21,200	20,500	17,200	n.a.	17,700	25,500	n.a.	21,000
Trade	15,700	17,900	12,100	24,200	13,800	19,200	24,700	17,200
Finance, insurance, realty	16,400	19,400	19,300	35,600	29,700	21,800	36,800	18,500
Personal service	15,300	13,100	22,700	25,900	18,100	15,000	2,050	15,000
Business service	17,300	22,100	17,800	25,400	22,400	21,000	21,000	21,000
Average (unweighted)	15,600	17,589	19,150	26,163	20,488	19,433	21,044	17,811
(Public)								
Transportation, communication, utilities	15,000	18,100	17,700	25,900	22,800	17,600	19,400	17,400
Education	13,000	13,100	13,000	31,300	15,300	16,000	19,200	14,600
Health, welfare	11,200	16,500	16,000	34,300	39,700	21,300	25,100	30,400
Federal administration	15,000	17,100	18,400	21,700	22,000	17,900	20,400	17,300
Provincial administration	13,100	16,200	16,600	24,100	23,300	16,300	18,800	16,200
Local administration	11,300	16,900	17,300	23,400	23,500	18,400	19,700	16,000
Average (unweighted)	13,100	19,355	16,500	26,783	24,433	17,917	20,433	18,650

						(female)		
(Private)								
Agriculture	n.a.	7,400	n.a.	13,700	n.a.	n.a.	n.a.	7,900
Mines, quarries, oil	8,600	9,600	n.a.	n.a.	n.a.	n.a.	n.a.	9,200
Durable manufacturing	7,800	10,300	n.a.	n.a.	n.a.	n.a.	30,700	9,200
Nondurable manufacturing	8,900	9,000	11,500	n.a.	n.a.	11,300	n.a.	9,300
Construction	n.a.	11,800	n.a.	n.a.	n.a.	n.a.	n.a.	10,100
Trade	7,300	9,400	8,900	n.a.	n.a.	9,900	n.a.	8,600
Finance, insurance, realty	10,200	9,700	n.a.	n.a.	n.a.	12,200	n.a.	10,000
Personal service	7,900	9,000	13,300	n.a.	n.a.	9,000	n.a.	8,800
Business service	9,900	10,700	15,700	n.a.	n.a.	10,000	13,900	10,400
Average (unweighted)	8,657	9,656	12,350	13,700	n.a.	10,480	22,300	9,278
(Public)								
Transportation, communication, utilities	9,500	10,600	9,100	n.a.	n.a.	11,900	n.a.	10,100
Education	10,900	10,800	10,300	20,000	11,200	13,100	15,600	11,200
Health, welfare	8,000	9,600	10,100	18,500	22,500	12,400	18,100	11,300
Federal administration	9,800	10,900	10,300	19,700	n.a.	14,000	17,600	11,000
Provincial administration	8,600	10,000	11,000	23,500	n.a.	13,100	18,300	10,500
Local administration	9,100	10,500	n.a.	n.a.	n.a.	12,000	n.a.	11,000
Average (unweighted)	9,317	10,400	10,160	20,425	16,850	12,750	17,400	10,850

Source: Highly Qualified Manpower Survey, Statistics Canada, 1973. Computed from table 29A, pp. 1 to 3 (microfilm).

Note: n.a.—Not applicable.

II. CHARACTERISTICS OF PROFESSIONALS

Professionals have a variety of characteristics that have important implications for their behaviour both in the public sector and private sector labour market. Many of these characteristics are those that help to define a professional; that is, professionals tend to have all or most of these characteristics. In a sense, many of the problems of professionals in the public service are associated with these characteristics. Specifically, problems arise because of the tensions created by the conflicts that occur between the demands of a large bureaucratic organization like the government, and the demands of professionalism, associated with the characteristics of professionals. This theme will be elaborated in the discussion of each of the defining characteristics of professionals.

Specialized Education and Training

Most professions involve a substantial investment in education and training, often to acquire a specialized degree or certificate, over and above a general university degree. Much of the training involves learning the language and jargon of the profession, and it is by definition fairly specialized, often involving education with a high investment and low consumption component.

Because of rapid knowledge obsolescence, retraining is often required, either through formal refresher courses or more informally by 'keeping up with the literature'. Conventions, seminars, and frequent contact with professionals in other institutional settings are also regarded by professionals as part of their continuous education process. Interruptions in professional careers are often irreversible, a fact that has severe implications for professionals who leave the profession to engage in administrative activities or for female professionals who leave to engage in household activities or the bearing and raising of children.

To a large degree professional activity involves constant discretion and judgment. This fact, and the fact that many professionals tend to deal with a constantly changing set of new issues and problems, have led to a fairly heavy emphasis on theoretical and conceptual issues in the training of professionals. This has been used to distinguish professionals from craft workers, who acquire their training more by experience, repetition of tasks, and learning-by-doing. Obviously the distinction is one of degree rather than kind, as the difference between many craftworkers and professionals is blurred.

In varying degrees, these educational characteristics of professionals have created tensions between public sector employers and their professional employees. A major cause of conflict is the question of who should bear the cost of the expensive and time-consuming education and retraining processes. Employers may pay in a variety of forms: allowing paid time off for courses, conventions or sabbaticals, allowing part-time students to complete a thesis, and allowing or paying for so-called business lunches are but a few examples.

While these forms of employer payment may be a convenient way of providing non-taxable compensation to professionals, public sector employers should also realize that paying for such education may not be warranted on efficiency grounds if the training is *generally* usable by the professional in other firms or institutions. In such circumstances the professional should pay for such education — perhaps by accepting a lower wage during the training period — because competition will ensure that the professional will reap the benefits in the form of higher remuneration afterwards. Only if the education or training is *specific* to the particular government agency itself, should the government bear the cost of such training if it is worthwhile. This may be the case, for example, with teacher training, since such training is usable only in the teaching profession; it would not seem to be the case, however, for language courses, at least to the extent such knowledge is valuable to private sector employers. If governments bear the cost of generally usable training, they may simply find themselves to be training grounds for the private sector.

The long training period and the threat of skill obsolescence also means that professionals will have a fairly short benefit period from which to recoup the costs of their skill training. In that time they will probably be intensely preoccupied with the particular perspective of their profession: this attitude will be reinforced by fairly lucrative professional rewards in these peak earnings years.

Educational requirements will also create conflicts *within* the profession itself. Issues of degree requirements — controversies that have recently been waged in the teaching, nursing and accounting professions — continue to divide the professions, especially the newer ones which seek status through high education standards. If formal requirements are created, then, there is the issue of what to do about existing professionals who have seniority but not formal education. (If a grandfather clause is allowed, does this not conflict with the alleged public interest of high standards of education?). There is also the perennial problem of the optimal mix of formal training and more informal experience and learning-by-doing, as well as theoretical versus practical education—problems that are reflected in the curriculum of various professional schools.

Professional Identification

Formal education requirements and the exclusive language and jargon of each profession, help foster professional identification. Professionals themselves find it in their self-interest to encourage such identification because it provides territorial security and sets them apart from the mass of other workers. It may also insulate them from competition to the extent that their identification gives them the exclusive-right-to-practise in their profession, or at least gives them a reserve-of-title certification.[5] With professional identification also comes group

---

[5] As the names imply, the exclusive-right-to-practise means that only those with the professional licence can practise, whereas professionals with the reserve-of-title are the only ones who can use the professionally certified title,

power—an important element in today's society of competing interest groups. Such power facilitates not only effective lobbying for the interests of the professional group but also a united front against outside criticism or threats.

From the perspective of the government as an employer, however, such professional identification creates some conflict. Other employee groups may resent any special treatment given to professional employees: in such circumstances employers may have to grant such special privileges to all workers in order to prevent discord. Narrow professional perspectives may also create conflict with the broader organizational imperatives of government bureaucracy, as for example when the organization requires an immediate product or service, but the professional employee wants time and resources to do only a first-rate 'professional' job.[6] Conflict may also occur when the professional employee places allegiance to the profession over that of the employing organization or when the professional values the respect of the profession more than that of the organization.[7]

To be sure, not all of these situations create conflict: an employee with a good professional image may well be highly valued by the organization. Nevertheless, the potential for conflict is great especially in the public sector where the professional may have a high degree of job security, and where it may be more difficult to reward or discipline employees who place their prime allegiance elsewhere.

Self Governing, Often with Licensing Powers

Professional services are allegedly somewhat unique in that it is difficult for consumers to evaluate their worth. In some cases, like a surgeon performing an operation, the client may not be around to shop elsewhere if the service is unsatisfactory. Only the professionals themselves are deemed fully qualified to judge if the service is necessary, and, if so, how much and what quality. Such a situation places professionals in the somewhat unique position of determining— or at least strongly influencing—the demand for their service, while at the same time supplying the service.

Allegedly to protect the public interest, in such circumstances professionals have often been granted self-governing powers[8] with a high degree of autonomy over their own internal affairs. The rationale is simply that no other group

---

although others can practise without the title. By way of example, architects have the exclusive-right-to-practise their prescribed field while town planners have only the reserve-of-title. The *Evolution of Professionalism in Quebec* (1976, pp. 14–16) lists some 38 professional organizations in that province, of which 21 have the exclusive-right-to-practise and 17 have the reserve-of-title.

[6] For a discussion of this point, see Goldstein (1954, p. 277).

[7] A specific conflict is illustrated by Goldstein (1955, p. 201): "The desire for recognition from colleagues, which traditionally involves publication, may be blocked by the employer's need to maintain a degree of secrecy over what is being done, because of national security or for the sake of competitive advantage."

[8] For a current discussion of the rationale for self-government see Tuohy and Wolfson (1978).

possesses sufficient knowledge to govern and regulate the profession; consequently it is given to the profession itself. One of the more common techniques used by self-governing professions to achieve high-quality service is to influence the number and the quality of those who practise in the profession.

This control is achieved through a variety of techniques ranging from registration where the practitioner must simply register somewhere, to certification where a certificate is granted to those who meet certain requirements but anyone can practise (i.e., holders of the certificate have a reserve-of-title but not the exclusive right-to practise), to licensing which is usually taken to mean only those with the licence can practise (i.e., they have the exclusive-right-to-practise). Needless to say, most professions for which the state has granted only a reserve-of-title for their members, seek the exclusive right-to-practise which would give them considerably more power and control over their profession. Other techniques for regulating entry into the profession are also employed, including the requirement of citizenship and residence qualifications, influencing the curriculum of education and training institutions, and influencing government policy on such things as immigration.

While this control of entry into the profession can certainly have an impact on the quality of practitioners and hence of the service received by the public, it also has the convenient property—convenient for the professionals themselves—of enabling professionals to restrict the supply of labour to their profession. This ability to restrict supply, along with their ability to increase the demand for their services (recall that only professionals were deemed qualified to determine how much of their service is required) puts them in the unique position of determining the basic labour market forces that affect their wages and employment opportunities. Such power—ostensibly granted by the state to protect the public—will be jealously guarded and eagerly sought after.

This self-government and autonomy creates conflicts with employers when they seek to use non-professional personnel or when they are pressured to grant similar powers to other groups. However, a more serious conflict occurs with the public interest since such self-government tends to be unnecessary when large numbers of professionals are employed on a salaried basis. While self-government *may* provide the public with a measure of protection in circumstances where the self-employed professional deals directly with an uninformed individual client, it does not seem necessary in cases where the client possesses a reasonable degree of sophistication concerning the need for professional services and the quality of service required. Employers who employ professionals on a salaried basis could be considered such clients, since they have both the incentive and the capability of hiring the appropriate amount of professional service. Thus for the large and increasing number of salaried professionals employed in the public sector—be it government, a not-for-profit institution, or a regulated utility—self-government is not necessary to ensure the public interest. Its continuance in such circumstances only perpetuates the disadvantages of self-government—excessive salaries and hence costs, excessive quality of the service, restriction of upward mobility of other persons who could do the tasks, and animosity of other workers who do not possess self-governing powers. In this sense, self-government is an anachronism for salaried professionals.[9]

Ethical Codes, Altruism, Community Responsiblity

Again, allegedly to protect the public interest, most professions have a code of ethics often involving statements of altruism and community responsibility. While this may guide the behaviour of some professionals in a socially desirable fashion and inspire the confidence of some clients, it also serves to insulate the profession from outside criticism and, most important, the code of ethics reduces internal competition by discouraging advertisement, price competition and the solicitation of customers. Fortunately for the professions, altruism and self-interest coincide: one cannot help but wonder which motive would prevail if they conflicted.

Strict adherence to the 'rules of the game' is a common social device to preserve the status quo for groups whose large numbers preclude the cartel-like behaviour that is possible when the number in the group is small. Employment of sanctions is facilitated by the homogeneous membership of each profession and by the fact that the notions of altruism and community responsibility serve to attach a higher social purpose to actions that otherwise might be interpreted as self-serving.

As with the other characteristics of professionals, the adherence to ethical codes, altruism, and community responsibility may create tensions between public sector employers and their salaried professionals. If these characteristics of professionals were truly designed to serve the public interest, then in theory there should be no conflict since the public sector should want its employees to act in the public interest. When these activities of professionals are mainly self-serving, even insofar as they simply create an aura of sanctity around the notion of professionalism, then conflict may and should occur.

Such could be the case, for example, where professionals refuse to do anything but expensive, first-rate work on the grounds that their code of ethics prevents them from doing otherwise, or where they leak confidential information on the grounds that the public has a right to know. Obviously in some cases their action may be in the public interest; nevertheless, it may create a conflict situation with a public sector employer.

---

[9] For an extensive discussion of this point see Beatty and Gunderson (1977).

III. CHARACTERISTICS OF PROFESSIONAL LABOUR MARKET

The characteristics of the market for professional labour also have important implications for the employment of professionals in the public sector. In particular, the professional labour market is often characterized as 'segmented'. It is also subject to important demand and supply trends and fluctuations, and other peculiarities of the market arise from the predominance of public sector employment.

Professionalism and Segmented Labour Markets

In the terminology of the dual or segmented labour market proponents, the professional labour market may be characterized as being within the primary or core market for labour.[10] This follows from the specialized education, professional identification and self-governing powers that define its participants. According to this type of analysis, the primary labour market is distinguished by high wages, low turnover and absenteeism, desirable working conditions, and opportunities for advancement, promotion and self-fulfillment. The secondary labour market has the opposite characteristics, and these characteristics are self-perpetuating in that they foster poor work habits which keep people locked into the secondary labour market.

In such circumstances, economic theory predicts that the forces of competition would operate to equalize the conditions in both markets. However, the basic point of segmented labour market theory is that such forces are inoperable: the markets will remain separate even though individuals in the secondary labour market may potentially be capable of doing the tasks of the primary labour market.

Market segmentation can be maintained by a variety of devices. In the case of professionals, the segmentation is maintained by controlling the use of paraprofessionals and others who could do professional tasks, and by maintaining a degree of insularity. The flow of new entrants is controlled by long and expensive education and training requirements, occupational licensing, immigration and residence requirements and the requirement that new recruits enter at well-defined ports-of-entry and move through the ranks in a well-defined manner. The use of paraprofessionals and substitute inputs is controlled by laws and regulations, as well as by the dictates of professionals themselves. The insularity of the profession is maintained by a variety of devices including their use of exclusive language and jargon, ethical codes preventing advertising and competitive actions, and a social contract that emphasizes the 'old-boy network' and restricts the profession to members of certain social classes. In this last vein, some who have extended the segmented labour market theory along more radical

---

[10] For a critical discussion of segmented labour market analysis and a review of that literature, see Cain (1975). Segmented labour market theory is contrasted with neoclassical theory and with a more radical analysis, in Gordon (1972). The 'classic' presentation of segmented labour markets is given in Doeringer and Piore (1971).

lines have argued that segmentation is also a function of class structure and that class structure would also foster segmentation.

The concept of professionalism is one that in a sense epitomizes the notion of a segmented labour market. Mobility from the secondary (non-professional) to the primary (professional) labour market is effectively controlled, with those fortunate enough to be in the primary market reaping the benefits of such segmentation. Because they gain from the segmentation, it is not in their self-interest to question it: rather their control of the occupation is usually justified under the guise of the public interest.

In the context of segmented labour markets in general and with respect to professional segmentation in particular, the key question to be analyzed is: how can such segmentation persist under the pressure of competitive forces? Alternatively stated, can the forces of competition consistently be suppressed by the forces creating the segmentation? To be sure, those who gain will contribute heavily to the continuation of segmentation, and they are probably a small, homogeneous, articulate group with considerable to gain. On the other hand, segmentation is costly to workers who are excluded from the primary labour market, and it is costly to consumers who ultimately pay for the higher-priced services. To the extent that both the latter groups are diverse and heterogeneous with little to lose from any one element of segmentation, they may not react adversely. Even then, however, there may be forces at work to represent their interest.

In a market economy with profit constraints, firms that utilize salaried professionals would be under cost-saving pressure to substitute cheaper labour from the secondary labour market. They may be under pressure from those in the primary labour market not to do so directly, but they could contract out or purchase inputs from firms that employ labour from the secondary labour market. They could also make use of paraprofessionals. If they were prevented from doing so they might be able to reorganize their production process so as to reduce their need for certain professionals. Because of the profit imperative, salaried professionals in the private sector may be unable to maintain the protective barriers that foster segmentation.

In the public sector, however,—where the vast majority of professionals work—segmentation may not conflict with a profit constraint. It may be fostered through separate bargaining units for professionals or unnecessary professional requirements. Rapid growth of the professional labour force in the public sector may thus be attributed to a hospitable climate for continuing segmentation.

In general, there are two alternative policy prescriptions that usually flow from the segmented labour market analysis. One is to try to break the barriers that lead to the segmentation: the other is to extend the benefits that were previously afforded only to those in the primary labour market to a larger array of workers, particularly to those in the secondary labour market. With respect to professionals, the latter policy prescription might imply the extension to non-professional labour markets of a variety of benefits previously reserved largely for professionals, such as sabbaticals, flexible working hours, workers' control, and job enrichment and job enlargement. Since these are more in the nature of fringe benefits than basic job rights or minimum standards, government policy on such issues should be neutral and passive: their costly introduction is best left to the normal process of collective bargaining, with its various trade-offs best known to the parties themselves.

Governments can have a more active role in the alternative policy prescription of breaking down the barriers that foster the segmentation of the professional labour market. The possible policies fall into two general categories. First, much of the segmentation arises because of state-granted monopoly power for the profession to self-regulate: this power can be reduced by various means including the requirement of public representatives on the regulatory boards, the disallowance of unnecessary citizenship, residence or even educational requirements, and the granting of less restrictive powers such as reserve-of-title rather than the exclusive-right-to-practise.

Second, the government can attempt to keep its own house in order—and its own house is the largest employer of professionals—in a variety of ways including the use of paraprofessionals when appropriate, and the use of 'buy not make' when the competitive market can provide the service more efficiently.[11] The government response need not always be one of standing up to the powerful interest group of professionals: simply utilizing its own professionals more effectively would go a long way to encourage the professional self-esteem that is so important to this group. Many of the government's internal employment problems with respect to professionals would be helped by the general injection of efficiency criteria and techniques in the public sector:[12] this would compel government agencies to utilize professionals more effectively and to break down the segmentation of the professional labour market when appropriate. This would also prevent the public sector from becoming a haven for salaried professionals who have priced themselves out of the private sector labour market, but who can find employment in the public sector, where the profit constraint is not as binding.

To a large extent the barriers that foster segmentation of the professional labour market, both in the private and public sectors, are under considerable pressure from a variety of supply and demand forces. The extent to which these forces—discussed in the following section—will break down the segmentation

---

[11] Obviously the procedure of buying from the private sector need not always be cost-saving, as could be the case, for example, if government 'inside' information on contracts were important, or if the government had slack resources, or if it were easier for the government to monitor the quality of the inputs rather than assess the quality of the output.

[12] Certain current practices are not conducive to the efficient utilization of professional, as well as other, personnel in the public sector. For example, the policy (discussed later in this paper) of granting departmental allocations in terms of specific number of personnel rather than in dollar terms, may encourage the overutilization of overqualified personnel. Judging the importance of a department and its administrator on the basis of the size and growth of its budget or the number of its personnel can encourage unnecessary employment expansion, as can incremental as opposed to zero-based-budgeting. Similarly, the policy of judging public sector output on the basis of inputs — so many dollars of high-level personnel devoted to the problem — can encourage overutilization of personnel.

remains an open question. Suffice it to say that to the extent that desegmentation is in the public interest these basic forces should be encouraged, or at least their impact allowed to work its way through the system.

Demand Trends and Fluctuations

Conventional wisdom seems to suggest that the demand for professionals will continue to grow, thereby providing ample employment opportunities at high salaries. While this may have been true in the past, there are signs that this sustained demand may be waning.[13] The public sector is under strong pressure to curtail its expenditure growth: since professionals constitute a large and expensive portion of the public sector labour force, they are logical candidates for cost-saving measures. This is especially the case if they are unorganized and hence could not provide a united front or if they have little public support because they already occupy a privileged position.[14]

Changes in the age structure of the population can also have a dramatic effect on the demand for professionals in the public sector, as evidenced by the decline in demand for teachers as the baby-boom population ages. Reorganization of public sector delivery systems can also have an impact, as evidenced by the shift to home-care and out-patient facilities in hospitals which can reduce the demand for hospital professionals.

Just as the public sector is coming under increased scrutiny so also are the professions themselves—especially those with self-governing powers.[15] Public questioning over the sanctity of professionalism has been heightened by the self-interest actions of many professional groups as they have engaged in legal and illegal strikes, organized into unions, and publicly engaged in internal quarrels.[16] In addition, there is questioning of the necessity of self-government especially in situations where large numbers of professionals are salaried.[17]

---

[13] Bird (1978) cites evidence to show that the fastest growth of public employment in Canada occurred in the 1950s and that, in the 1970s, public employment has levelled off and may even have declined. Internationally, a waning demand for professionals in the public sector has been noted in ILO (1977, p. 43): "In many countries the major cutbacks in employment in the public service and education, which are generally the largest employers of research workers, specialists and highly qualified personnel, have sharply reduced the employment opportunities for this group of workers".

[14] One way of effecting cutbacks of government professional employment is through the currently favoured policy of 'buy, not make' for some government services. As observed above, if professionals are overutilized in the public sector, total demand for professional labour might be reduced when actual production is transferred to the private sector. As also noted above, however, buying from the private sector need not necessarily be cost-saving; it may not even reduce the total demand for the services of professionals. In some cases, the practice may simply imply a relocation of professionals from the public to the private sector.

[15] In the legal context, this is evidenced by the recent extension of anti-combine legislation to professions, by the establishment of the Office of Professions in Quebec to oversee the professions in that province, and, in Ontario, by the evaluation of various professional charters by the Professional Organization Committee of the Ministry of the Attorney-General.

[16] For example, teachers have increasingly used the strike weapon, education and health personnel are increasingly turning to unionization, and engineers have engaged in internal quarrels over the pros and cons of unionization.

[17] This issue is discussed in Beatty and Gunderson (1977) where it is concluded that self-government is inappropriate for salaried professionals.

Professionals in the public sector may thus be under a double-barrelled scrutiny both by virtue of their being in the public sector and by being professionals.

Professionals in the public sector, or in any organization for that matter, are also subject to the pressure that even if they can control entry into the profession, it is difficult for them to prevent the organization from substituting away from their services if they are priced too high. Firms can reorganize their production process to use more paraprofessionals or other inputs in place of professional labour, and salaried professionals can do little to prevent this, even if they have the exclusive-right-to-practise their professional task.

Not only are there signs of a possible waning of the long-run demand for professionals, but also short-run fluctuations in the demand for professionals may occur. To the extent that professionals are employed in the public sector they are subject to short-run changes in government expenditures. Such changes can be dramatic when government expenditures are used to combat business cycles or when expenditure priorities respond to the key issues of the day, be they the environment, cities, crime, medicare, legal aid, or wage-price controls. To be sure, professionals engaged in such programs may have employment security, although it may not always be in the job nor with the same employment expectations under which they were hired.

Contrary to conventional wisdom, then, the market for professionals in the public sector can be subject to adverse demand conditions, both long-run and short-run.[18] The problem is particularly acute when favourable demand conditions give rise to soaring expectations, expectations that are dashed when the trend or cycle reverses. In such circumstances—as perhaps exist now in the academic, teaching and nursing labour markets—professional discontentment will heighten, and professionals become ripe for organizing and unionization.

Supply Trends and Fluctuations

Even if they can control entry into their occupation, professionals can be subject to various supply trends and fluctuations that can have a dramatic impact on their labour market situation. In the long-run, exogenous factors may be at work to increase the supply of services that are akin to those provided by some professionals. For example, the dramatic increase in the education of the labour force means more groups aspiring to professional status. That, in turn, often implies a diminution of the virtues of being considered a professional. In addition, increased specialization means an increase in the number of

---

[18] As summarized by Oppenheimer (1975, p. 38): "Pressure upon the services sector generally, and the public sector in particular, to become more accountable and prove productive now overlays the deterioration of incomes and job opportunities that are linked to an overexpansion of education, and the levelling-off of population. This phenomenon, which can no longer be described as a merely cyclical factor, is attributable to what some economists have labelled the 'fiscal crisis of the state' — in short, the inability of the public sector to generate revenues to meet its increasing expenditures."

paraprofessionals equipped to do some of the specific tasks previously done by other professionals.

Supply fluctuations can also be prevalent as evidenced by the 'cobweb' cycle that often characterizes professional labour markets.[19] Because of the long training period, supply responses may overreact to a short-run wage increase. This creates a glut in the market which in turn lowers salaries dramatically. Entrance into professional programs then drops, creating the conditions for the next shortage and resulting salary increases. Again the potential for soaring expectations followed by unfulfilled aspirations becomes obvious, and professional discontent heightens.

Peculiarities of Public Sector Employment

There are features of the public sector labour market that create particular problems for salaried professionals. While many of these features are not unique to the public sector,[20] they are present in sufficient degree to merit careful scrutiny.

The absence of a formal profit constraint may reduce the pressure to utilize professionals to their full potential. While the absence of such pressure may be welcome relief to most workers, professionals may not find the situation sufficiently challenging or rewarding, after years of intensive education and training.

Under-utilization of the potential of professionals may also occur to the extent that public sector managers may have an incentive to hire overqualified personnel.[21] This occurs when department hiring allocations are specified in terms of number of personnel rather than dollar amounts.[22] In such circumstances, department heads have an incentive to hire overqualified personnel: they may hire professionals for jobs that could be done by less-qualified people. Again, professionals may find themselves unable to fully utilize their professional training.

Pressure to act as a model employer, and concern over public criticism of high salaries, may compel public sector employers to compress the wage structure. To the extent that professionals would otherwise be near the top of the wage structure, they would obviously lose by such a policy.

Public sector output tends to be difficult to evaluate and, consequently, inputs are often used as a measure of output, with little regard for the production process that connects the two. Thus, government attempts to deal with certain

---

[19] For an empirical application of the cobweb model to the labour market for lawyers, see Freeman (1975).

[20] For a discussion of the peculiarities of the public sector labour market and their implications for wage determination see Gunderson (1977a).

[21] Evidence that this may be an international phenomenon is given in ILO (1977, p. 45): "Besides being more vulnerable to unemployment nowadays, professional workers also run the risk of having to take a job for which they are overqualified. This seems to be becoming more and more common in many countries, the industrialized as well as the developing." The study then cites empirical evidence to this effect.

[22] I am indebted to Neil Swan of the Economic Council of Canada for suggesting this point to me.

public sector problems are often measured in terms of the inputs or resources devoted to the problem. Again, this provides a perverse incentive to hire overqualified personnel to give the impression that the government is doing something about the issue. Professionals, who find themselves mere window-dressing in such situations, will obviously have their professional aspirations unfulfilled. They may have the easy life, but that doesn't always accord with their training and conditioning.

The fact that public sector output is difficult to evaluate, coupled with the observation that professional services are complex and difficult to evaluate, also creates certain conflicts between salaried professionals and public sector employers. Authorship of documents and reports can be a contentious issue, with professionals seeking authorship for professional recognition. Patent rights can be an important issue for scientists and engineers. Conflicts may also arise when professionals want to do basic research of a theoretical nature, since such research often has public good characteristics — the results are available to the whole community and it is not possible to exclude users who don't pay. Even public institutions may have little incentive to encourage such research. Monitoring of moonlighting and outside activities is often an issue, and a difficult one to resolve because of the problem of measuring the effect of such activity on the professional's prime job. To a certain extent moonlighting enables professionals to achieve their competitive earnings in public institutions that tend not to reward according to merit or market forces: yet the potential for abuse is obvious, in such situations, where job security in the primary job is virtually guaranteed.

Obviously, not all of these issues are peculiar only to professionals in the public sector. Nevertheless, the public sector labour market does have a variety of peculiarities that create unique problems — unique in degree if not in kind — for professionals in the public sector.

IV. UNIONIZATION OF PROFESSIONALS

In response to some of the recent changes in the professional labour market as well as to the tensions that arise between the characteristics of professionals and the bureaucratic demands of public sector employment, salaried professionals have increasingly turned towards unionization as a way to solve their problems.[23] Alternative forms of organizations have evolved, each with their own characteristics as well as impact. In addition, a variety of legal issues has emerged over such things as the appropriate bargaining unit and appropriate bargaining agent.

---

[23] The economic dimensions of professional unionism, with particular emphasis on its causes and consequences, are discussed in Gunderson (1978).

Reasons for Unionization of Professionals

Professional characteristics of autonomy, identification with the profession, insularity, community responsibility, and concern with full utilization of professional training may create serious conflicts with the demands of the large bureaucratic employer, so characteristic of the public sector. Such requirements often involve hierarchical authority structure, rigid work schedules, and immediate policy-oriented objectives; they are accompanied by formal salary structures with emphasis on seniority over merit.

Finding themselves treated like production workers or other white-collar workers, professionals have often followed the successful response of such workers — they have sought to present a united front, often in the form of unionization.

The unionization of production workers was essentially a response to job insecurity and to the arbitrary whims of management, associated with rapid industrialization and the dictates of a market economy. Faced with rigid managerial directives and with job insecurity associated with recent supply and demand conditions, salaried professionals are prone to have the same security response. This is especially the case when they find themselves in the position of being excluded from managerial decisions, and yet not afforded the job security of many organized workers.

Salaried professionals have also found themselves to be in a declining economic and social position. They are no longer a unique group, set apart from the rest of their workforce by their education and autonomy. Their social and economic position has often been diluted by the increased education of the whole workforce, and the large influx of persons into the existing professions and into new professions and quasi-professions. This has been compounded by the actions of many professional groups, as they have engaged in worker-type activities such as unionization, picketing and strikes. Thus the once-lofty image of professionalism no longer serves as an insurmountable barrier to unionization — especially if it can be called by some other name.

Salaried professionals have also seen their power base eroded by other groups who have successfully organized to present a united front. This includes not only blue- and white-collar unions, but consumer groups, community action groups and employers' associations. Often finding little sympathy within their own professional associations when they are dominated by self-employed professionals, salaried professionals have often organized if for no other reason than to be heard amongst the countless other organized groups. Where individual action may have been sufficient when they were a small and select group, it is often no longer sufficient in today's society of competing interest groups.

Thus, university professors organize to have sufficient bargaining power so that they will not be forgotten, as administrators respond to the pressures from other interest groups including students, legislators, alumni, non-teaching staff, research and teaching assistants, and community groups. Engineers in the U.S. began organizing in the 1940s and 1950s to avoid being engulfed in the bargaining units of production workers' unions that were having marked success. Social workers engage in organizing to have a say in their own job position, as community groups put pressure on budget allocators. Teachers and hospital professionals organize to have a say in education and health budgets, as they are no longer expanding so rapidly.

Extent of Professional Unionization in the Public Sector

Unfortunately, comprehensive data on unionization by occupation are not readily available, so it is not possible to document the extent and growth of professional unionism in either the private or public sector.[24] The problem is compounded by the fact that the organization of professionals takes on a variety of alternative forms, and not all of these forms use the label of a union.

At the federal level, almost all professionals bargain collectively under the *Public Service Staff Relations Act*. The provincial and local picture is more complicated because of the variety of separate provincial labour relations acts and because public sector employees are often covered by separate statutes. In either case, professionals are often, but not always, excluded from coverage under the relevant acts. In the teaching and health care professions, separate labour relations legislation usually prevails. In both cases, collective bargaining through the union or professional association is prominent. Even doctors bargain collectively through their professional associations for their fee structure under medicare.

Alternative Forms of Professional Unionism

Collective action on the part of professionals generally occurs through a professional association, a union, or both. Professional associations sometimes act as mere sounding boards for their members (as is often the case for engineers), and sometimes engage in full-fledged collective bargaining (as is often the case for pilots, and medical associations that bargain with the government over the fee structure for doctors under medicare).

Trade union affiliation may involve being subsumed in the bargaining unit of existing production or white-collar unions, as is often the case with social workers, health personnel, librarians and many professionals in the provincial and local civil service. Or, it may involve separate bargaining units of professional employees, either as independent unions or with national or international affiliation, as is often the case with teachers, university faculty,

---

[24] This is also true for the U.S. For example, Hoffman (1976, p. 41, 42) states: "No one is exactly sure, however, how many professionals are members of labour organizations . . . . . one estimate of the membership level of all professions places it at approximately 40 per cent of the organizable potential . . . . . Forty per cent of the organizable potential is a better showing than the 25 per cent unions have recorded for the labour force as a whole . . . . . A recent spurt to organization, dating from the 1960s, has involved teachers, college professors, and government-employed professionals."

musicians, and professionals in the federal civil service of Canada. Some professions, like teaching, university faculty, and engineering, have run the gamut of all of the alternative forms of collective action.

As Muir (1968) illustrates, the case of public school teachers in Canada provides an interesting portrayal of the evolution of collective action. Prior to World War I, most teachers were involved in education associations with broad social purposes relating to the relationship of education to society. Around World War I most teachers broke away from educational associations to form professional associations to foster their own economic and occupational interests concerning salaries, pensions and status. During the 1920s and 1930s, these professional associations generally achieved voluntary recognition as the bargaining representative for teachers. Wage cuts during the 1930s exposed the ineffectiveness of voluntary recognition and most associations sought compulsory recognition with statutory membership so that all teachers were members of the association and fees are automatically deducted. In recent years, voluntary bargaining has also given way to compulsory bargaining, with teachers employing regular union tactics including picketing and the strike. The evolution from a social organization with nebulous social objectives, to a union-like organization with specific economic goals, has been gradual but steady.

For many other professions, a similar evolution is present, with the professional association more and more taking on many of the characteristics of a trade union.[25] The McGill report (1973), for example, documents this evolution, for the Professional Institute for the Public Service of Canada.

The evolution is particularly prominent for professions dominated by salaried professionals. In cases where the associations represent both salaried and self-employed professionals, tensions have often arisen. Whether such associations can and will adapt to the needs of their salaried members remains an open question. If they do adapt, they will probably do so only by taking on the characteristics of a trade union.

Characteristics of Professional Unionism

Under whatever form it occurs, professional unionism can be expected to acquire some interesting characteristics with respect to the age and militancy of its members and its attitude towards other unions.

Support for professional unionism will probably come from both younger and older professionals. Older workers will gain most from seniority provisions and from formalized pension and retirement schemes. Having less mobility, they stand to gain the most from improvements in their existing job. Older workers

---

[25] Hoffman (1976, p. 47) states: "The first stage of growth for the societies is the consolidation of their membership. The next series of actions furthers interests through legislative lobbying, manpower studies, and the guidelines. The final stage involves bargaining." She also provides an excellent summary of the step-by-step changes in the structure, function, membership and leadership attitudes in the professional societies as they follow this evolution.

may also be more disenchanted with their declining social and economic status: many entered the profession as a select elite, only to have their status undermined by a large influx of new professionals, many with more current training. Older workers have also been exposed longer to the bureaucratization of their work, and have lost any idealism that their earlier professional status would serve them well as salaried employees.

On the other hand, as Barnes (1975, p. 14) points out, younger workers tend to be more militant and not as imbued with notions of proper professional conduct. In addition, they may be the first to be laid off or bumped down the job ladder during economic declines. In some cases — non-tenured university faculty, probationary teachers, doctors in residence, and articling lawyers — they stand to gain from due process in their promotion procedures.

As Oppenheimer (1975, p. 38) points out, however, the emphasis on what the union should seek to accomplish, will differ for younger and older workers:

> "Older, technologically more obsolescent workers become less employable in professional-technical jobs as younger, more up-to-date (and cheaper) workers enter the labour force. The younger tier is therefore advantaged relative to the older. At the same time, the younger worker is entering a situation in which he/she is likely to be overeducated for jobs that are becoming more segmented, less autonomous, and less professional. The likely payoff is that both tiers move toward unionization in order to deal with their respective problems — though young workers will tend to emphasize issues related to on-the-job decision making, while older workers will be more concerned with job security, pay, pensions, etc.".

The attitude of professional unions towards other unions, especially of blue-collar workers, will probably continue to be one of aloofness, in spite of many of their common problems. Professional unions have no history of working class struggle; their members come from social backgrounds that are vastly different than most manual or even white-collar unionists; and, the occupational prestige of professionals rests on their being able to distinguish themselves as something apart from other workers. Rather than solidify the labour movement by extending its influence to higher income and education groups, the unionization of professionals may well inject schisms, especially along political grounds.

Expected Impact of Professional Unionization

Like any union, the potential impact of a professional association or union depends upon the elasticity of the demand for its labour, and on its own power and ability to set wages above the competitive norm, either directly by collective bargaining or indirectly by reducing the supply of labour.

When the demand for union labour is inelastic or insensitive to wage changes, the adverse employment effect of a wage increase will be small. In such circumstances unions will be less inhibited in their wage demands and the potential wage impact of unionism will be large. The demand for union labour is inelastic where there are few good substitutes for union labour, when there are few good substitute products or services for those produced by union labour, and when the ratio of union labour cost to total cost is small.

Since most professional unions have different combinations of the three factors that determine their demand elasticity, it is not possible to make *a priori* judgments about the potential impact of professional unionism. Nevertheless, analysis suggests that the demand for many types of professional labour is relatively inelastic, and in such circumstances professionals should be less constrained in their wage demands than are many other types of labour.

AVAILABILITY OF SUBSTITUTE INPUTS

With respect to the availability of substitute inputs, professional unions have an element of control to the extent that they influence the use of paraprofessionals (especially if they have the exclusive right-to-practise), and to the extent that professional personal contact and discretionary judgment can be maintained as important. The complexity of the subject matter of many professions means that in many cases only professionals themselves know how the job can be done — a factor that is not conducive to their being replaced by other inputs. Often being responsible for their own recruiting, professional in-breeding is an obvious possibility.

University professors, for example, are largely responsible for their own recruiting, they often decide on the combination of inputs that are optimal for their teaching, research and administrative functions, and they usually influence the extent to which paraprofessionals (teaching assistants, demonstrators) and other inputs (closed circuit television, larger lecture halls, books) can be utilized.

In spite of the ability of many professions to influence the substitutability of alternative inputs, this ability is not infinite, especially since the substitution can take subtle forms and can involve alternative production processes. For example, university administrators and budget-conscious governments can encourage the building of satellite teaching campuses with low staff/student ratios; hospital delivery systems can be altered towards out-patient clinics and surgical day-care, which involves more clinics but fewer night-care personnel; and governments can contract-out ('buy, not make') if their own professional staff becomes too expensive.

AVAILABILITY OF SUBSTITUTE OUTPUTS

Professionals also have some control over the availability of alternative outputs or services, and therefore they can pass on wage increases to consumers or taxpayers without having to worry about large reductions in the demand for the service, and hence in the derived demand for professional labour. In essence, professionals can impart a degree of price inelasticity for their services.

Because of the complexity of many of their services, professionals themselves are often relied upon to recommend both the quantity and quality of the service they should provide. This can be the case with doctors under medicare, lawyers under legal aid, and teachers in special-education programs. More generally, the difficulty of evaluating the output of the public sector applies to the value of professional services therein: since the value of output is undefined, so is the value of the marginal product of labour, and hence the derived demand for labour.[26]

To the extent that services are in the public sector because they are essential or because they are produced by natural monopolies, consumers or taxpayers may not be able to shop elsewhere if the cost of these services becomes too high. Education and health as well as many general government activities are often regarded as essential services that are carried out largely by professionals, and for which alternative services are not readily available. Much of the transportation-communications-utilities sector is considered a natural monopoly[27] where consumers are restricted to one or a few firms that are usually publicly regulated.

This does not mean that there is no relationship between professional salaries and the demand for their services. Rather, in such circumstances it simply may be easier for professionals themselves to define the value of their output, and hence the derived demand for their services. Needless to say, there may be a temptation to value their own output highly so that it, and their services in providing the output, become indispensable. This could be the case with government engineers and scientists, social scientists advising on socio-economic policy, as well as social workers, teachers and highly-skilled medical personnel.

There are constraints on the output side, however, even in the public sector. The public may not know how to value a space program, but it can reveal its preferences for space program expenditures, versus social welfare expenditures, versus private consumption via tax cuts. Moreover, it may shift its demands in response to the price and tax burden of a particular program. Each of these alternatives has profound implications for the employment of particular groups of public sector professionals.

It is also the case that many outputs of the public sector are thought of more as frills than as essential items: in the short-run at least they are regarded as postponable. This may be true for higher education, advanced medical treatment, and social work, as well as basic research on the part of physical and social scientists. In addition, the ability of the public to survive a number of recent strikes in essential services has cast doubt on the essentiality of much public sector output, and hence on the derived demand for professional labour that produces the output. As with their ability to control substitute inputs, it is hazardous to generalize about the price elasticity of demand for the output produced by professionals.

---

[26] I am indebted to Ralph Turvey of the International Labour Organization for making this point to me.

[27] A natural monopoly occurs when the demand for the service is not sufficiently large in a given market to exhaust the economies of scale so that the industry could sustain more than one firm. Since competition is thereby restricted, the monopoly is usually regulated by the government.

RATIO OF LABOUR COST TO TOTAL COST

With respect to the ratio of labour cost to total cost, a similar picture emerges — a *priori* generalizations are not possible. In some professions — teaching, health care, social work — the cost of professional services are a large portion of the total cost of providing the final output. In others — pilots, air traffic controllers, legal, architectural and engineering services — only a few professionals may be involved and their services are only a small share of the total cost.

SUMMARY OF ELASTICITY OF DEMAND CONDITIONS

Clearly, generalizations concerning the elasticity of derived demand for professional labour as a whole are not possible. Nor is it usually possible to generalize about any given profession. The demand for teachers or skilled health personnel may be inelastic because of the unavailability of alternative inputs or because of the essentiality of the service: however, it may be elastic because of the high ratio of professional labour cost to total cost. Research scientists may be a small portion of the total cost of providing a certain output, but the output itself may not be regarded as necessary. Some professions, like social work, seem to have little bargaining power because the derived demand for their services will probably be elastic for all three reasons. Others, like airline pilots and controllers, may have more bargaining power because of an inelastic derived demand for their services.

Although no generalization could cover every possibility, one may, nonetheless, register an impressionistic overall view — a view that may, perhaps, not be shared by others. More than most types of labour, professionals in the public sector probably face a fairly inelastic demand for their services. This occurs in part because they are public sector employees, and hence the absence of an immediate profit constraint reduces the speed at which substitute inputs or outputs are found; it occurs in part because professionals have a large say in the destiny of their own profession and in the use of substitute inputs and outputs.

POWER TO SET WAGES

Even if many professionals faced an inelastic demand for their labour, they would not be able to take advantage of that situation, in their wage demands, if they could not put forth a united front. As with the influences on elasticity of demand, it is not possible to make an unambiguous generalization concerning the ability of professional unions to put forth a united front and therefore to set wages above the competitive norm.

On the one hand, their professional identification, exclusiveness and homogeneous social attitudes gives them an identity and solidarity. Their influence over entry into the profession gives them an element of power only rivalled by the powerful craft unions with their apprenticeship systems and hiring hall.

On the other hand, the individualistic orientation of many professionals often makes them averse to collective action and union tactics of strikes, walkouts, picketing, work-to-rule and confrontation. This attitude is reinforced by their identification with management and the fact that they may feel their promotion possibilities are jeopardized by union-like activity. Those who are members of a professional association dominated by self-employed professionals may find little support for any collective bargaining process for the salaried members. Those who are members of a larger bargaining unit of nonprofessionals may have little power over professional issues. This weakness would be compounded by lack of support from the trade union movement itself with its emphasis on egalitarianism.

Within professional unions rifts may occur amongst those of a different age, sex or skill level, over the appropriate issues to emphasize. Such problems can and do occur in all unions; yet they may be more prevalent in professional unions because of the importance to career development of different policies. Thus, as noted earlier, older workers want pensions, job security and seniority recognition, because they fear career obsolescence. Younger workers may want merit increases and a greater say in job decisions. Females may want flexible working hours or provisions providing job security or retraining should professional careers be interrupted. Highly-skilled professionals want patent rights, authorship, job selectivity and the exclusive right to do certain jobs: less-skilled technicians and paraprofessionals want the right to do the more skilled work.

Legislation may also make it difficult for many salaried professionals to put forth a united front or even to bargain collectively. At times, professionals are excluded from the labour relations act of their particular jurisdiction.[28] Others are classified as managerial and hence unable to join a union, or union certification is refused on the grounds that the union contains some professionals who do managerial functions. Many professionals in the public sector do not have the right to strike or are required to provide the essential elements of their service during a strike. Needless to say, such conditions are not conducive to their bargaining power.

Clearly, there are a variety of offsetting factors that influence the ability of professional unions to put forth a united front, and hence to have the power to set wages above the competitive form. Perhaps the only generalization that can be made — and even this view may not be widely shared — is that, over time, salaried professionals increasingly have been willing to act like unionists more

---

[28] The Canadian situation, as of 1974, is summarized by Fraser and Goldenberg (1974, p. 458): "Collective bargaining is provided for professional employees, including engineers of the Canadian government, under the provisions of the *Public Service Staff Relations Act* . . . . . As for the provinces, only Ontario and Manitoba still exclude the members of engineering and other professional associations from the bargaining rights accorded to other civil servants. Public service legislation in Quebec and New Brunswick, like the *Public Service Staff Relations Act* at the federal level, provides for separate professional bargaining units (though not necessarily confined to members of a single profession), as does the recent *Public Service Labour Relations Act* in British Columbia. The remaining provinces have no professional exclusions in their public service legislation."

than like individualistic professionals. Whether this will be sufficient to solidify them collectively and strengthen their power base remains an open question.

Legal Questions

A variety of legal questions concerning salaried professionals has already been indicated. It is beyond the scope of this paper to analyze these questions, or even to suggest answers.[29] However the main questions and policy alternatives can be outlined. They pertain to the determination of the appropriate bargaining agent, bargaining unit, scope and structure of bargaining, and dispute resolution procedures.

On the issue of the bargaining agent, the key policy question is: should professional associations be allowed to bargain for their salaried members if at the same time they control the supply of labour to the occupation, through some form of occupational licencing? Alternatively stated, should the self-governing licencing body, which was created for the alleged purpose of protecting the public, also act as a bargaining agent for its salaried members, in which case it will act in their economic self-interest? Or should these functions be separated and delegated to different bodies? There is also the larger question of the necessity to grant self-governing powers to professions dominated by salaried employees who may be compelled by market forces to act in the public interest.

On the appropriate bargaining unit, there are a number of policy questions. Should there be a single bargaining unit for all professionals within an organization, or a separate one for each profession? Should paraprofessionals be included in the bargaining unit? Can professionals who have some managerial function be included in the bargaining unit? Can professionals be part of a larger bargaining unit consisting largely of nonprofessionals?

On the scope and structure of bargaining the key issues revolve around the potential conflict between management rights and professional standards and ethics, perhaps as outlined in a professional charter. In addition, there is the question of the scope for individual bargaining.

The dispute resolution questions often hinge on the compatibility of professionalism and strikes, and on the larger issue of the right-to-strike in the public sector, where most professionals work. If the powers of self-government are granted to professionals in order to protect the public interest, is it consistent also to grant them the right-to-strike?

Answers to many of these questions hinge upon the answer to one overriding question: are salaried professionals sufficiently unique to merit special consideration under existing or new labour relations laws, or can they be accommodated under the existing statutes? If they can be accommodated then most of the legal issues are ones that have already been dealt with in labour board

---

[29] These issues are discussed thoroughly by Dave Beatty in Beatty and Gunderson (1977). I am indebted to this source for this material, and to Dave Beatty for further elaboration and discussion.

decisions. The others will be dealt with in the give-and-take of collective bargaining and internal union trade-offs.

V. CONCLUDING OBSERVATIONS

Throughout this paper, a variety of public policy issues emerged and a variety of questions were posed. While it would be presumptuous to suggest answers to most of these questions, some personal reflections may be in order by way of conclusion.

To a large extent professionals and even paraprofessionals are a privileged group, economically and socially. In this regard, public policy should be more concerned with the public interest than the employment interest of professionals, and, contrary to professional protestations, the two need not coincide. Professionals will take care of themselves: public policy should ensure that this does not come at the expense of the public interest.

At the policy level this calls for an opening of the professions, perhaps by restricting the powers of professional bodies to registration or at most certification, rather than licencing of exclusive-right-to-practise. In the legal context, salaried professionals could be treated like other workers, and when organized they should have the rights and responsibilities of other trade unionists. In this context it seems best to separate the trade-union function and the self-governing licencing function of many professional associations that have both salaried and self-employed members. Allowing both licencing and union representation functions grants them an inordinate amount of power — a power that *may* be necessary when self-governing professionals deal with an uninformed client but is not necessary when professionals are employed on a salaried basis.

In terms of keeping its own house in order — and its own house is the largest employer of professionals — a public sector employer would be well advised to inject efficiency criteria into public sector decisions, for example, by granting agencies dollar budget allocations rather than personnel allocations, since the latter encourages the use of overqualified personnel. Special privileges granted to professionals will also be emulated by other groups and may lead to costly changes with little returns. On the other hand, some privileges — like authorship — should be encouraged because they are costless, they will not be emulated by other groups, and they encourage professional responsibility.

The issue of an appropriate salary policy for professionals is complex because an egalitarian wage policy may conflict with efficiency needs of recruitment. Rather than agonize over such issues as private sector comparability or total compensation, however, public sector employers could simply monitor the disequilibrium quantity signals[30] — queues or shortages of applicants — to

---

[30] The argument for using disequilibrium signals, together with a discussion of other criteria for public sector wage determination, is given in Gunderson (1977b).

see if they are paying the appropriate wage. More strongly stated, the appropriate wage is the minimum that the public sector employer can get away with, without experiencing recruitment problems. While such a market-oriented policy may not be acceptable for low-wage workers because it subjects them to the vicissitudes of the market, it is certainly more acceptable for salaried professionals who are already in a strong market position.[31] This is probably one of the few cases when public policy can be guided by efficiency criteria, without having to worry considerably about the distributional results.

An appropriate salary policy for professionals is important in the public sector because it may be necessary to come to grips with a key question: why has professionalism grown so fast in the public sector? We have a variety of reasons to explain the growth of the public sector itself, but these do not add up to an explanation of the growth of professionalism within the public sector. The key question is: why have we not conserved on the use of the scarce and expensive professional input in the expansion of the public sector itself?

It may be a technological fact of life that substitution for professional labour is simply difficult, and that our growing demands on the public sector could only be met with proportionately more professionals. Or it may be that *self-employed* professionalism increasingly became an unsatisfactory and expensive way of serving various public wants:[32] having a knowledgeable public sector employer serve as an intermediary between ill-informed clients and professionals may be a more sensible way of ordering production.

Alternatively, professionals may have created their own demand, and this may go unchecked by a salary policy that encourages more professionals to seek employment in the public sector. The appropriate policy response in such a situation is to restrict the powers that enable professionals to create their own demand and to follow a salary policy that pays attention to disequilibrium signals of queues or shortages.

Such policies need not be contrary to the interests of professionals — at least for those 'true professionals(?)' who obtain tremendous satisfaction from the nature of their work itself. They may well be better off by having paraprofessionals and others doing many of their tasks, and by having colleagues whose main interest is in their work rather than their artificially high remuneration. In addition, such policies would go a long way to discourage other groups from viewing professionalism mainly as a socially acceptable means of attaining a high and secure income.

---

[31] Given the cobweb cycle that was discussed earlier as characterizing many professional labour markets, the utilization of disequilibrium quantity signals may mean that professionals' wages would fluctuate quite dramatically. However, if wages do not fluctuate accordingly, the excess supplies or demands would persist, leading to costly shortages or excesses of professional labour. If it were desirable to lessen the cobweb cycle, the government could provide advance information on the expected supply responses, and it could attempt to iron out demand fluctuations. In addition, it could alter professional supply responses by its control or influence over such factors as university education and occupational licencing.

[32] One could speculate — and at this stage it is simply speculation — that self-employment is unsatisfactory for reasons mentioned earlier in the text. That is, many self-employed professionals can affect both the supply of and demand for their services, and they may use this to further their own ends at the expense of the public interest. If this were the case then there may be public pressure to utilize salaried rather than self-employed professionals.

REFERENCES

Barnes, W. (1975) *The Changing Stance of the Professional Employee*, Research Monograph 29 (Kingston: Queen's University Industrial Relations Centre).

Beatty, D. and M. Gunderson (1977) "The Employed Professional: Accountants, Architects, Engineers and Lawyers in Ontario", Professional Organization Committee, Ministry of the Attorney-General, Toronto.

Bird, R.M. (1978) "The Growth of the Public Service in Canada", Chapter Two in David K. Foot (ed.) *Public Employment and Compensation in Canada: Myths and Realities* (Toronto: Butterworth & Co. for The Institute for Research on Public Policy).

Cain, G.G. (1975) "The Challenge of Dual and Radical Theories of the Labor Market to Orthodox Theory" *American Economic Review* (Papers and Proceedings) 65:2, 16–22.

Doeringer, P.B. and M.J. Piore (1971) *Internal Labour Markets and Manpower Analysis* (Lexington, Mass.: Heath).

Evolution of Professionalism in Quebec (1976) (Quebec: Office des Professions Du Quebec).

Fraser, D. and S. Goldenberg (1974) "Collective Bargaining for Professional Workers: The Case of Engineers" *McGill Law Journal*, 20, 456–74.

Freeman, R.B. (1975) "Legal 'Cobwebs': A Recursive Model of the Market for New Lawyers" *Review of Economics and Statistics* 57, 171–79.

Goldstein, B. (1954) "Unions and the Professional Employee" *Journal of Business* 27, 276–84.

Goldstein, B. (1955) "Some Aspects of the Nature of Unionism Among Salaried Professionals in Industry" *American Sociological Review* 20, April, 199–205.

Gordon, D.M. (1972) *Theories of Poverty and Underemployment: Orthodox, Radical and Dual Labor Market Perspectives* (Lexington, Mass: Lexington Books).

Gunderson, M. (1977a) "Public-Private Sector Differences and Implications for Wage Determination", Research Branch, Anti-Inflation Board, Ottawa.

Gunderson, M. (1977b) "Criteria for Public Sector Wage Determination", Research Branch, Anti-Inflation Board, Ottawa.

Gunderson, M. (1978) "Economic Aspects of the Unionization of Salaried Professionals", in M. Trebilcock and P. Slayton (eds.) *The Professions and Public Policy* (Toronto: University of Toronto Press).

Hoffman, E. (1976) *Unionization of Professional Societies*, Conference Board Report 690.

ILO (1977) *Conditions of Work and Employment of Professional Workers* (Geneva: International Labour Office).

McGill Report (1973) "The Professional Employee in the Public Service of Canada" *Journal of the Professional Institute* 52, 4–28.

Muir, J. (1968) *Collective Bargaining by Canadian Public School Teachers*, Task Force on Labour Relations Study No. 21 (Ottawa: Information Canada).

Oppenheimer, M. (1975) "The Unionization of the Professional" *Social Policy* 5, Jan./Feb., 34–40.

Tuohy, C. and A. Wolfson (1978) "Self-Regulation and Who Qualifies", in M. Trebilcock and P. Slayton (eds.) *The Professions and Public Policy* (Toronto: University of Toronto Press).

Chapter Five

Comparative Public Sector Growth: A United Kingdom Perspective

by
*Peter M. Jackson**

> "Agreement on what is the wisest total, and pattern, of government spending is a goal men are never likely to reach".
>
> C. Lowell Harriss

Public expenditure and its counterpart, taxation, are topics of popular discussion and common concern. Increases in public expenditures and taxes are held high on press headlines as if to convey to the reader that the government of the day has acted imprudently or unwisely. Seldom do such headlines suggest that increases in public spending, and increases in the taxes to pay for them, might be a sign of a prosperous society, a society which can afford to enjoy the benefits that these public expenditures provide. Of course not all increases in public expenditures are signals of a prosperous nation. Standard Keynesian policies, which expand aggregate demand through the public budget, may be the reason for rising public expenditures.

For many people it is not the absolute increase in public expenditure which is of interest or concern, but rather the growth of the public sector relative to other sectors of the economy. To these people an expansion in the relative size of the public sector means an increase in government control over Mankind's destiny and a corresponding reduction in the power of the individual to determine his/her own fate.

Discussions about public expenditure, its importance and role in economic affairs, its distributional and allocative effects, and its appropriate level are usually conducted in an atmosphere of confusion. Public expenditure is not a simple statistic to handle: it means many things to different people and it is wide open to abuse and misuse. This paper attempts to sort out some of the relevant

Editor's Note: **Peter M. Jackson** is Director of the Public Sector Economics Research Centre, University of Leicester, Leicester, England.

*The author wishes to note valuable editorial assistance received from Professors R. Bird and M. Bucovetsky, both of the University of Toronto.

questions. Its point of reference is the United Kingdom, a country often held forth as the 'horrible example' toward which Canada — and other countries — are relentlessly proceeding.

The paper is divided into four parts. Section I considers the basic questions of measurement: what is public expenditure? how has it behaved over time? can an interpretation be placed on its behaviour? In section II public sector growth in a number of countries is examined and compared, with emphasis placed on the U.K., Canada, and the U.S.A.. In section III structural changes in labour markets are considered. Growth in public expenditures has, unsurprisingly, been closely related to growth in public sector employment. The growth in public sector employment appears to reflect two more fundamental structural changes in the developed industrialized economies: a growth in the demand for the product of the services sector of the economy, and a growth in the employment of married females by that sector.

Recently, a good deal of attention has been given to the alleged implications of the relative size of the public sector of the U.K., especially in the post-1970 period. This change in the structure of the U.K. economy has been used by a number of persons to explain the economic problems (or 'British Disease') experienced by the U.K. during the 1970s. Some have recently seen the on-coming signs of a similar 'Canadian Disease'.[1] Section IV of the paper considers these claims critically.

I. MEASURING THE SIZE OF THE PUBLIC SECTOR

Individuals have long been concerned about the power and the influence of the State over their personal freedom to act in accordance with that which best serves their own self interest. Fear of the spread of Leviathan has caused commentators to search out indices which reflect the size and the influence of government. Most of the summary measures used, however, are not without ambiguity, and the pitfalls in using them are many.

In recent years several works drawing attention to the undesirable spread of the influence of government and the concomitant erosion of personal freedom have employed indices and measures of the size of government with an unquestioning authority wholly unwarranted by the measures themselves. Thus, when referring to the U.K. economy, economists like Bacon and Eltis (1976) or Friedman (1976) refer to the 60 per cent of GNP which is 'absorbed' by the public sector. But what does such a statement mean and is it a fact of life about which the ordinary citizen should be concerned?

A great deal of confusion surrounds the measurement of the relative size of

---

[1] Two commentators have recently drawn attention to such a possibility. First, Eltis (1977c, p. 7) "... there is a distinct possibility that Canada is following the British trend with a time lag of around seven years". Second, Johnson (1977, p. 10) also identifies one of Canada's economic problems to be "... the growth of the government sector itself ... the absorption of labor, especially educated and technically skilled labour, away from production into a form of unproductive consumption".

government, and understanding of these problems is not aided by such unqualified blanket statements. One must consider quite carefully both what it is that is to be measured and the inherent properties of the measure itself. The lack of attention given to the properties of the measure has contributed to much of the confusion. No physical scientist would consider accepting the results of his experiments without being sure of the limitations of his measurement equipment.

We must, therefore, be more prepared to think carefully about what statements referring to the relative size of the public sector really mean. Do the indices which we adopt accurately reflect the relative size of government; what is meant by government; do the measures reflect the influence of government? These are not idle questions posed by academics, who might be thought to be taking up a 'Profession Joad' position of answering a question by calling for a definition. The questions are fundamental to our understanding of the role of government and to the influence that possible answers to them might have on economic policy.

Government Expenditure Ratios

One summary measure frequently used to illustrate the relative size of government is the ratio of such aggregates as total government expenditure to national income. Which national income concept should be used (GDP, GNP, at market prices or factor cost, etc.?) has been adequately and extensively discussed by, amongst others, Bird (1970) and Prest (1972). The value of the ratio will obviously (by simple arithmetic, not economics!) vary with the national income aggregate, yet this simple remark is frequently ignored by those who use such ratios. This is not to imply that the choice of the appropriate national income aggregate is a trivial exercise dependent only on arithmetic. Bird (1970) has demonstrated quite clearly that the use of factor cost or market price measures of aggregate output depends upon the views taken about the shifting of indirect taxes. An appreciation both of the arithmetic and the economics involved in constructing government expenditure ratios would greatly enrich the debate and may reduce the frequency with which outrageous statements are made.

The choice of numerator is also problematical. What is government expenditure? Once again this might seem to be a trivial question. Surely government expenditure is defined in the national income accounts. But such a remark only removes the question one stage. Is the national income accountant's choice of definition suitable? These questions cannot be considered in isolation from what must be the fundamental question — why is a measure of the size of government required?

Individuals require a measure of the size of government for a variety of reasons. They might be interested in the volume of resources absorbed by the public sector, or the size of the tax bill, or the number of persons employed in the public sector. There are often good economic reasons for being interested in these questions: the government's actions, as a participant in the labour, capital goods, and money markets will, for example, influence the behaviour of prices and quantities in these markets. If the government is a sufficiently dominant influence then the behaviour of government and the behaviour of markets are difficult to separate out.

The government also has an influence upon economic behaviour by virtue of the effects of taxation. These effects — incentives and disincentives on work effort, savings, risk taking, etc. — are well documented in the literature. But does a summary measure such as the ratio of government expenditure to GNP adequately reflect concern for the market effects outlined above? The answer must be no. Such ratios fail to reflect the 'structural' aspects of government, and it is usually these which are of interest and importance. The aggregation of government expenditures fails, for instance, to distinguish between exhaustive expenditures on goods and services, and transfers. Since exhaustive expenditures and transfers have different economic effects, discussions about the desirability, or otherwise, of these effects (and hence of the size of government) cannot be conducted in terms of total government expenditure aggregates. A similar argument may be made against using the ratio of total tax revenue to GNP for analytical purposes: this ratio does not distinguish the structure of taxation, and different tax structures have different economic consequences.

Thus the general argument against using aggregate government expenditure or tax ratios is that they are insufficiently rich in information to be of much value when discussing the effects of government. Since it is the *effects* of the relative size of government which must be central to the discussion then alternative ways of carrying out the debate must be sought. In part this is already done by those who draw attention to the distribution of public expenditures between exhaustive and non-exhaustive items and who distinguish between alternative tax structures.[2] Another area of concern which is frequently debated is how are the benefits and the costs of government action distributed amongst members of the community. Again, the government expenditure ratio cannot begin to answer this incredibly complex question.

In short, individuals are generally concerned about the *consequences* or the effects of government activity. The *size* of government, however, is only a poor proxy for these effects and so government expenditure ratios are of limited value in relation to these concerns. Nevertheless, government expenditure ratios may be of some value if employed with caution, with understanding, and applied only to a limited number of clearly formulated questions. Even then, there are several problems of particular concern:

(1) *Transfers and Double Counting.* Total government expenditures (defined in its widest sense to include transfers) does not represent the public sector's absorption of real resources. Exhaustive public expenditures represent the value of goods and services absorbed by the public sector when performing its role as a producer. Transfer payments, on the other hand, represent

---

[2] For example, see Bird (1970) and Prest (1972).

government's power within the economy. Even then certain transfer payments may be double counted. Is a transfer payment of $100, which is then spent by a consumer, an item of consumer expenditure or an item of government expenditure? The answer given to this question will influence the size of the government expenditure ratio.

(2) *Tax Expenditures.* Public expenditures on transfers are direct payments to households. But, for example, child benefits can either be paid out in cash transfers or the same benefit can be given to the household by means of a tax credit or deduction. (In Canada, all three routes are followed simultaneously!) In the first case total public expenditures would be greater than in the last two. The same argument applies to investment grants and investment allowances. Changes in the method of financing such activities will, therefore, change the size of the government expenditure ratio, but clearly do not change the volume of activities performed by government.

Since transfers, subsidies, tax expenditures (and some intergovernmental transfers of intermediate products) are not included in GNP, the numerator of the ratio of government expenditures to GNP is not comparable to the denominator. Nevertheless, all these items have to be financed, so that the ratio of government expenditure to GNP is perhaps most useful as indicating the total financing burden implied by the activities of government.

Changes in Government Expenditure Ratios

Very rapid changes in government expenditures and in the ratio of government expenditure to GNP do not necessarily reflect permanent changes in the size of government. This obvious truism is emphasized by recent events in the U.K.. In 1970, total public expenditure constituted 42.9 per cent of GDP at market prices.[3] By 1975 it was 52.7 per cent. This rapid increase in the ratio reflected various factors including

---

[3] The precise numerical value of such 'public expenditure ratios' will depend upon whether GDP or GNP is used as denominator. However, whilst there will be a *slight* difference in the numerical values of the two ratios it should be appreciated that the time trends in the ratios, whatever the denominator, will move in the same direction.

The value of the ratio will also depend upon the definition of public expenditure used in the numerator. For example, U.K. national income accounts data on public expenditure differ from OECD and Canadian National Accounts definitions insofar as the U.K. definition included (prior to 1976) gross fixed capital formation by government-owned enterprises. The importance of such expenditures can be seen by comparing the U.K. public expenditure ratios for 1970 and 1975 with and without these capital expenditures:

Ratio of U.K. Public Expenditure to GDP
(at market prices)

	1970	1975
When public expenditure includes domestic fixed capital formation of government enterprises	42.9%	52.7%
When public expenditure excludes domestic fixed capital formation of government enterprises	39.7%	48.7%

- a decline in the rate of increase in GDP due to the world recession and therefore an increase in unemployment;
- an expansion in public sector transfer payments to the personal sector in the form of unemployment benefits and increase in net lending by the public sector to the business sector in order to prop up ailing businesses that might otherwise have gone bankrupt, thereby adding to the unemployment; and
- an expansion in subsidies and the money value of all transfer payments in an attempt to offset the rapid inflation which followed the quadrupling of world oil prices, the failure of world agricultural harvests, the rapid increase in primary commodities, the decision to float the pound sterling and the downward float of the pound following a succession of speculative runs on it.

Given that so many factors influence both the numerator and the denominator of any public expenditure ratio in the short run, it is extremely difficult to look behind all of these influences to find out what is happening to the structure and nature of government in the longer term. Despite these problems, however, many commentators persist in using short run changes in the ratio to infer longer term implications.

Another difficulty in interpretation arises because exhaustive public expenditures represent expenditures on inputs whereas GNP, measured at market prices, is a hybrid of expenditures on inputs and outputs. Insofar as output price changes reflect productivity increases, output prices will tend to increase less rapidly than will the prices of inputs. Thus, in the short run, if government does not adjust its volume of inputs the *value* of the ratio of public exhaustive expenditure to GNP will rise as a consequence of changing relative prices. However, there is nothing inevitable about a rise in the G/Y ratio[4] as a result of relative price changes: the final outcome must depend on the influence of the relative price changes on the actual process of collective choice, including the taxpayers' reaction to the increase in government expenditure and taxation. In any case, it is clear that the ratio of government expenditure to GNP can rise even though government doesn't produce any additional output and doesn't hire any additional resources.

Government Expenditure Ratios and the 'Latter Day Physiocrats'

Considerable prominence has recently been achieved by a group of writers who may not inaccurately be labelled the 'Latter Day Physiocrats'. The study by Bacon and Eltis (1976) is perhaps the best-known work along these lines. This new breed of Physiocrats, not unlike their 18th century predecessors, dislike the services sector of the economy and the services of the government sector in

---

[4] G/Y is the generalized economist's shorthand for the ratio of exhaustive government spending to one of the measures of total national expenditure.

particular. The economy is divided, roughly, into producers (i.e. those who produce manufactured output) and non-producers (i.e. those who produce services and government output). Eltis (1977a), for example, argues that "those who produce and sell finance everything" . . . "not all workers are producers". . . . "millions of non-producers are needed and wanted, but they have to be paid for and that is where the strains arise". It is hard to follow this argument since in no relevant economic sense is the government a nonproducer or its workers non-productive. Indeed, much of the government's output can be considered as final output, examples being defence, administration of justice, health and education. In the majority of remaining cases public sector products are intermediate goods which are essential complements to private sector productive activity, as is the case with communications and transportation.[5] In short, households who sell their labour to government are no different from households who sell their labour to business firms.

It is even harder to follow most of the discussions on public expenditure in this literature, in part because exhaustive and transfer expenditures are seldom distinguished. In effect, the reiterated complaint about workers and producers financing an ever-increasing burden of public expenditures is a complaint about the degree of redistribution which takes place in society — a complaint which completely ignores the benefit side of such redistribution. Moreover, to claim that it is only those employed in the productive sector of the economy who finance such transfers is to fail to appreciate that those employed in the public sector pay taxes also.

The new Physiocratic thesis, as elaborated in Bacon and Eltis (1976), is a mixture of the obvious, the banal, and the absurd. And yet the issues implicitly raised are important.

- How can society arrange its institutions so that it gets the correct (i.e. acceptable) mix of goods and services, including government services?
- What are the effects of government expenditures and taxation on incentives, inflation, the balance of payments, and growth?
- Does a shift in production towards services affect the balance of payments; i.e. does it reduce the marginal propensity to export whilst maintaining the same marginal propensity to import?
- Can an economy live beyond its means for long?

Unfortunately, the approach taken in these studies does little to come to grips with the real issues. The influence of government upon economic behaviour and personal freedom is a fascinating question — but no answer will be found by staring at crude G/GNP ratios unless they can be used as keys to open the doors to greater understanding.

---

[5] These and other flaws in the argument of the 'Latter Day Physiocrats' are convincingly demonstrated in Ginzberg (1976).

II. INTERNATIONAL COMPARISONS OF THE GROWTH OF PUBLIC EXPENDITURES

This section considers the growth that has taken place in the public sectors of Canada, the U.S.A. and the U.K. — and in other countries of the OECD — in historical perspective, but with particular attention to the decade following 1965.

20th Century Trends: U.K., Canada, U.S.A.

Since the beginning of the 20th century there has been a secular upward trend in the ratio of total public expenditure to GNP at market prices. This upward trend is shown in Table 5.1, for the U.K., Canada and the U.S.A. Although the size of the U.K.'s public sector, as measured by the public expenditure to GNP ratio, has been consistently larger than that of both Canada and the U.S.A., the growth of government spending relative to GNP was fastest in the U.S.A., followed by Canada and the U.K. The result of these differential growth rates is that the relative U.K. public sector in 1975 was 27 per cent greater than that of Canada, compared to a 43 per cent margin in 1900, while that of the U.S. had risen from 72 per cent of Canada to 91 per cent.

In each country public expenditure at current prices has risen faster than GNP at current market prices. For example, in the case of Canada public expenditure grew at an annual compound rate of 9.0 per cent, between 1926 and 1973, as compared to an annual growth of 6.9 per cent in GNP. In the U.K. a similar picture emerges: public expenditure grew at 7.3 per cent per annum, between 1900 and 1975, whilst GDP grew at 5.3 per cent. The lack of data on original absolute levels of American public expenditures prevents similar calculations being made — however, Borcherding (1977, p. 27) does draw attention to the same phenomenon in the U.S.A.

It is clear from the ratios of public expenditure to GNP that the growth in the relative size of the public sector has not been even. For some periods public expenditures were rising very much faster than GNP, as shown for the U.K. and Canada in Table 5.2. In particular, growth rates have accelerated in the post-war period, especially in the post-1960 period. The more recent period is therefore considered in more detail in the next sections.

TABLE 5.1

THE RISE OF PUBLIC EXPENDITURES: CANADA, THE U.S.A. AND THE U.K., 1900-1975
Total Public Expenditure as a Percentage of GNP (at market prices)

	YEAR										1975 ratio divided by 1900 (or 1902) ratio
	1900	1902	1938	1940	1950	1955	1960	1965	1970	1975	
Canada	9.5		23.8		22.2	26.3	29.8	29.9	36.4	41.4	4.4
U.S.A.		6.8		21.0	24.8	27.4	30.0	29.8	33.8	37.8	5.6
U.K.	13.6		27.5		34.0	36.9	36.9	39.7	42.9	52.7	3.9

Sources:

Canada. 1900: Bird (1970), Appendix C, Table 25; 1938-1970: *National Income and Expenditure Accounts*, Statistics Canada, #13-531 (1975), Vol. 1, Tables 2 and 43; 1975: *Economic Review*, Department of Finance (April 1978), Tables 2 and 51.

U.S.A. 1902-1960: Borcherding (1977), Table 12; 1965-1975: C.L. Schultze "Federal Spending Past, Present and Future", Table 8-1, and E.M. Sunley "State and Local Governments", Table 9-1, both in H. Owen and C.L. Schultze, eds., *Setting National Priorities: The Next Ten Years* (Washington: Brookings, 1976).

U.K. 1900-1950: Peacock and Wiseman (1967), Table A-5, and C.H. Feinstein, *Statistical Tables of National Income, Expenditure and Output of the U.K. 1855-1965* (Cambridge: Cambridge University Press, 1972), Table T8; 1955 to 1975: *Economic Trends Annual Supplement: 1976* (HMSO), Tables 8 and 114.

TABLE 5.2

ANNUALIZED RATES OF CHANGE IN GOVERNMENT EXPENDITURE AND GNP
(in current prices)

	Change in Government Expenditure (per cent)	Change in GNP (per cent)
United Kingdom, 1900 to 1975		
1900 to 1935	4.1	2.7
1955 to 1960	7.4	7.4
1960 to 1970	9.8	8.0
1970 to 1975	25.6	21.9
Canada, 1926 to 1975		
1926 to 1935	3.7	2.2
1950 to 1960	12.1	8.5
1960 to 1970	10.6	9.3
1970 to 1975	17.0	14.1

Source: As for Table 5.1
Note: Percentage changes refer to annual compound rates of growth.

Post-War Growth in Public Spending

To make further comparisons of public sector growth in these three countries — and in other countries — we shall make use of OECD data rather than the national income accounts of each country (as was done immediately above). The national income accounts data are obviously closely related to the OECD data since they provide the basis of the OECD accounts. The difference lies in the uniform classification system which has been adopted. Starting from a set of general definitions for each sector of the economy, the OECD system translates the indigenous national accounts data into a consistent classification among countries. The items most likely to be affected in this process of translation are transfer payments. But there are other respects in which the definition of public expenditure used in the OECD accounts is narrower than that employed in national income accounts. For example, with respect to the United Kingdom OECD public expenditure excludes the nationalized industries; essentially, its concept of 'government' comprises central and local government and the social insurance funds.

A consistent historical series is available, from the OECD, for Canada and the U.S.A. over the period 1950/1975, and for the U.K. from 1960/1975. The

TABLE 5.3

GOVERNMENT FINAL CONSUMPTION EXPENDITURE[1] AS A PROPORTION OF GDP (at market prices) CANADA, U.S.A., AND U.K.
(per cent)

	1950	1955	1960	1965	1970	1975
I. Expenditures and GDP evaluated at Current Prices						
Canada	10.2	13.9	13.6	14.9	19.2	20.1
U.S.A.	12.2	16.0	17.2	17.0	19.1	19.3
U.K.[2]	—	—	16.5	16.9	17.7	22.2
II. Expenditures and GDP evaluated at Constant 1970 Prices						
Canada	15.2	19.2	16.7	16.8	19.2	19.0
U.S.A.	16.1	19.2	19.6	18.3	19.1	18.1
U.K.[2]	—	—	18.9	18.3	17.7	19.2

Source: *National Accounts of OECD Countries, 1975*, Vols. I and II (Paris: OECD, 1977).

Notes:

[1] Government Final Consumption Expenditure is equal to total government spending on goods and services, excluding fixed capital formation.

[2] The source does not provide data for the U.K. for 1950 and 1955.

top half of Table 5.3 shows the ratios of government current expenditure to GDP at market prices, all expressed in current values. It is clear, as before, that the public sector of each of the three countries has grown significantly when measured at current prices.

Changes in the ratio of government expenditure to GDP are of course affected by differences in the rates of change in the prices which affect the numerator and those which affect the denominator. Although the economic interpretation of the 'relative price effect' requires care, insofar as the real volume of inputs to the public sector is maintained over time the ratio of G/Y, at current prices, will tend to rise. The differences in the rates of change in the GDP deflator and the implicit government final consumption expenditure deflator are presented in Table 5.4. It is seen that in all cases growth in the deflator for GDP is less than that for government expenditure.[6]

---

[6] Auld (1976) lays stress on the relevance of this phenomenon to Canada.

TABLE 5.4
RATES OF CHANGE IN PRICE DEFLATORS
FOR GOVERNMENT FINAL CONSUMPTION EXPENDITURE AND THE GDP
CANADA, U.S.A., AND U.K.[1]
(per cent)

	1965 to 1966	1966 to 1967	1967 to 1968	1968 to 1969	1969 to 1970	1970 to 1971	1971 to 1972	1972 to 1973	1973 to 1974	1974 to 1975
Canada										
G. Deflator[2]	6.7	6.8	5.7	8.3	5.8	6.1	7.7	8.7	13.1	13.3
GDP Deflator	4.4	3.9	3.2	4.3	4.7	3.1	5.1	9.3	14.5	10.7
U.S.A.										
G. Deflator[2]	5.0	4.7	5.2	5.8	7.9	7.4	7.1	7.0	9.9	9.6
GDP Deflator	3.2	3.0	4.4	4.0	5.2	5.1	4.1	5.7	9.7	9.5
U.K.										
G. Deflator[2]	5.8	4.7	5.9	6.4	10.8	10.7	9.3	9.4	21.5	32.1
GDP Deflator	4.5	2.9	4.4	5.6	7.4	8.9	8.0	7.9	13.4	27.8

Source: As for Table 5.3.

Notes:

[1] Year on year percentage changes

[2] G. Deflator refers to price deflator for Government Final Consumption Expenditure.

Table 5.4 also illustrates the rapid inflation of the 1970s and shows clearly that the U.K. suffered much greater price rises than did Canada and the U.S. The especially rapid inflation in the U.K. public sector over the period 1973/1975 is also clear.

When the government expenditure ratio is measured at constant 1970 prices, the increase in the relative size of the public sector appears considerably more modest: see the lower half of Table 5.3. The relative size of the public sector also displays more variability. In the case of Canada, for example, there was a rapid increase in the size of the public sector relative to GDP between 1950 and 1955 followed by a decline in its relative size between 1955 and 1960 and a rise between 1965 and 1970. The U.S.A. showed a similar but not identical pattern, over the 1950s and 1960s, and a decline in the relative size of the public sector between 1970 and 1975. This is a marked contrast to the experience of the U.K. where the relative size of the public sector showed a marked increase between 1970 and 1975 following gradual decline between 1960 and 1970.[7]

Changes in the ratio of G/GDP arise from changes in both the numerator and the denominator. Table 5.5 shows more clearly what was happening. The large increase in the relative size of the real public sector of the U.K. during the 1970s was not due to a massive explosion in public expenditure, but rather resulted from the 'continued' increase in public expenditure combined with a slump in GNP especially over the period 1973/1975.

Whilst there appeared to be a more severe slump in the U.S.A. for the same period, 1973/1975, earlier reductions in public expenditure (1969/1970), and the lower growth rate in public expenditure during the 1970s (as compared to Canada and the U.K.) ensured that the G/GDP ratio fell.

Finally, Canada's growth in real public expenditure was, on average, above that for the U.K. during the 1970s. However, the growth in Canada's GDP during the 1970s was also faster than that in the other two countries and marginally faster than the rate of increase in Canadian public expenditure. Whilst Canadian GDP slowed down during 1973/1975, it did not experience the same severe effects as befell that of the U.S.A. or the U.K.

The picture which emerges so far is that throughout the 20th century the public sectors in Canada, the U.S.A., and the U.K. have increased in size relative to their GDP's, when measured at current prices. However, this upward trend has not been smooth. Apart from very large increases in the public sector's relative size, due to wars and recessions,[8] there have been many variations in the relative size of the public sector around its long term trend, reflecting variations in the relative rates of change of both the numerator (G) and the denominator

---

[7] Beck (1976) has emphasized the relative decline in real public expenditures in the U.S. Care should, however, be used when interpreting Beck's results since he employs the questionable procedure of using the deflator for exhaustive public expenditures for transfers also.

[8] See Peacock and Wiseman (1967), who identify their now celebrated 'displacement effect', and Bird's (1970) subsequent critical evaluation of that effect.

TABLE 5.5

YEAR ON YEAR CHANGES IN GOVERNMENT FINAL CONSUMPTION EXPENDITURE AND GNP[1] CANADA, U.S.A., AND U.K.

(per cent)

	1965 to 1966	1966 to 1967	1967 to 1968	1968 to 1969	1969 to 1970	1970 to 1971	1971 to 1972	1972 to 1973	1973 to 1974	1974 to 1975
Canada										
G.[2]	9.3	7.2	7.6	3.7	10.3	4.1	2.6	4.4	6.9	3.6
GNP	7.0	3.4	5.6	5.2	2.6	6.6	5.6	7.2	3.2	0.5
U.S.A.										
G.[2]	10.4	8.3	3.1	-0.2	-1.3	1.8	-1.8	1.0	2.1	1.8
GNP	6.0	2.7	4.5	2.6	-0.1	2.9	5.8	5.4	-1.6	-1.6
U.K.										
G.[2]	2.8	5.7	0.3	-1.8	1.5	2.9	4.3	4.1	2.5	4.9
GNP	2.0	2.6	3.5	1.3	2.3	2.5	2.6	6.0	0.3	-1.3

Source: As for Table 5.3.

Notes:

[1] Government Final Consumption Expenditure and GNP both measured in current prices.

[2] G. refers to Government Final Consumption Expenditure.

(GDP). The rapid increase in the relative size of the public sector is moderated substantially when the ratio of G/GDP is expressed in terms of constant prices.

Changing Composition of Public Expenditures

The composition of public expenditures has changed over time in all three countries. Detailed data on the composition of public expenditure is not available on an OECD basis, so direct comparisons are not feasible. It is, however, possible to examine and to compare the trends which have taken place within the public sector budgets of each country.

In each country, for example, there has been a marked decline in defence expenditure as a proportion of both public expenditure and GNP (see Table 5.6). Although the absolute level of expenditure on defence has increased due to

TABLE 5.6
DEFENCE EXPENDITURE
AS A PROPORTION OF GNP AND TOTAL PUBLIC SPENDING
CANADA, U.S.A., AND U.K.

	1950[1]	1975
Canada		
Per cent of GNP	3.8	1.7
Per cent of total		
public expenditure	12.1	4.1
U.S.A.		
Per cent of GNP	10.5	5.9
Per cent of total		
public expenditure	44.6	21.3
U.K.		
Per cent of GNP	9.8	5.0
Per cent of total		
public expenditure	24.5	9.5

Sources:

Canada. *Economic Review*, Department of Finance (April 1978), Table 51.

U.S.A. 1950: F.M. Bator, *The Question of Government Spending* (New York: Harper, 1960); 1975: J.A. Pechman, ed., *Setting National Priorities: The 1978 Budget* (Washington: Brookings, 1977), Table 4.1.

U.K. *National Income and Expenditure* (HMSO, 1976), Table 10.1.

Note: For the U.K., first column is 1953.

inflation, general wage increases and so on, a greater proportion of successive increments to GNP has been allocated to non-defence public sector programmes. Presumably this generalized decline reflects a change in the perception of what constitutes an adequate level of external security, a change in the set of international relations and also a change in each society's preferences for the mix between defence and non-defence services.

The decline in defence spending has been rapidly filled by expenditures on social programmes. These may be divided into programmes commonly identified with exhaustive expenditures, such as education and health services, and those consisting of transfer payments, such as social security benefits and social assistance grants. In the U.K. and Canada, at least, between 1963 and 1974 there appears to have been a slight shift towards transfer payments as a proportion of total current expenditures.[9] The increase in transfer payments reflects such factors as improvements in the level of 'real' benefits received, adjustments to inflation, and increases in numbers of beneficiaries. As inflation proceeds, for example, subsidies on food and housing will rise.[10] Similarly, as unemployment rises the rate of increase of GNP will decline and the rate of increase of public expenditure will rise.

The increase in payments made for retirement pensions has also contributed to the expansion of social security benefits and social security grants. The observable increase in the number of persons aged 65+ in each country, a reduction in participation rates of older people in the work force, and an increase in the number of inactive persons aged 65+, all suggest an increased demand for an expansion in the absolute amount paid out in pensions. Over and above these demographic factors, the real value of pensions has also improved over time. This in part reflects the 'insurance element' in pension payments, since contributions to the pension scheme are closely related to improvements in wages and salaries.[11] However, there has also been an increase in the extent to which intergenerational transfers contribute to pensions. Finally, in all three countries changes have taken place in the eligibility rates for those who might claim pensions.

The other demographic factor of particular importance to the trend of public expenditures is the number of young persons in the economy.[12] Many public sector services are orientated towards serving this particular client group; e.g. maternity, clinics, child allowances, education, libraries, and certain cultural activities. In the U.S.A. and the U.K. the number of students at school or college

---

[9] In the OECD definitions, 'Government Final Consumption Expenditure' is equivalent to government current expenditure on goods and services. See Notes in *National Accounts of OECD Countries, 1975*, Vol. I (Paris: OECD, 1977).

[10] Only under a fully indexed system would such increases be automatic. Instead, in the case of the U.K., such increases in public expenditures reflect deliberate policy decisions.

[11] Canada has had 'insurance' pensions only since 1966, and the U.K. since the early 1970s.

[12] A discussion of the influences of demographic factors on public expenditures can be found in Denton and Spencer (1977).

increased by 3 per cent per annum, over the period 1963/1971. In Canada the comparable increase was closer to 5 per cent, which may reflect policy factors as well as demography.[13]

European Comparisons

The growth in the relative size of public sectors seems ubiquitous. In this section a brief comparison will be made between levels of government spending and the burden of taxation in industrially advanced economies. In Table 5.7 it is seen that public expenditure as a proportion of GNP (at factor cost) has, for all countries shown in the table, increased over the period 1964/1973.[14] Apart perhaps from Japan,[15] no single country is dramatically dissimilar to the others. Whilst each country has its own particular social/political/economic structure, the overall result, in terms of the broad public expenditure aggregates, is a striking similarity. It may be observed that the increase in the public expenditure ratio for the U.K. was below the average for the eleven European countries.

Data on total social or welfare benefits, which include those provided by both private and public employers, are shown in Table 5.8. Benefits in kind in addition to cash payments are included. These data must be interpreted with caution because of variations in the way in which different countries use tax expenditures. For example, in the U.K., tax allowances are made for the number of children each taxpayer has, whereas in other countries direct public expenditures are provided for children. Nevertheless, that proviso should not change the overall picture too much.

The variation in ratio of tax revenue to GNP is shown in Table 5.9. For most countries their tax ratio is close to their expenditure ratio, though in recent years Italy and the U.K. have been running larger budget deficits. For the eleven European countries, the ratio of indirect tax to GNP displayed less variation than the ratio of direct tax. Between 1964 and 1973 the ratio of direct tax rose more than did the ratio of indirect tax. This increase in the direct tax ratio is presumably mainly due to the automatic properties of the tax system during periods of increases in real GNP and/or during periods of inflation.

---

[13] See *Public Expenditures on Education* (Paris: OECD, 1976), Statistical Annex III.

[14] The relationship of the national income accounts data on public expenditure of the various countries to that of the OECD data has already been noted. However, in Table 5.7 further differences should be noted. First, the statistical compatibility of the various data sources has been checked; they were found to be sufficiently similar to allow trends to be compared. Second, the year 1973 has been chosen as the terminal date for the comparisons since this was the last year of relatively high employment. Third, OECD data on GNP are measured at factor cost and not at market prices. There is, therefore, a difference between Table 5.7 and other tables in this chapter. Fourth, Table 5.7 omits payments of property income since there are differences between different countries in the extent to which governments own or rent their own buildings.

[15] On Japan, see Patrick and Rosovsky (1976).

TABLE 5.7
INTERNATIONAL COMPARISON OF PUBLIC EXPENDITURE, 1964, 1970 AND 1973
(Per cent of GNP at Factor Cost)

	Expenditure on Goods and Services			Current Grants			Subsidies			Total Expenditure		
	1964	1970	1973	1964	1970	1973	1964	1970	1973	1964	1970	1973
European Countries												
Austria	21.8	23.6	24.6	14.3	15.3	14.8	2.2	1.6	1.3	38.3	40.5	40.7
Belgium	17.8	19.3	20.4	12.5	16.5	18.2	1.1	1.5	1.6	31.4	37.3	40.2
Denmark	20.1	30.0	31.8	9.2	14.5	15.5	1.2	1.8	0.8	30.5	46.3	48.0
France	n.a.	19.2	19.6	n.a.	19.3	20.5	n.a.	2.1	1.6	n.a.	40.6	41.7
Germany	22.4	23.0	24.5	12.7	12.8	13.6	1.1	1.6	1.7	36.2	37.4	39.8
Ireland	19.3	21.1	23.6	7.6	10.8	13.0	4.1	5.6	5.2	31.0	37.5	41.8
Italy	18.4	16.9	18.9	13.0	16.3	18.9	1.5	1.7	2.7	32.9	34.9	40.5
Netherlands	21.1	23.4	22.8	n.a.	19.8	24.1	1.0	1.5	1.9	n.a.	44.7	48.8
Norway	n.a.	23.0	24.9	n.a.	16.7	19.9	n.a.	6.2	6.3	n.a.	45.9	51.1
Sweden	25.4	31.0	32.3	9.6	13.2	16.3	1.1	1.2	1.4	36.1	45.4	50.0
United Kingdom	23.2	26.2	26.1	8.1	10.3	10.6	1.7	2.1	2.3	33.1	38.5	38.9
Non-European Countries												
Canada	21.9	26.8	26.4	7.5	9.8	11.2	1.0	1.0	1.1	30.4	37.6	38.7
Japan	15.1	14.1	16.1	4.5	4.7	5.1	0.6	1.2	1.0	20.2	20.0	22.2
United States	n.a.	25.5	24.8	n.a.	3.6	10.0	n.a.	0.5	0.4	n.a.	34.6	35.2
Unweighted average of European Countries	21.2	23.3	24.5	10.9	15.0	16.9	1.7	2.4	2.4	33.7	40.8	43.8

Source: *National Accounts of OECD Countries, 1962-1973*, Vols. I and II (Paris: OECD, 1975).

TABLE 5.8

BENEFIT EXPENDITURES, PUBLIC AND PRIVATE, IN THE NINE E.E.C. COUNTRIES, 1972[1]

(per cent of GNP at factor cost)

	Sickness	Old Age	Invalidity	Employment Injury	Unemployment	Maternity	Family Benefits	Misc.[2]	Total Expenditure
Belgium	4.9	7.8	1.8	1.1	1.1	0.1	3.6	2.1	22.4
Denmark	7.0	9.0	3.4	0.4	0.9	0.4	3.8	1.1	26.0
France	5.8	8.3	0.3	1.0	0.2	0.3	3.7	4.3	24.0
Germany	6.9	10.8	1.7	1.1	0.2	0.2	1.9	2.4	25.1
Ireland	4.9	6.2	1.7	0.1	1.0	0.3	2.2	5.7	22.1
Italy	6.2	8.5	3.4	0.9	0.4	0.4	2.0	6.6	28.3
Luxembourg	3.7	11.9	1.5	1.3	—	0.1	2.3	1.9	22.7
Netherlands	6.9	9.9	4.5	n.a.	1.1	0.1	3.2	1.5	27.2
U.K.	5.1	9.3	1.6	0.3	1.0	0.4	1.4	1.4	20.4
Unweighted average of all countries	5.7	9.1	2.2	0.8	0.7	0.3	2.7	3.0	24.2

Sources: Benefits expenditures from *First European Social Budget (1970-1975)* (Brussels: E.E.C., November 1974). GNP at factor cost: as for Table 5.7.

Notes:

[1] All benefits and voluntary payments from the state and public and private enterprises are included, so long as no return from the beneficiary is involved. Insurance by private households is excluded.

[2] 'Misc.' includes administrative and other costs as well as transfers not classified elsewhere.

TABLE 5.9
INTERNATIONAL COMPARISON OF TAXATION, 1964, 1970 AND 1973[1]
(per cent of GNP at factor cost)

	Direct Taxes			Social Security Contributions			Indirect Taxes			Total Taxes		
	1964	1970	1973	1964	1970	1973	1964	1970	1973	1964	1970	1973
European Countries												
Austria	13.5	14.3	14.1	8.0	9.4	9.8	17.2	18.5	19.0	38.7	42.2	42.9
Belgium	9.3	12.4	15.0	9.8	11.6	12.5	13.7	14.5	12.9	32.8	38.5	40.4
Denmark	14.6	25.2	30.6	2.0	2.2	1.3	15.8	20.3	20.3	32.4	47.7	52.2
France[2]	n.a.	7.6	7.4	n.a.	15.2	15.8	n.a.	18.4	17.9	n.a.	41.2	41.1
Germany	12.2	12.0	14.0	9.8	11.4	13.2	16.3	15.1	15.1	38.3	38.5	42.3
Ireland	6.9	9.6	10.7	1.9	2.9	3.5	19.0	23.0	22.3	27.8	35.5	36.5
Italy	6.9	6.9	7.5	12.1	12.8	13.1	13.7	13.4	12.0	32.7	33.1	32.6
Netherlands	13.8	15.3	17.3	11.2	16.2	18.8	11.0	12.7	13.3	36.0	44.2	49.4
Norway[2]	n.a.	15.4	17.7	n.a.	11.0	16.1	n.a.	21.3	21.0	n.a.	47.7	54.8
Sweden	17.9	23.2	22.2	6.0	8.7	9.9	12.5	14.3	17.4	36.4	46.2	49.5
United Kingdom	12.2	18.2	15.2	4.9	6.1	6.1	14.6	18.6	15.1	31.7	42.8	36.4
Non-European Countries												
Canada	12.1	16.7	18.0	1.8	3.3	3.3	15.8	16.3	16.1	29.7	36.3	37.4
Japan	8.4	9.4	10.7	3.2	4.0	4.1	8.4	8.1	7.7	20.0	21.5	22.5
United States[2]	n.a.	14.4	14.9	n.a.	6.4	8.0	n.a.	10.6	10.5	n.a.	31.4	33.4
Unweighted average of European countries	11.9	14.6	15.6	7.3	9.8	10.9	14.9	17.3	16.9	34.1	41.6	43.5

Source: *National Accounts of OECD Countries, 1962-1973*, Vols. I and II (Paris: OECD, 1975).

Notes:

[1] A new system of national accounts ('New SNA') was introduced by the United Nations in 1968. Of the countries in this table, the old system ('Former SNA') is still used by the following: Austria, Belgium, Germany, Ireland, Italy and Japan. Differences are not big enough to upset comparison of the levels and patterns of tax. The main differences are the following: motor vehicle licence duties paid by households are counted as taxes on expenditure in Former SNA and as taxes on income in New SNA; taxes on capital gains are treated as capital transfers (and excluded from taxation) in Former SNA, but counted as taxes on income in New SNA; conversely, compulsory fees, fines and penalties are included in Former SNA and excluded in New SNA.

[2] n.a. — Not available.

In section I, a number of conceptual issues were discussed in connection with the problem of measuring the public sector. The components of the data which define the public sector, in an accounting or in a statistical sense, vary from country to country. However, insofar as the ratio of G/GNP is a rough measure or indicator of the degree of government involvement and intervention in an economy, then Table 5.1 shows that the U.K. government plays a more dominant role than do the governments of Canada or the U.S.A. — and Table 5.7 shows this role is about the same as in other European countries.

There are many reasons why this intercontinental difference exists. Many of the goods and services provided wholly or in part by the private market in Canada and the U.S.A. are produced completely by the public sector in the U.K. and Europe. Included in the list of services which are distributed differently are health care, old age pensions and insurance and education. Canada is mid-way between Europe and the United States in most of this.

Of course, which organizational structure is the best is not determined by crude measures such as the ratio of G/GNP. Because the G/GNP ratio is greater for the U.K. does not automatically imply that the U.K. economy performs worse (or better) than the other two economies, nor does it imply that the U.K. is a less (or more) desirable place to live. The criteria used to judge the desirability of alternative ways of organising the production and distribution of goods and services in a society depend upon a complex interaction of technical considerations (e.g. incentive and disincentive effects of taxation) and upon individual tastes and preferences. That the ratio of government expenditure to GNP is not a useful guide to judging either the performance or the desirability of an economy/society can be seen clearly by looking at the G/GNP ratios for Canada and the U.S.A. in 1970. The two ratios for that year were very similar but mere consideration of this figure alone tells nothing about the relative efficiency or performance of the two economies, about how the two economies deal with their poor and underprivileged, or about anything else of real interest. The G/Y ratio at most gives us a quick capsule indicator of the relative importance of government in the economy. Beyond that, it tells us little.

III. STRUCTURAL CHANGES IN THE LABOUR MARKET

In developed economies employment growth has been concentrated in the services sector of the economy (see Bell (1973) and Ginzberg (1976)): Table 5.10 illustrates this trend, which many think will continue in the future.

Sectoral differences in the relationship between output, employment, and the growth of the capital stock will result in differences in the distribution of labour between the various sectors. Employment in the primary sector declined sharply during the period 1962/1974 for each of the three countries examined, for example, despite a modest expansion in output and growth of the capital stock. This suggests that investment in the primary sector was mainly aimed at factor substitution. The share of total employment accounted for by the secondary sector (manufacturing), also fell because of the high rates of technical progress in

TABLE 5.10
DISTRIBUTION OF CIVILIAN OCCUPIED MANPOWER:
CANADA, U.S.A, AND U.K.
(per cent of total)

	1962	1970	1974
Canada			
Agriculture, Forestry, Fishing	12.1	8.2	6.3
Manufacturing	34.7	32.3	31.1
Other	53.2	59.5	62.6
U.S.A.			
Agriculture, Forestry, Fishing	8.2	4.6	4.1
Manufacturing	32.8	33.7	31.1
Other	59.0	61.7	64.8
U.K.			
Agriculture, Forestry, Fishing	4.0	2.9	2.8
Manufacturing	48.0	46.8	42.3
Other	48.0	50.3	54.9

Source: OECD, *Economic Observer* (1964, 1971 and 1977).

this sector where both the expansion of output and the capital stock were strongest. The tertiary sector (i.e. mainly services), in contrast, accounted for most of the increase in total employment, reflecting both rising output demand and the relatively limited scope for factor substitution and technical progress.

These trends are not confined to Canada, the U.K. or to the U.S.A. They are to be found in all major industrialized European countries. In Germany, for example, between 1964 and 1974 the number of persons as a proportion of the working population, employed in community, social and personal services increased from 18.0 per cent to 20.8 per cent and in financing, insurance, real estate and business services from 3.5 per cent to 4.9 per cent.[16]

Another significant trend in the post-war period has been a marked change in the participation rate of women in the labour force: see Table 5.11. Labour market statistics demonstrate that the female role as homeworker and child-rearer has changed. For example, women now bear fewer children. Moreover, provision of education for women has increased and job opportunities have expanded. One contributing factor was the labour shortage during the second world war that opened up new fields of female employment. More important, structural changes in the economy, especially expansion of demand for the

---

[16] See *Labour Force Statistics 1960/71* (Paris: OECD, 1973), and *Labour Force Statistics 1964/75* (Paris: OECD, 1977).

TABLE 5.11

WOMEN AS A PROPORTION OF CIVILIAN EMPLOYMENT
(per cent of total)

	1956	1966	1973
Canada	23.6	30.3	34.2
U.S.A.	32.0	35.6	38.4
Belgium	30.2	32.0	34.3
U.K.	33.9	35.7	37.0
Germany	36.6	36.8	36.8
Denmark	34.7	35.3	41.1
Norway	30.2	30.9	n.a.[1]

Source: *Labour Force Statistics 1956/66* (Paris: OECD, 1968), Graph 5, and *Labour Force Statistics 1962/73* (Paris: OECD, 1975), Graph 4.

Note:
[1] n.a. — Not available.

TABLE 5.12

PROPORTION OF FEMALE LABOUR FORCE EMPLOYED
IN THE SERVICES SECTOR: 1960-1972
(per cent)

Country	Year	Per cent in Services	Year	Per cent in Services
Australia	—	—	1971	75.0
Belgium	1960	60.0	1968	64.7
Canada	1962	72.6	1972	76.8
Denmark	1965	68.8	1970	69.7
Finland	1960	53.6	1970	58.8
France	1960	49.4	1968	60.4
Italy	1960	33.3	1968	41.7
Japan	1960	40.0	1972	51.8
Sweden	1960	64.7	1971	79.5
United States	1960	80.3	1970	82.8

Source: M. Darling, *The Role of Women in the Economy* (Paris: OECD, 1975), Table 2.

products of the services sector, have provided a higher permanent demand for female labour. Increasingly, women in their middle years return to work when their family responsibility lessens.[17]

Table 5.12 brings together the two major changes which have taken place in the labour markets of industrialized nations in the post-war period — the growth in the female labour force and the growth in the services sector. These figures suggest that a great deal of the growth in demand for labour by the services sector must have been satisfied by the growth in the participation rates of females.

Trends in Public Sector Employment

Public sector employment has followed a trend very similar to that of the service sector as a whole. Public sector employment as a share of total employment has increased in the post-war period, and a growing proportion of the increase in employment is accounted for by female workers. Detailed analysis of the trends in public sector employment in Canada, the U.S.A. and the U.K. are to be found in Bird (1978) and Foot, Scicluna and Thadaney (1978) for Canada; Ehrenberg (1972), Sunley (1976) and Gustely (1974) for the U.S.A.; and Jackson (1977) for the U.K. Findings from these studies are summarised in this section.

Relative public sector employment for the years 1961 and 1975, as shown in Table 5.13, serve to illustrate the post-war trend in Canada, the U.S.A. and the U.K. In all cases total public employment as a percentage of the total working population has increased over the whole period. A great deal of care, however, has to be taken when interpreting such statistics. For example, the U.K. and Canada data have not been adjusted to full-time equivalent employees. Part-time and full-time employees are therefore treated on the same basis to the extent that the former are included. The U.S. data is on a full-time equivalent basis, and therefore is not directly comparable.

The data in Table 5.13 indicate a relative decline in defence employment for the U.K. and for Canada (the decline in Federal employment was due to the contraction in civilian defence employees). In all these cases the growth in employment at lower levels of government greatly exceeded that of higher levels.

---

[17] The changing role of women in the Canadian economy is described in Cook (1976). For example, on page four: "Evidence in this book suggests that women are increasingly curtailing their life-long wife-housewife-mother roles in various ways, even though they are continuing to marry at the same rate and perhaps at a slightly younger age. This adaptation reflects a response to a number of factors: more tolerant attitudes toward women who do not play the full-time wife-housewife-mother roles; increased opportunities outside the family; and economic pressures for two income earners in the family''.

TABLE 5.13

PUBLIC EMPLOYMENT AS A PERCENTAGE OF TOTAL EMPLOYMENT

	Canada		U.S.A.		U.K.	
	1961	1975	1961	1975	1961	1975
Total Government and Government Enterprises[1]	22.2	23.8	18.9	20.6	22.4	27.4
Total National Government and Enterprises	7.5	5.7	8.8	6.9	14.6	15.9
Civilian, Government	3.3	3.3	3.1	2.7	3.4	6.4
Armed Forces	1.9	0.8	4.6	3.1	2.0	1.4
Government Enterprises	2.2	1.6	1.2	1.1	9.2	8.1
Total Sub-national Government and Enterprises	14.7	18.0	10.1	13.7	7.8	11.5
Education	4.9	6.2	4.5	6.7	3.2	5.9
Other, Government	8.3	9.9	5.0	6.1	4.6	5.6
Government Enterprises[2]	1.6	1.9	0.6	0.9	—	—

Sources: For Canada, R.M. Bird and D.K. Foot, "Bureaucratic Growth in Canada: Myths and Realities", paper presented to the Conference on Methods and Forums for the Public Evaluation of Government Spending, Carleton University, October 1978.

For U.S.A, *The National Income and Product Accounts of the U.S., 1929-1965, Statistical Tables* (1966), and *Survey of Current Business* 57 (July 1977).

For U.K., *Economic Trends* (February 1977).

Notes:

[1] Columns may not add exactly, because of rounding.

[2] In the U.K. there are no separately identifiable government enterprises at the local level. Such enterprises are included at the central level of government.

The composition of public employment is also of interest. Jackson (1977) has shown, in the case of the U.K., that much of the growth of employment by local governments has been due to the employment of part-time employees, especially women. For example, between 1952 and 1973 part-time male and female employees increased in number at an annual compound rate of growth of 5.5 per cent and 6.2 per cent respectively. (The comparable growth rates for full-time employees were 1.6 per cent for males and 2.8 per cent for females.) These trends in public sector employment are in keeping with the general trends that were observed for the services sector as a whole, especially the increase in the number of part-time female employees.[18]

The growth of public sector employment by service category is more difficult to deal with and is the subject of much current research in Canada, the U.K., and the U.S.A. Preliminary data for the U.K. are presented in Table 5.14.

The growth of current government expenditures, at constant prices, in part reflects this expansion in the number of persons employed in government. Other contributing factors include the growth in real wages and salaries paid. At first sight it might appear that the growth of public sector employees, as a percentage of the total work force, is inconsistent with the smaller increase in deflated expenditures as a percentage of GNP, noted earlier. If productivity increases in the public sector are small relative to those in the private sector, however, then the trend in employment share is not a reliable indicator of the trend in public expenditures as a percentage of GNP at constant prices.

---

[18] Whilst data on part-time government employment in Canada is fragmentary and data on female employment is incomplete, Foot, Scicluna and Thadaney (1978) have shown that at the federal government level the proportion of female employment went from 26.3 per cent of the total in 1961 to 32.6 per cent in 1975.

TABLE 5.14
COMPOSITION OF PUBLIC SECTOR EMPLOYMENT
UNITED KINGDOM: 1966 and 1976
(numbers employed, in thousands, at mid-year)

	1966	1976	Per cent change: 1966 to 1976
Post Office	414	434	4.8
Health and Social Services	904	1,467	62.3
Civil Service—industrial employees	236	184	−22.0
—non-industrial employees	442	586	32.6
Other Central Government	48	88	83.3
Education	1,013	1,569	54.9
Local Authority Construction	133	173	30.1
Local Authority Transport and Communication[1]	109	34	−60.8
Restaurants, canteens, entertainments etc.[2]	18	—	—
Police Service—Police	98	127	29.6
—Civilians	28	59	110.7
Water Authorities[3]	27	—	—
Other Local Government[2]	604	739	22.4
Nationalized Industries[4]	1,425	1,256	−11.9
Other Public Corporations[1] [3]	123	261	112.2
Total (excluding Defence)	5,623	6,978	24.1

Source: Estimates supplied by U.K. Department of Employment.

Notes:

[1] Some Transport employees were included in 'Other Public Corporations' after 1970.

[2] From 1971 'Restaurants, etc.' were included in 'Other Local Government'.

IV. "THE BRITISH DISEASE: DOES CANADA ALREADY HAVE IT?"

Recently, Eltis (1977a, b, c) has put forth the thesis that the increase of employment in the public sector in particular and the non-marketed sector in general has in some sense brought about the problems of the British economy — and that Canada seems to be following the British route to economic morbidity. The purpose of the present section is to analyze the nature of the 'British Disease', its possible causes, and whether or not the patient is responding to treatment.

The first important point to note is that many of the fundamental problems of the British economy are of long standing[19] — much longer than the recent increase in the public sector or the emergence of the services sector. It is true that the long term underlying growth rate of the British economy — at just over two per cent per annum from 1970 to the present — is much lower than that of North America or northern Europe (see Denison, 1967). Over the period 1960/1974 the average annual growth rate of output was 2.7 per cent for the U.K. and 5.7 per cent for the average of all OECD countries.

A number of reasons have been advanced to explain this relatively poor performance. A list of reasons would include

- low productivity of labour;
- high propensity to strike of British labour;
- labour possessing the wrong skills for current demand;
- sluggish industrial investment;
- use of sterling as a reserve currency and overvalued pound sterling;
- decline in world markets;
- lack of a large pool of labour.

Arguments like these have been around for years. However, the recent disastrous short term performance of the British economy has brought forth new attempts to explain the short run situation. During the 1970s the British economy has been characterized by 'slumpflation', i.e. by the simultaneous existence of both high rates of inflation and a depression in the product and labour markets. Real output fell in both 1974 and 1975, for example, while the general price level rose by 16 and 28 per cent, respectively.

While dealing with the problems of the U.K. economy in the mid-1970s, it is, therefore, necessary to distinguish between the lingering long term aspects of the problem and the more immediate short term problems arising from the severe shocks to the world economy in the 1970s.

Some of the long term problems of the British economy were outlined

---

[19] Phelps Brown (1977) in an extremely stimulating essay places the problems of the British economy within an historical perspective and shows that the widely held commonplace view of the British predicament is part myth. Post-war Britain has enjoyed unprecedented improvements in real per capita economic growth, the standard of living, and productivity. However, whilst the absolute growth rate has been good compared to previous time periods, the rate of growth relative to other countries has not been impressive. This is where the problem lies and the answer according to Phelps Brown is to be found in a deeper understanding of the role played by socio-economic institutions.

above. Each has a different weight of plausibility associated with it. The contribution of each factor to the final outcome, namely a poor economic growth record, is difficult to establish. One factor which does seem to stand out in relation to the rest, however, is Britain's poor investment record. The U.K. has a very low ratio of investment to GNP in comparison with other countries. In 1970, gross domestic fixed capital formation in the form of plant and machines, as a percentage of total GDP (at 1963 prices) was 7.8 per cent in the U.K. compared to 13.0 per cent in Germany, 12.1 per cent in France, 8.7 per cent in Italy, and so on. This situation has persisted throughout the post-war period. The result of this low rate of investment is that the age of the capital stock in the U.K. is greater than that of other competing countries. In a recent OECD Report (1976) the average life of the U.K.'s stock of plant and machinery was placed at 34 years, or almost double that of countries like France, Germany, Sweden, and the U.S.A., and almost treble that of Japan. Thus it could be argued that the low labour productivity is due to a lack of adequate investment.

The balance of payments has for years acted as a severe restraint to economic growth in the U.K. and has produced the familiar 'stop-go' cycle so characteristic of the U.K. economy. Prior to 1976 Britain operated a system of fixed exchange rates with Sterling as a reserve currency. The value of the pound in the foreign exchange markets was therefore very sensitive to the dealings in Sterling balances. Since the Bank of England had to step in to stabilize the pound, economic policy towards growth was sensitive to the speculative dealings of holders of Sterling balances who feared the worst (i.e. a devaluation) when the value of imports exceeded that of exports. Since the floating of the pound sterling in 1976 another problem has emerged. Those who hold to the monetary theory of the balance of payments will recognize that a fall in the exchange rate (for any reason, such as an expansion in domestic demand via imports) will feed back into the economy in the form of higher prices and so on. The result is that the exchange rate will continue to rise.

During the 1970s the quadrupling of the price of oil led to a rapid increase in the current account of the balance of payments. The non-OPEC countries generally had deficits to match the OPEC surpluses, so in this event the U.K. was not alone. However, the deficits on the balance of payments current account coincided with large public sector deficits. The public sector deficits were brought about by a number of factors including the increase in public expenditure and loss in tax revenue resulting from unemployment, the use of subsidies to hold down prices during the rapid inflation, a reluctance to increase taxes, especially indirect taxes, and the increase in the money value of public expenditure due to the general inflation.

Thus on two major accounts in the economy, namely the public sector and the external accounts, the U.K. was in deficit — or, some might argue, living beyond her means. The 'crisis' in the mid 1970s for the U.K. economy thus resulted from long standing structural weaknesses which were stressed to breaking point by a combination of events: the world depression in 1973/74, the quadrupling of world oil prices, the failure of primary commodity markets and the rapid rise in commodity prices, and the floating of the pound sterling.

The considerable increase in public expenditure appears to have been a *reaction* to a situation caused originally largely by external factors: it is difficult to argue that it was the prime cause of the problem. The *structure* of the public sector, however, probably did little to ease the situation. This is certainly true in the case of the personal tax system, whose marginal rate structure was found to be wanting during periods of low growth in real incomes and rapid rates of inflation. The system of public expenditure planning and control, a system designed for conditions of high economic growth and low rates of inflation, was also found to be deficient for an economic climate of zero growth and rapid inflation.

The structural weaknesses of the public sector were thus thrown into sharp relief during the general crisis of the 1970s. Observation of these weaknesses resulted in changes being made. In order to deal with the short run situation public expenditure growth was halted. In 1976 new public expenditure plans took £1 billion off the public expenditure account (at constant prices) for 1977/78 and a further £1.5 billion for 1978/79. The result was that the public sector borrowing requirement (PSBR)[20] fell to 7.7 per cent of GNP in 1976 and to four per cent in 1977.

These cut backs in public expenditure are of course cuts in *planned* public expenditure. They represent the postponement of programme expansions. If this proves to be adequate then further cut backs, this time into ongoing programmes, will not be necessary. Public expenditure savings have also been made as a result of the introduction of 'cash limits' for each department (with the exception of health and social security) in April 1976. The results of the financial year 1976/77 reveal that most departments did not spend up to the limits and had made a conscious attempt to save on staff costs by relying on natural wastage and reducing the propensity to appoint new staff. It will be interesting to see if these economy measures show up in the employment data. Jackson (1977) has already shown that in the case of Scottish local governments, staff savings were made between July 1976 and September 1976.

These savings, following the introduction of cash limits, have contributed to the reduction in the PSBR. Another factor which has contributed to that objective is that wage costs in the public sector have been held back. The reduced rate of increase in money wages is a result of the successive incomes policies which have been in force in the U.K. throughout the 1970s. The £6 per week voluntary incomes policy, introduced in August 1975, was followed, in August 1976, by a five per cent limit and in 1977/78 by a ten per cent upper limit (on 'average').

---

[20] The U.K. public sector borrowing requirement (PSBR) is a statistic of the net borrowing requirement of the public sector and as such is a consolidated PSBR (i.e. any net indebtedness between parts of the public sector have been netted out). The PSBR is not simply defined as government borrowing, but is net of transactions in certain assets; thus, for example, the sale of foreign currency from the reserves results in sterling finance for the government and is included with borrowing. Purchases of commercial bills, other than during open market operations, for example to assist industry or help exports, increase the borrowing requirement.

The U.K. government is currently negotiating a five per cent limit for 1978/79. These pay policies have resulted in substantial reductions in the growth of nominal incomes, a reduction in the real absolute levels of higher income groups, who have not been allowed any increases, and an erosion of pay differentials, especially net of tax, due to the effects of the tax system during periods of inflation. The number of people falling into the 'poverty trap' has also increased; i.e. those people whose income remains static over a range, despite the fact that they might move from unemployed to employed status, because of the combined effects of lower social benefits and higher tax liabilities.

The British economy is not yet through the crisis although the economic indicators are showing signs of 'relative' improvement. What happens to a small open economy, such as the U.K., to an extent depends upon economic performance in the rest of the world. A slowing down in the growth rates of economies such as West Germany or the U.S.A. will obviously affect the level of economic activity in other countries. This fact was recognised when the heads of state of the major economies met in July 1978, at the Bonn Summit. The most recent (second quarter 1978) economic indicators for the U.K. show that GNP is estimated to have risen by one per cent in the first quarter of 1978 and that the index of industrial production was 1½ per cent up on the previous quarter. Stock building was positive in the first quarter following two quarters of destocking. Large month to month fluctuations in the trade figures for the first few months of 1978 (alternating deficits and surpluses) have so far resulted in a £100 million surplus for the first quarter of 1978. The production of oil from the North Sea has had an important influence upon the U.K. exchange rate and upon the balance of payments. This has strengthened sterling and attracted foreign capital into the U.K.; to the extent that North Sea oil reduces imports, the direct benefit to the current account of the balance of payments has been estimated at £2½ billion for 1978.

Inflation in the U.K. continues to fall and for the year up to end-July 1978 is estimated to be running at seven per cent per annum. This means that the rate of retail price inflation has now been reduced to around the level of early 1973. This reduction in the inflation rate is partly due to successful incomes policies and the reduced rate of increase in the world price level following the onset of a recession in world economic activity.

Unemployment continues to fall and has done so for eight successive months up to May 1978. Unfilled vacancies continue to rise. However, the U.K. government is nervously awaiting the figures which will show the degree to which the economy will absorb the 1978 school leavers. A failure to take up this important section of the population could easily reverse the unemployment trends.

The public sector borrowing requirement (PSBR) in the first quarter of 1978 was just under £2 billion (seasonally adjusted). This brought the PSBR for the financial year 1977/78 well below the government's original ceiling of £8½ billion.

If Canada is suffering from the same disease as Britain, as Eltis has argued, then the symptoms are very different indeed. Canadian real output did not experience the same shock during the world recession as did that of the U.K. The Canadian rate of inflation was certainly affected by the increase in world oil prices and primary commodity prices but not to the same extent as that of the U.K. Unemployment in Canada remains high but will fall once world trade picks up. As in the U.K., there are doubtless long term structural weaknesses in the Canadian economy — lack of research and development, foreign control, whatever you want — but they are quite different ones from those in the U.K. It is also difficult to argue convincingly that in either country the problems are due specifically to a rise in government expenditure and employment. There are problems; they may not be *helped* by government expenditure; but they are not in any fundamental sense due to government expenditure.

The public sector has grown relative to the manufacturing sector of the major industrialized nations of the world. This phenomenon has not, however, been the 'cause' of the economic ills faced by those economies during the 1970s. These causes must be sought elsewhere. The use of broad aggregative indicators, such as the ratio of public expenditure to GNP, to argue the case of cause and effect in economics has an extremely limited value. Summary measures may sometimes be useful indicators of a phenomenon worthy of further study, but it is then necessary to proceed with deeper, more searching analysis.

There is a well-established body of thought and a stock of empirical results which provides the basis of an informed discussion of the impact of the public sector at both the micro and the macro levels. Ultimately it is an evaluation of the *effects* of the public sector which is of interest. As yet neither the theory nor the empirical results are sufficiently unambiguous to enable us to make definitive pronouncements on these matters. Ultimately, the optimal mix of public sector services, private sector services, and manufacturing output remains a matter of informed judgment.

Until evidence to the contrary is produced, and it has not as yet been done, there is only a weak case in support of the claim that the ailing U.K. economy is the result of a growing public sector. The patient is certainly ill but not from the disease that has been diagnosed. Will the cure kill?

REFERENCES

Auld, D.A.L. (1976) *Issues in Government Expenditure Growth* (Montreal: C.D. Howe Research Institute).

Bacon, R. and W. Eltis (1976) *Britain's Economic Problem: Too Few Producers* (London: Macmillan).

Beck, M. (1976) "The Expanding Public Sector: Some Contrary Evidence" *National Tax Journal* 29:1, 15–21.

Bell, D. (1973) *The Coming of Post-Industrial Society* (Harmondsworth: Penguin Books).

Bird, R.M. (1970) *The Growth of Government Spending in Canada* (Toronto: Canadian Tax Foundation).

Bird, R.M. (1978) "The Growth of the Public Service in Canada", Chapter Two in Foot (1978).

Borcherding, T.E. (1977) "One Hundred Years of Public Spending, 1870-1970", in T.E. Borcherding, ed., *Budgets and Bureaucrats: The Sources of Government Growth* (Durham: Duke University Press) 19–44.

Cook, G.C.A. ed. (1976) *Opportunity for Choice: A Goal for Women in Canada* (Ottawa: Information Canada).

Denison, E.F. (1967) *Why Growth Rates Differ* (Washington: Brookings).

Denton, F.D. and B.G. Spencer (1977) "Demographic Change and Government Expenditure in Canada: An Analysis and Projections" Working Paper 77-19 (Hamilton, Ontario: McMaster University Department of Economics).

Ehrenberg, R. (1972) *The Demand for State and Local Government Employees* (Lexington, Massachusetts: D.C. Heath).

Eltis, W. (1977a) "Will Canada make same economic errors as U.K.?", *The Globe and Mail*, Toronto, June 28.

Eltis, W. (1977b) "Britain learned a labour lesson, but has Canada?", *The Globe and Mail*, Toronto, June 29.

Eltis, W. (1977c) "Are Canada and the United States Following Great Britain?" *New International Realities* 2:July, (Washington: International Division of the National Planning Association).

Foot, D.K., ed. (1978) *Public Employment and Compensation in Canada: Myths and Realities* (Toronto: Butterworth & Co. for The Institute for Research on Public Policy).

Foot, D.K., E. Scicluna and P. Thadaney (1978) "The Growth and Distribution of Federal, Provincial and Local Government in Canada", Chapter Four in Foot (1978).

Friedman, M. (1976) "The Line We Dare Not Cross" *Encounter*: October.

Ginzberg, E. (1976) "The Pluralistic Economy of the U.S." *Scientific American*, 235: Dec., 25–29.

Gusteley, R.D. (1974) *Municipal Employment and Public Expenditure* (Lexington, Massachusetts: D.C. Heath).

Jackson, P.M. (1977) "The Growth of Public Sector Employment: The Case of the U.K.", in *Fiscal Policy and Labour Supply* (Institute for Fiscal Studies, Conference Series No. 4).

Johnson, H.G. (1977) "Schools Should Train for Jobs" *The Globe and Mail*, Toronto, Feb. 19.

OECD (1976) *The Measurement of Capital* (Paris: OECD).

Patrick, H. and H. Rosovsky (1976) *Asia's New Giant: How the Japanese Economy Works* (Washington: Brookings).

Peacock, A.T. and J. Wiseman (1967) *The Growth of Public Expenditure in the United Kingdom* (London: George Allen and Unwin).

Phelps Brown, Sir Henry (1977) "What is the British Predicament?" *The Three Banks Review*, 116: Dec., 3–29.

Prest, A.R. (1972) "Government Revenue, the National Income, and all that", in R.M. Bird and J. Head, eds., *Modern Fiscal Issues* (Toronto: University of Toronto Press).

Sunley, E.M. (1976) "State and Local Governments", in H. Owen and C.L. Schultze, eds., *Setting National Priorities: The Next Ten Years* (Washington: Brookings).

Chapter Six

Bureaucrats and Elections

by
*Richard Johnston**

INTRODUCTION

Can public servants determine elections? Some observers allege that they try and other observers contend that they succeed. I shall review such arguments, discuss factors affecting the power of civil servants as an electoral bloc, and test those factors where possible on Canadian data.

From theory, one can argue that the very existence of a public service will lead to its further growth. To the extent a civil servant's income is a function of the size of the public sector, the quantity of public output a private citizen demands should increase if he becomes a bureaucrat. As public employment grows proportionately to private employment, the distribution of preferences for public output will therefore shift toward greater quantities. The median preference, which determines the amount of public output actually provided (Downs, 1957), will shift upward commensurately. Thus, it is argued, the public service will grow over time, its growth halting only when public servants' marginal income from such growth is exactly offset by the marginal tax on their salaries. At every point in this process, the quantity of public output will be greater than that demanded by voters outside the public service. From this analysis, one might conclude that bureaucrats should be barred from voting (Bush and Denzau, 1977; Borcherding, Bush and Spann, 1977).

Although the assumptions giving this argument much of its force are violated in real electoral politics, there may still be cause for alarm. It is true that more than two parties compete in most Canadian elections and that the single dimension of quantity of public output rarely governs voters' choices between parties. Further, parties must gain pluralities not of votes, but of seats. Public

Editor's note: **Richard Johnston** is Assistant Professor in the Department of Political Science at the University of British Columbia. An earlier version of the present chapter was circulated as Working Paper Number 7719 of the Institute for Policy Analysis of the University of Toronto.

*The author acknowledges the contribution of Richard Bird, David Foot, and Morley Gunderson to his thinking on the subject matter of this chapter. Nonetheless, the author accepts full responsibility for the final product.

servants may still determine elections, however, and, in so doing, appropriate more of the total product for themselves than the rest of us would prefer. Such a possibility may have emerged in the 1977 Ontario general election, in the course of which a Toronto *Globe and Mail* editorial observed:

> Mr. Darrow [the president of the Ontario Public Service Employees Union] now wants to retain the job security but also play politics. . . . It is logical says Mr. Darrow, for civil servants to try to ensure that political decisions favor them. Favor *them*, not the electorate. . . . It is painfully obvious that a group of 60,000 civil servants, tightly organized, could hold so much political power so close to the seat of power that they could blackmail governments into serving them, not the public. (May 27, 1977)

Friends and kin may add to civil servants' electoral leverage. Writing on the New York City fiscal crisis, Gramlich (1976, p. 417n) remarks that:

> . . . .there are now about 450,000 full and part-time city government employees in New York City. If each was married, lived in the city, and had one close friend or relative who would vote alike on city issues, conceivably 1,350,000 votes, 30 per cent of the entire voting age population and roughly half of the probable number of voters, could be marshalled in favor of some strategic concession to, or dealing leniently with, unions.

The problem would be compounded still further if, as some allege, civil servants turn out and vote at markedly higher rates than do private citizens (Bush and Denzau, 1977; Borcherding, Bush, and Spann, 1977; Halter, 1972; Lipset, 1960).

The contemporary fear that bureaucrats are sufficiently numerous, co-ordinated, and participant to swing elections in their favour differs from earlier concerns about civil service political activity. Formerly, civil servants were feared not as an interest group in their own right but as passive agents of the *political* executive. Where appointment to office was by patronage, adept politicians could potentially corner the market: use their power of appointment to buy a critical mass of votes in each election and keep themselves in power indefinitely. With open voting, the ministry could monitor the behaviour of actual and potential appointees. In restricted nineteenth century electorates, the number of civil servants may well have been great enough to swing seats in the ministry's favour. To avert this, customs and excise workers were disenfranchised in 1844, most postal workers in 1851, and crown land agents in 1855 (Hodgetts, 1973). The *Canada Elections Act* of 1874 rescinded these prohibitions, however, leaving judges as the only public servants ineligible to vote. The nexus between offices and votes was finally broken in national politics by the *Civil Service Act* of 1918. But in reducing patronage and granting bureaucrats (in effect) tenure, the 1918 Act created the very conditions that vex contemporary observers: the possibility that a bureaucracy, entrenched by the merit system, will use elections to pursue ends its members have determined for themselves.

Is the fear that public servants carry disproportionate weight in elections justified? Underlying this question is the proposition that a group of voters is more powerful the greater is its probability of casting the deciding votes. The closer the group is to determining the outcome, the greater the return to a party of investing resources in attracting the group's votes. The greater, then, should be the resources the party is willing to invest in the group. What factors affect the probability of determining the outcome? At least five occur to me, of which three were suggested above. First, a group will be more powerful the larger the proportion of its members who actually turn out and vote and who participate politically in other ways. Second, a group will be more powerful the more homogeneous are preferences within it. Third, a group will be more powerful the less committed are the party preferences of its members. Fourth, a group will be more powerful the more its members are concentrated in relatively marginal constituencies. This consideration applies only in single-member plurality electoral systems, of course. Fifth, a group will be more powerful the larger it is. I shall consider each factor in turn.

POLITICAL PARTICIPATION

For public servants, the benefits from voting should be relatively great and the costs relatively small. On the benefit side, party differences over many policies, including the size and composition of public employment itself, could affect the livelihood of civil servants profoundly. At the same time, the costs to public servants of assessing the connection between issues and parties should be relatively small. Civil servants enjoy above-average levels of education. In dealing with public questions as a matter of course, bureaucrats should have made many of the intellectual investments necessary to detect the policy consequences of the vote. Thus, government employees should be more likely than non-government employees to vote. A government/non-government difference should persist even after controlling for educational differences.

The government/non-government difference should vary across kinds of elections. The lower the general level of interest and involvement in an election, the greater should be the impact of factors affecting turnout. Outside Quebec, provincial elections attract less interest and turnout than do national elections. Everywhere, municipal elections attract the lowest voter turnout of all. The general lack of interest in municipal politics is compounded by the absence of political parties at that level. Parties lower the cost of voting in at least two ways. First, they help voters assess the relations between issues and candidates (Downs, 1957). Second, they assist voters physically in getting to the polls. I expect, then, that turnout differences will be greater in provincial elections than in federal ones, and greater still in municipal elections.

The difference should vary across kinds of participation. The more costly and difficult the activity, the more weight factors affecting participation should carry. In any election, then, the government/non-government difference may be even greater in canvassing, giving money, attending rallies, and the like than in simple voting. Further, the relatively demanding activities help sway less active citizens even as they create policy obligations in the parties. Thus, to the extent that civil servants participate relatively greatly in activities beyond voting, their ability to determine elections is compounded. But a prediction that civil servants will be relatively likely to do such things is clouded by legal restrictions on bureaucrats' political activity. Although many federal civil servants may attend politial rallies, give money to parties and seek leave to run for office, they may not otherwise campaign actively for a party (Kernaghan, 1976). Even though federal bureaucrats may engage in more political activity than strictly permitted, a situation tolerated by the tacit mutual consent of the parties (Kernaghan, 1976, p. 447), the regulations may still inhibit such activity.

I shall test the propositions in this and the following sections against data from a national probability sample survey done shortly after the 1968 general election.[1] In the data, I identified three occupational categories corresponding to significant groups of public employees: educators; health and welfare workers; and an otherwise undifferentiated 'government' category. All other respondents, whether or not they were in the labour force, are coded as non-governmental. Public employees represent just over 12 per cent of the sample. This is smaller than the public sector proportion of total employees, according to tax returns (Foot and Thadaney, 1978), but is so principally because the sample represents all adults rather than the labour force alone. About 4½ per cent of respondents are educators, just over three per cent are health and welfare workers, and 4½ per cent are other government employees. For regression purposes, I created four dummy variables, one for each of the three specific public employment categories and one for all forms of public employment. These variables are designated in the tables as 'educator', 'health', 'govjob2' (public sector workers other than in education and health and welfare), and 'govjob' (all public employees). A respondent's education (denoted 'educ') is indexed by his or her number of years of schooling.

My only participation variables indicate whether or not the respondent claimed to have voted in the 1968 national election and in the last previous provincial election. Unfortunately, the 1968 survey failed to ask about other forms of participation, including voting in municipal elections and participating in ways other than voting. Each dependent variable is dichotomous, and, as such, not strictly appropriate for ordinary least squares (OLS) analysis. Other researchers' work with dichotomous dependent variables suggests, however, that OLS will suffice for most purposes (see, for instance, Gunderson, 1974). In any case, the crudity of the available data would mock more demanding techniques. The constant terms in Tables 6.1 and 6.2 indicate one weakness in my data. For example: turnout as reported greatly exceeds actual turnout in 1968. While 89.1

---

[1] The principal investigator for the 1968 survey was John Meisel of Queen's University. The tape was made available by the Canadian Consortium for Social Research. Neither the principal investigator nor the Consortium is responsible for anything in this paper. Comprehensive national election surveys exist for 1965 and 1974, but neither permits the identification of civil servants as an employment group. The 1965 survey asked for respondent's occupation, but not for his or her industry. The 1974 survey has an extremely detailed occupational code on which some categories were clearly public sector and some private sector. But most categories were ambiguous in this respect. The 1974 survey does have an 'industry' question, but asked it only of non-manual respondents.

per cent claim to have voted in the election, only 75.7 per cent actually did so according to official returns. The self-reported provincial turnout is similarly too high. The overestimation of turnout may come in part from the oversampling of relatively participant groups. Most of it, however, probably comes from bias toward the socially-approved response. The bias should work against rejecting the null hypothesis in the regression equations.

Table 6.1 presents evidence for turnout in the 1968 national election. Not one government employment coefficient differs significantly from zero. The only one which even threatens to do so is the 'educator' coefficient in equation two. In spite of the positive association between education and government employment, such employment exerts no significant effect even when education is not controlled (as in equations one and two). Even if one interprets at least the sign of the 'govjob', 'govjob2', and 'educator' coefficients as consistent with the theoretical predictions, Table 6.1 indicates that this effect is essentially the result

TABLE 6.1

**GOVERNMENT/NON-GOVERNMENT TURNOUT DIFFERENCE,
1968 NATIONAL ELECTION[1]**

Variable[2]	Equation			
	(1)	(2)	(3)	(4)
Govjob	0.029 (1.471)	—	0.009 (0.045)	—
Govjob2	—	0.028 (0.890)	—	0.005 (0.164)
Educator	—	0.055 (1.776)	—	0.018 (0.570)
Health	—	−0.006 (−0.161)	—	−0.028 (−0.754)
Educ	—	—	0.010 (4.904)	0.009 (4.928)
Constant	0.887	0.887	0.796	0.797
R^2	0.0009	0.002	0.012	0.012

Notes:

[1] Number of observations equals 2322. Entries in parentheses are t-statistics.

[2] See text for variable definitions.

of government/non-government education differences rather than of factors peculiar to the job.

Table 6.2 presents much the same pattern as Table 6.1 for the last provincial election prior to 1968. Here, however, one 'educator' coefficient (in equation two) does creep over the margin of significance, though this significance vanishes when the education variable is introduced. Whether education is controlled or not, government employees, as a whole, are not more likely than others to vote in provincial elections. Teachers may be an exception, but apparently not because of their status as provincial employees but because of their high education level.

Why are the effects weak or non-existent? One problem may be with the data. Respondents claiming erroneously to have turned out may mask real differences. But turnout differences may truly be weak. In Canada, the costs of voting in federal and provincial elections are so low that factors affecting ability to bear such costs have little scope. In national elections and in every province but British Columbia, the responsibility for registration rests with the state (Qualter, 1970). Where individuals must register themselves, marked turnout differences appear (Kelley, *et al.*, 1967).

TABLE 6.2
GOVERNMENT/NON-GOVERNMENT TURNOUT DIFFERENCE, LAST PROVINCIAL ELECTION to 1968

Variable	Equation			
	(1)	(2)	(3)	(4)
Govjob	0.013 (0.812)	—	−0.0008 (−0.046)	—
Govjob2	—	0.0007 (0.027)	—	−0.010 (−0.391)
Educator	—	0.057 (2.174)	—	0.039 (1.443)
Health	—	−0.029 (−0.949)	—	−0.040 (−1.286)
Educ	—	—	0.005 (3.012)	0.005 (2.849)
Constant	0.924	0.924	0.877	0.880
R^2	0.0003	0.002	0.004	0.006

Note: See notes to Table 6.1.

HOMOGENEITY OF PARTY PREFERENCES

Other things equal, a group should be more likely to cast the deciding votes in an election the larger the proportion of its members supporting the same party. The more a group can 'deliver' its votes, the greater the incentive on parties to invest resources in it. How homogeneous will the civil service vote be? This question points to a more fundamental one: what do civil servants want? Undoubtedly, the desires of public employees are many and complex, but some ought to be more basic than others.

Civil servants probably want the same things as the rest of us. Bureaucrats' administrative behaviour, according to common sense and scholars' observations, is usually self-regarding. So should be their political behaviour. Not every bureaucrat is interested exclusively in pay and security, of course. Many emphasize rewards inherent in their work (Beattie, *et al.*, 1972, Chapter Seven). But even such a work emphasis is self-regarding inasmuch as it refers to rewards accruing to the individual bureaucrat, rather than to the rest of us. I suspect, too, that even a truly public-regarding bureaucrat would resemble a self-regarding one in his actual political behaviour. For example, both a personally greedy agricultural researcher and one wanting only better research would probably want more money spent in the area.

But self-interest is hardly an infallible guide to party preference. Bureaucrats' definitions of self-interest will vary with their attitude to risk. Even where all agree on such a definition, interests may conflict and drive contending bureaucrats to different parties. Lurking behind all of this is the constant attraction of the party in power. Let me consider each of these problems.

One definition of bureaucratic self-interest was suggested in this paper's introduction: the maximizing of power, income, and prestige. By this definition, bureaucrats are entrepreneurs, seeking to maximize their present value. Such a goal requires attention to one's income and opportunities and to the income streams attached to each point on the opportunity chain. An obvious preference should be for a party advocating higher civil service salaries. An only slightly less obvious preference should be for a party favouring growth in the public sector in general and in the civil service in particular. Civil servants may seek to capture rents by raising barriers to entry, and should for the same reason advocate growth in demand for public employees. Growth in such demand should raise the salaries attached to each point in the system, and, at the same time, should permit incumbents to advance relatively rapidly, while forcing no incumbent to lose ground absolutely (Tullock, 1974; Niskanen, 1971).

But, in the accepted view, many who seek public employment do so for its convenience and security. Most civil servants are probably not risk-takers even in bureaucratic games. Bureaucratic settings, be they private or public, engender rules whose intent, if not always whose consequences, is to improve response to routine situations. Both individuals and bureaux build up sunk costs in current procedures. In general, then, a public servant might reasonably want a relatively stable administrative environment (Downs, 1967, pp. 18-19, 88). This could lead him to prefer a party which opposes innovation in the public sector. It might even lead him to oppose too rapid a growth in public employment and remuneration.

Individual bureaucrats may differ in the relative weights they attach to career enhancement and administrative stability. A pattern of individual differences in these weights has been suggested by Downs (1967). The older the bureau in which a civil servant works, the more he should emphasize administrative stability. He is more likely to emphasize stability the lower is his probability of promotion, aggrandizement, and jumping between bureaux, the older he is and the longer he has been in his present position. If he is out of the promotion 'mainstream', he should be more concerned with stability the longer he has been in the bureau and the more authority and responsibility he has (Downs, 1967, pp. 98 ff.).

Where this leaves the distribution of bureaucrats' preferences is not totally clear. We should expect bureaucrats to prefer higher quantities of public expenditure than the rest of the electorate. But this will be less true the larger the proportion of bureaucrats weighting administrative stability relatively highly.

Even by itself, career enhancement is not an unambiguous guide to party preference. There are potentially serious conflicts within the public service over income and opportunities, especially when there is little overall growth in public employment. An obvious conflict in the Canadian federal service is over the language of work. Change in language rules may represent a considerable transfer of career opportunities between language groups. Education requirements confer differential benefits quite as much as do language requirements. Poorly or inappropriately educated employees might suffer from the general upgrading of the educational level of the public service. Conflicts could be most severe over income differences themselves. Should wage and salary increases be proportional or flat rate? Do some civil servants lose rather than gain through public sector collective bargaining? And, of course, Canada does not have one public service, but several. Growth at one level is not necessarily independent of shifts in employment at other levels. In short, even if all public servants agreed on the general merits of growth, there remains ample scope for conflict.

Self-interest may dictate that a bureaucrat support the party in power, whatever the level of public output it advocates. Of course, with a secret ballot, the costs to parties of monitoring individual voting are high (although not infinite). But the costs are not so high for more overt acts. The bureaucrat may also reveal himself through the advice he gives on policy. Although bureaucrats typically are protected against partisan dismissal, they may find promotion chances to vary directly with enthusiasm for the incumbent party. Where this is true, the proportion favouring incumbents should be greater the more senior the rank, other things equal. This will come about not just through the active use of partisan criteria and not just as candidates for advancement reveal their conformity with the policy preferences of their seniors, but as individuals preferring parties other than the one in power fail to present themselves for advancement.

In short, self-interest can push bureaucrats in different directions. Some bureaucrats should prefer the party advocating the greatest public employment growth. Another, probably smaller group, should prefer the party promising the most stable administrative environment. Some will be drawn to the party advocating growth in their own sector, or advocating recruitment and promotion criteria from which they, in particular, benefit. Finally, some will be drawn to the incumbent party, whatever its policies. Where this leaves summary predictions for civil servants as a voting bloc is not clear.

Table 6.3 presents some evidence from the 1968 national election study.[2] Government employees, broadly defined, were modestly more likely than non-government respondents to vote Liberal and slightly less likely to support each other party. Government employees were thus slightly more homogeneous politically than all others. Government/non-government differences sharpen as the occupation breakdown becomes more specific. Government employees, narrowly defined, are substantially more Liberal and, thus, more homogeneous politically than non-government respondents. As only some respondents in the government category are federal employees, this is especially striking. Health and Welfare workers are modestly more Liberal, at the expense of the NDP and Social Credit, and thus politically a bit more homogeneous than non-government

TABLE 6.3
PARTY PREFERENCE BY OCCUPATION, 1968
(per cent)

Party Preference	Non-Government	Government (excluding Education, Health and Welfare)	Education	Health and Welfare	All Government
Liberal	44	65	36	51	51
Conservative	31	18	34	34	28
NDP	17	13	23	10	16
Social Credit /Creditiste	8	4	7	5	5
Number of Observations	1986	112	110	76	298

Source: 1968 Election Survey (see text).

[2] Entries in Table 6.3 were adjusted, by successive row and column multiplications, to become consistent with the party composition of the 1968 popular vote according to official returns. The adjustment, necessitated by the survey's gross overestimation of the Liberal vote, exactly preserves the level of association between occupation and party preference in the original data. For a description and justification of the procedure, see Mosteller (1968).

respondents. Teachers are the least Liberal and the most New Democratic, and by far the least homogeneous, of all our groups. Of course, teachers' career interests are not at stake in a federal election.

Table 6.3 gives a suggestion of bloc-like behaviour. Indeed, the table may underestimate the partisan homogeneity of the group most affected by national elections, federal employees. Federal employees might appear even more distinct politically were they separated from provincial and municipal ones. But Table 6.3 may overstate bureaucrats' power, relative to other groups, as a bloc. The table makes non-government respondents seem politically very heterogeneous, but does so by averaging the party preferences of several, possible quite distinct, sub-groups. To assess bureaucrats' relative homogeneity, I should compare them with each other possible interest group. Many of these groups may actually be more politically homogeneous than civil servants.

Can I extract any conclusions from this section? Although the data in Table 6.3 are fragile and limited, they suggest a markedly Liberal orientation among government employees, not including teachers, in at least one national election. Whether the Liberals were attractive as the party advocating government growth or simply as the incumbent is not clear. A full and proper account would require evidence that neither I nor others have produced: party preference data spanning several elections comparing civil servants with each other group struggling for power. Short of such evidence, arguments portraying bureaucrats as a uniquely monolithic voting bloc are premature. Thinking about bureaucrats' political motives leads me to suspect that such arguments may be not just premature, but positively misbegotten.

VARIABILITY OF PREFERENCES

Is the civil service vote relatively available for transfer between parties? The literature on voting points to a citizen's amount of political information as a factor in the variability of his vote. As I have already argued that public servants should be, on the average, more informed than private citizens about political questions, I should be able to extract some predictions from the literature. Unfortunately, the literature itself is ambiguous on the question.

Students of voting typically have observed that the more information one has the more stable is one's response to the party system (Berelson, *et al.* 1954; Butler and Stokes, 1969). But those who observe this tendency fail to distinguish between switching directly between parties, on the one hand, and dropping in or out of the electorate, on the other hand, as alternatives to voting consistently for the same party. Usually, they completely ignore consistent abstention. In fact, all forms of individual-level transition from one election to the next combine two processes: variation in turnout and variation in party preference. Explanations of findings typically refer to factors affecting variation in party preference, but the observers could easily have been using arguments about preference to explain variation in turnout.

In any case, the usual explanation takes the following form: voting (and otherwise acting on behalf of) a party is a form of commitment. A voter may gather information *after* commitment and in order to buttress it. The information will be screened for its supportive content and the more (supportive) information received, the more the original commitment is reinforced. Thus, the more information one has, the more stable one's preferences will be.

At least as plausible an argument yields exactly the opposite prediction. Commitment to a party and information about politics are not complements, as the first argument suggests, but substitutes. The more costly information-processing is for a citizen, the more incentive he has to transfer the burden of it elsewhere. Among the agencies to which the costs may be transferred is the party. By this argument, the less information the citizen has, the more intense and stable his party preference should be. Conversely, the more information one has the less need one has for party loyalty and the more variable one's preferences should be (Downs, 1957).

Both arguments have merit. For many voters, information only reinforces initial party commitments. For many others, new information potentially weakens such commitments. The net relationship between the amount of political information and the stability of party preferences must depend on the relative proportions in the electorate of each type of voter. I have no *a priori* basis for predicting the dominance of one or the other type. The proportion under the control of the information-investment process may, however, be greater among public servants than among others. To the extent that public servants are restricted from acts on a party's behalf they are cut off from some of the mechanisms by which party commitment is typically built up. If so, public servants should be relatively likely to report vote switching.

Tables 6.4 and 6.5 indicate no such effect. Separately for federal and provincial elections, the respondent was asked which party, if any, he or she consistently supported.[3] One-half the sample reported never having switched between parties in national elections and 55 per cent claimed never to have switched between parties in provincial elections. A score of zero was assigned to consistent partisans and a score of one to respondents claiming to have switched between parties. Thus, the equations predict the probability of switching. No coefficient is significantly different from zero and the only ones which even strain toward significance are those for 'govjob2' in equations two and four of Table 6.4 and for 'educ' in equations three and four of Table 6.5. At the individual level, then, public servants appear to be no more available than others for switching between parties.[4]

---

[3] Respondents were asked (Question 42a): "Have you always voted for the same party in federal elections, or have you voted for different parties?". The question (Question 44a) for voting in provincial elections was essentially the same.

[4] The overestimation of the Liberal vote in 1968 (see note two above) deterred me from trying to compare bureaucrats and others in terms of aggregate vote-switching.

TABLE 6.4
**GOVERNMENT/NON-GOVERNMENT DIFFERENCES
IN REPORTED SWITCHING BETWEEN PARTIES
OVER PREVIOUS FEDERAL ELECTIONS, 1968**

Variable	Equation			
	(1)	(2)	(3)	(4)
Govjob	0.047 (1.502)	—	0.038 (1.145)	—
Govjob2	—	0.091 (1.830)	—	0.083 (1.649)
Educator	—	0.040 (0.792)	—	0.026 (1.511)
Health	—	−0.003 (−0.055)	—	−0.011 (−0.186)
Educ	—	—	0.003 (1.085)	0.003 (1.100)
Constant	0.503	0.503	0.471	0.471
R^2	0.001	0.002	0.001	0.002

Note: See notes to Table 6.1.

GEOGRAPHIC DISTRIBUTION OF PUBLIC EMPLOYEES

Votes are more useful in some constituencies than in others. In a single-member plurality electoral system, the geographic distribution of a group affects profoundly its ability to decide elections. The optimum distribution of a group varies with the group's size: the larger the group, the more dispersed over space its members should be, if they are to maximize their impact. Whatever a group's size, its members should be located in districts which are relatively closely contested (Johnston and Ballantyne, 1977).

How efficiently distributed are civil servants? I cannot do much more than speculate at this point, but some things come immediately to mind. To the extent that public employees are concentrated in a capital area, their votes are distributed inefficiently. The group would have many more votes in the few capital area seats than necessary to swing them and too few elsewhere. As it happens, however, public employees seem quite dispersed. In 1971, according to Hodgetts (1973, p. 220), fewer than one-fourth of federal civil servants worked

TABLE 6.5
GOVERNMENT/NON-GOVERNMENT DIFFERENCES IN REPORTED SWITCHING BETWEEN PARTIES OVER PREVIOUS PROVINCIAL ELECTIONS, 1968

Variable	Equation			
	(1)	(2)	(3)	(4)
Govjob	0.058 (1.709)	—	0.040 (1.141)	—
Govjob2	—	0.031 (0.586)	—	0.017 (0.315)
Educator	—	0.074 (1.374)	—	0.050 (0.909)
Health	—	0.073 (1.159)	—	0.059 (0.934)
Educ	—	—	0.006 (1.829)	0.006 (1.806)
Constant	0.440	0.440	0.382	0.383
R^2	0.001	0.001	0.003	0.003

Note: See notes to Table 6.1.

in the National Capital Region. Although information is lacking, I expect that provincial employees would be no more concentrated than federal ones in their respective capitals. Indeed, the importance at the provincial level of natural resources and services directly to citizens suggests that provincial public employees will be quite dispersed. This should be especially true if teachers and hospital employees are counted as provincial employees.

Are public servants located in marginal constituencies? Again I have no information, but I shall speculate a little. One criterion governments use in distributing benefits is the political return on the policy investment. Conferring benefits on marginal seats nets a greater return than conferring them on less closely contested seats. The probability that a few extra votes will change the outcome is simply greater in the marginal seat. A government seeking its own re-election may thus be moved to locate operations, many of them quite labour-intense, in marginal areas (see, for instance, Munro, 1975). Should the employees of the operation also happen to be natural supporters of the party in power, so much the better. But public employees need not always fit this description. Thus, in seeking to maximize its chances of re-election, a government may act, ironically, to increase the political leverage of its employees.

Of course, other criteria enter location decisions, for example, organizational imperatives, the location of resources, and the location of clients. Further, some operations are not popular locally, however many economic benefits they provide the district. Finally, governments entertain other political considerations than swinging marginal seats. Cabinet Ministers, for example, may capture favours, regardless of the marginality of their seats (see Blake, 1976). Still, had we the appropriate data, we might detect a pattern working to enhance the political efficiency of public employees' geographic distribution.

NUMBER OF CIVIL SERVANTS

The more numerous a group, the greater should be its ability to determine elections, other things equal. But complications arise. First, the more bureaucrats there are, the less distinct their interests may be from the interests of other groups. The image of bureaucrats as producers of public output appropriating revenues from other sectors breaks down as their numbers grow. Bureaucrats themselves become an increasingly important consumer group and pay an increasing proportion of total government revenues. At some point, their loss in taxes may offset income gains through increased public output. Of course, we do not know just where that point is. Second, recent bureaucratic growth has changed the public service's composition. Composition changes may have altered the bureaucracy's position on other factors affecting ability to determine elections: government/non-government turnout differences; the relative homogeneity of bureaucrats' party preferences; and the geographic distribution of employees. Judgments on the net political effect of employment growth must take into account these indirect compositional effects. I shall consider them in the paragraphs to follow.

Growth in public employment may have changed the government/non-government voting turnout difference. According to Hodgetts and Dwivedi (1974, p. 13), bureaucratic growth has come disproportionately in white collar grades, ones requiring relatively great amounts of schooling. Growth, then, should have brought an aggregate upgrading in public servants' turnout. But educational upgrading has pervaded the private sector as well, and it is not clear that the private-public turnout difference has changed. Further, it is not even clear that the aggregate upgrading of the population has increased its turnout. The education system may not actually teach participative skills so much as sort individuals on the basis of the prior possession of such skills. If the latter is true, aggregate shifts in educational attainment need produce no corresponding shifts in turnout. On the question of growth and turnout, then, the evidence at hand warrants no particular conclusion.

Should the growth in public employment have had much effect on the homogeneity of party preferences? Two aspects of the recent growth strike me as especially pertinent here. First, recent federal government growth has worked in part to redress earlier French-Canadian under-representation.[5] But as French-Canadians have increased their numbers, so too has conflict over language of work. If anything, the conflict will have made federal employees' party preferences more heterogeneous than before. Growth, then, may have reduced federal employees' ability to respond uniformly to parties. Second, total public growth has come disproportionately outside the federal service (Foot and Thadaney, 1978, Table 3.2). Now, institutional[6] employees dominate the distribution of public servants to almost exactly the same degree that federal government employees did in 1947. Although concentration in one category could be said only to have been replaced by concentration in another, the category now dominant may be geographically more diverse than the one dominant before. And, of course, provincial, municipal, and educational employment have grown relative to federal employment. If employees in one category perceive conflict or indifference between their interests and the interests of employees in another category, then the growth in employment will have made the preferences of the total body of civil servants even more diverse and less coordinated than before. Both the displacement of employment away from the federal service and the increased linguistic heterogeneity of the federal service itself should have *reduced* the capacity of civil servants to determine the outcome of elections, other things equal. This may have offset any increase in bureaucrats' power from overall employment growth.

What has growth done to the geographic distribution of public employees? The outstanding change has been the marked increase in the proportion of all public employees living in Quebec (Foot and Thadaney, 1978, Table 3.2). Ontario is no longer as pre-eminent a locale as before, but the two central provinces together now contain a rather larger proportion of total public employment than before. Whether this has enhanced or decreased civil servants' potential for determining elections is not obvious. In any case, talk of the efficiency of the distribution of votes would be idle if, as public employees' numbers have grown, their political coordination has become more difficult.

To conclude that bureaucrats have grown powerful out of proportion to their numbers as their numbers have grown would be premature. But so would be the rejection of such a conclusion. First, the effect of growth on private-public turnout differences is not known and may not be knowable. Second, growth may

---

[5] See Canada, Royal Commission on Bilingualism and Biculturalism, *Report* (Volume 3A, p. 220) where it is remarked that evidence available just before publication (1969) indicates that 38 per cent of public servants aged 20 to 24 claimed French as their mother tongue and that young francophones "were receiving pay increases (and promotions) at a rate faster than those in the other language groups".

[6] 'Institutional' employees work for hospitals, charitable and religious organizations, clubs, and other non-profit organizations. The category is derived from the occupational classification in *Taxation Statistics*; see Foot and Thadaney (1978). Institutional employees correspond roughly to the 'health and welfare' category in the 1968 political survey.

have made bureaucrats' party preferences more heterogeneous than before and, thus, less readily 'delivered' to a party. Even this is speculation, however. Third, the geographic distribution of public employees has changed as their numbers have grown, but the effect of the change on bureaucrats' power is not obvious. Finally, one must ask how much civil servants would truly benefit from overall growth in their numbers. Public employment may have reached the point at which the tax effects from further growth offset the income effects. This may be true at least among bureaucrats with high marginal tax rates. Thus, the assumption that bureaucrats will at least agree on the general merits of growth may no longer be warranted. A proper account of the matter would require data not just on the aggregate public service income effects of government growth but on the distributive effects. The possibility of such distributive effects has not, to my knowledge, been recognized in work on the electoral motives of bureaucrats.

SUMMARY AND IMPLICATIONS

I considered five factors affecting the power of bureaucrats to determine elections. The conclusions the data permit are not very frightening. As often as not, however, I could draw no clear conclusion. As predicted, civil servants turn out and vote at a higher rate than private citizens, but, almost without exception, the differences were not significant. Such turnout differences as appeared were explicable by private-public differences in educational attainment. I was unable to test hypotheses on turnout in municipal elections and on participation in ways other than voting. My data on the relative homogeneity of bureaucrats' and others' party preferences were extremely faulty. Such as they are, the data indicate some party preference differences between bureaucrats and all others. The evidence on the variability of party preferences was limited, but indicated that bureaucrats were no more volatile in this respect than the rest of us. I could produce no data on the geographic distribution of bureaucrats, but speculated that parties in power might, for their own reasons, locate bureaucrats in a way that incidentally enhances bureaucrats' ability to swing elections. Finally, I speculated on the political effects of bureauracies' size and growth, but again could produce no data.

A full and proper treatment of the question requires more and better data, especially on occupation, political activity, and geographic location. Civil servants should have been differentiated by level of government, possibly by department or policy area within levels, and by status in the bureaucratic hierarchy. Bureaucrats may have an especially great impact on municipal elections and so information at that level would be important. So too would be data on forms of participation beyond voting, especially if such activity greatly affects party strategy and the preferences of less active voters. My speculation on bureaucrats' location fairly begs for employment data aggregated by parliamentary constituency. In the absence of data such as those described in this paragraph, blanket statements about bureaucrats' power as a voting bloc would be premature and irresponsible.

REFERENCES

Beattie, Christopher, Jacques Desy and Stephen Longstaff (1972) *Bureaucratic Careers: Anglophones and Francophones in the Canadian Public Service* (Ottawa: Information Canada).

Berelson, Bernard, Paul Lazarsfeld and William McPhee (1954) *Voting* (Chicago: University of Chicago).

Blake, Donald E. (1976) "LIP and Partisanship: An Analysis of the Local Initiatives Program" *Canadian Public Policy–Analyse de politiques* 2, 17–32.

Borcherding, Thomas E., Winston C. Bush and Robert M. Spann (1977) "The Effects on Public Spending of the Divisibility of Public Outputs in Consumption, Bureaucratic Power, and the Size of the Tax-Sharing Group" in Thomas E. Borcherding (ed.) *Budgets and Bureaucrats: The Sources of Government Growth* (Durham: Duke University Press) 211–28.

Bush, Winston C. and Arthur T. Denzau (1977) "The Voting Behavior of Bureaucrats and Public Sector Growth" in Thomas E. Borcherding ed. *Budgets and Bureaucrats: The Sources of Government Growth* (Durham: Duke University Press) 90–99.

Butler, David and Donald Stokes (1969) *Political Change in Britain* (New York: St. Martin's).

Canada, Royal Commission on Bilingualism and Biculturalism (1969) *Report, Volume 3A. The Work World* (Ottawa: Queen's Printer).

Downs, Anthony (1957) *An Economic Theory of Democracy* (New York: Harper and Row).

Downs, Anthony (1967) *Inside Bureaucracy* (Boston: Little, Brown).

Foot, David K. and Percy Thadaney (1978) "The Growth of Public Employment in Canada: The Evidence from Taxation Statistics, 1946-75", Chapter Three in David K. Foot (ed.) *Public Employment and Compensation in Canada: Myths and Realities* (Toronto: Butterworth & Co. for The Institute for Research on Public Policy).

Gramlich, Edward M. (1976) "The New York City Fiscal Crisis: What Happened and What is to be Done?" *American Economic Review* (Papers and Proceedings) 66:2, 415–29.

Gunderson, Morley (1974) "Retention of Trainees: A Study with Dichotomous Dependent Variables" *Journal of Econometrics* 2, 79–93.

Halter, G.M. (1972) "The Effects of the Hatch Act on the Political Participation of Federal Employees" *Midwest Journal of Political Science* 16, 723–29.

Hodgetts, J.E. (1973) *The Canadian Public Service: A Physiology of Government: 1867-1970* (Toronto: University of Toronto Press).

Hodgetts, J.E. and O.P. Dwivedi (1974) *Provincial Governments as Employers* (Montreal and London: McGill-Queen's University Press).

Johnston, Richard and Janet Ballantyne (1977) "Geography and the Electoral System" *Canadian Journal of Political Science* 10, 857–66.

Kelley, Stanley, Richard Ayres and William Bowen (1967) "Registration and Voting: Putting First Things First" *American Political Science Review* 61, 359–79.

Kernaghan, Kenneth (1976) "Politics, Policy, and Public Servants: Political Neutrality Revisited" *Canadian Public Administration* 19, 432–456.

Lipset, Seymour Martin (1960) *Political Man* (New York: Doubleday).

Mosteller, Frederick (1968) "Association and Estimation in Contingency Tables" *Journal of the American Statistical Association* 63, 1–28.

Munro, John M. (1975) "Highways in British Columbia: Economics and Politics" *Canadian Journal of Economics* 8, 192–204.

Niskanen, William A. (1971) *Bureaucracy and Representative Government*, (Chicago: Aldine).

Qualter, Terence H. (1970) *The Election Process in Canada* (Toronto: McGraw-Hill).

Tullock, Gordon (1974) "Dynamic Hypothesis on Bureaucracy" *Public Choice* 19, 127–31.